D0292120

MACARTHUR'S
AIR FORCE

MACARTHUR'S AIR FORCE

American Airpower over the Pacific and the Far East, 1941–51

BILL YENNE

OSPREY PUBLISHING
Bloomsbury Publishing Plc
PO Box 883, Oxford, OX1 9PL, UK
1385 Broadway, 5th Floor, New York, NY 10018, USA
E-mail: info@ospreypublishing.com
www.ospreypublishing.com

OSPREY is a trademark of Osprey Publishing Ltd

First published in Great Britain in 2019

A catalog record for this book is available from the British Library.

ISBN: HB 978 1 4728 3323 5; PB 978 1 4728 3324 2; eBook 978 1 4728 3322 8;
ePDF 978 1 4728 3320 4; XML 978 1 4728 3321 1

19 20 21 22 23   10 9 8 7 6 5 4 3 2 1

Maps by Bounford.com
Index by Angela Hall

Typeset by Deanta Global Publishing Services, Chennai, India
Printed and bound in Great Britain by CPI (Group) UK Ltd, Croydon CR0 4YY

Front cover: (top) General MacArthur aboard the B 17F *Talisman*, September 5, 1943 (USAAF);
(bottom) A pair of Douglas A-20Gs striking Japanese positions at Kokas on the Vogelkop Peninsula,
July 22, 1944. (USAAF)
Back cover: (left) A B-25D Mitchell bomber departing Simpson Harbor at Rabaul (USAAF);
(right) *Amatsukaze* is attacked by a B-25 off the coast of Amoy on April 6, 1945. (USAAF)

Osprey Publishing supports the Woodland Trust, the UK's leading woodland
conservation charity.

To find out more about our authors and books visit **www.ospreypublishing.com**.
Here you will find extracts, author interviews, details of forthcoming events
and the option to sign up for our newsletter.

Contents

The Pacific Ocean Areas and South West Pacific Area, 1942–44

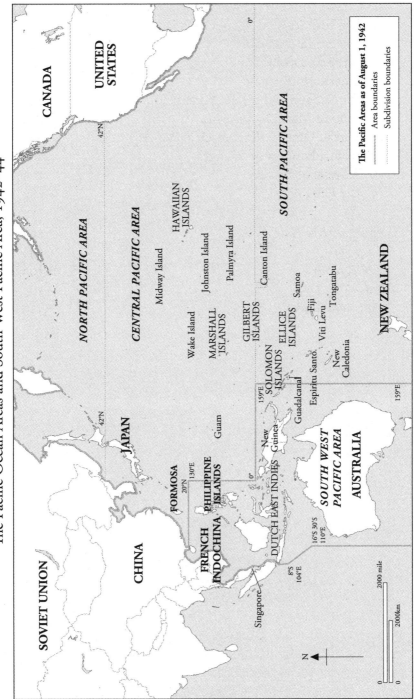

SOVIET UNION

CANADA

UNITED STATES

CHINA

JAPAN

NORTH PACIFIC AREA

42°N

FORMOSA

130°E

20°N

PHILIPPINE ISLANDS

FRENCH INDOCHINA

Guam

CENTRAL PACIFIC AREA

HAWAIIAN ISLANDS

Midway Island

Wake Island

Johnston Island

Palmyra Island

MARSHALL ISLANDS

Canton Island

0°

DUTCH EAST INDIES

New Guinea

159°E

SOLOMON ISLANDS

Guadalcanal

Espiritu Santo

GILBERT ISLANDS

ELLICE ISLANDS

Samoa

Fiji

Viti Levu

Tongatabu

New Caledonia

SOUTH PACIFIC AREA

Singapore

8°S
104°E

16°S 30'S
110°E

SOUTH WEST PACIFIC AREA

AUSTRALIA

159°E

NEW ZEALAND

N

2000 mile

0

2000km

0

The Pacific Areas as of August 1, 1942
———— Area boundaries
············ Subdivision boundaries

The South West Pacific Area, 1942–44

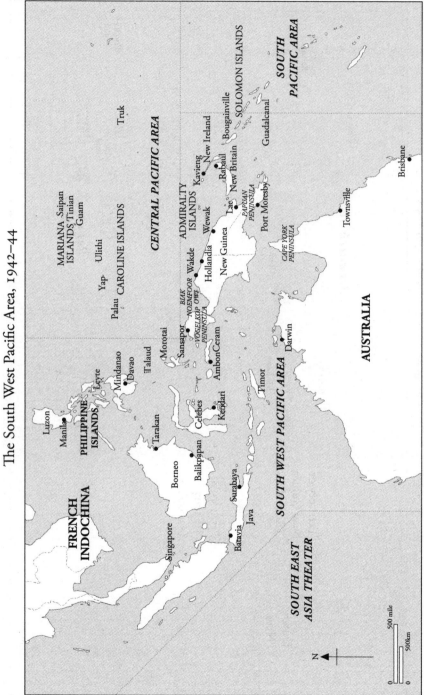

FRENCH INDOCHINA

Singapore

Borneo

Tarakan

Balikpapan

Surabaya

Batavia

Java

Timor

SOUTH EAST ASIA THEATER

SOUTH WEST PACIFIC AREA

AUSTRALIA

Darwin

CAPE YORK PENINSULA

Port Moresby

PAPUAN PENINSULA

New Guinea

Lae

Wewak

Hollandia

Wakde

Sansapor

VOGELKOP PENINSULA

BIAK

NOEMFOOR

OWI

Morotai

Ambon

Ceram

Kendari

Celebes

Talaud

Mindanao

Davao

Leyte

PHILIPPINE ISLANDS

Luzon

Manila

ADMIRALTY ISLANDS

CENTRAL PACIFIC AREA

MARIANA ISLANDS

Saipan

Tinian

Guam

Yap

Ulithi

Palau

CAROLINE ISLANDS

Truk

Kavieng

New Ireland

Rabaul

New Britain

Bougainville

SOLOMON ISLANDS

Guadalcanal

SOUTH PACIFIC AREA

Townsville

Brisbane

N

500 mile

500km

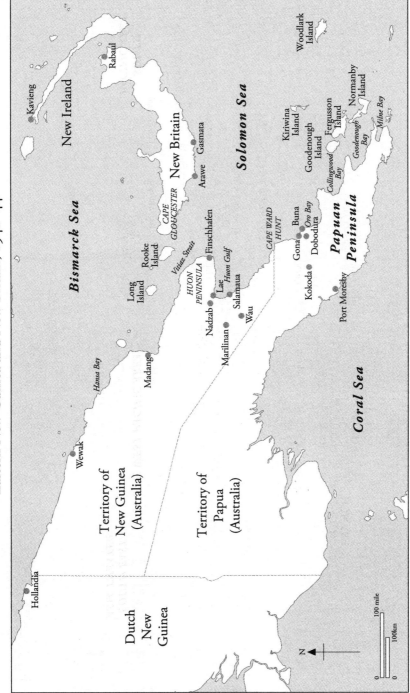

Eastern New Guinea and New Britain, 1942–44

Bismarck Sea

Solomon Sea

Coral Sea

New Ireland

New Britain

Kavieng

Rabaul

Gasmata

Arawe

CAPE GLOUCESTER

Rooke Island

Long Island

Vitiaz Strait

Finschhafen

HUON PENINSULA

Huon Gulf

Lae

Salamaua

Wau

Nadzab

Marilinan

Madang

Hansa Bay

Wewak

Hollandia

Dutch New Guinea

Territory of New Guinea (Australia)

Territory of Papua (Australia)

CAPE WARD HUNT

Gona

Buna

Oro Bay

Dobodura

Kokoda

Port Moresby

Papuan Peninsula

Woodlark Island

Normanby Island

Milne Bay

Kiriwina Island

Goodenough Island

Fergusson Island

Collingwood Bay

Goodenough Bay

N

100 mile

100km

0

The Philippines, 1941–45

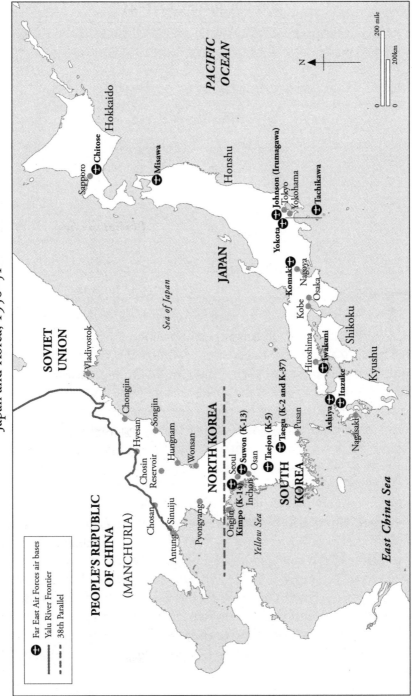

Japan and Korea, 1950–51

Legend:
- ⊕ Far East Air Forces air bases
- Yalu River Frontier
- 38th Parallel

PEOPLE'S REPUBLIC
OF CHINA
(MANCHURIA)

SOVIET
UNION

NORTH KOREA

SOUTH
KOREA

JAPAN

Sea of Japan

Yellow Sea

East China Sea

PACIFIC
OCEAN

N

200 mile
200km

Hokkaido
Sapporo
⊕ Chitose
⊕ Misawa
Honshu
Yokota ⊕ Johnson (Irumagawa)
Tokyo
Yokohama
⊕ Tachikawa
⊕ Komaki
Nagoya
Osaka
Kobe
Hiroshima
⊕ Iwakuni
Shikoku
⊕ Ashiya
⊕ Itazuke
Kyushu
Nagasaki

Vladivostok
Chongjin
Songjin
Hyesan
Hungnam
Chosin
Reservoir
Wonsan
Chosan
Antung
Sinuiju
Pyongyang
Ongjin
Seoul
⊕ Kimpo (K-14)
Inchon
Osan
⊕ Suwon (K-13)
⊕ Taejon (K-5)
⊕ Taegu (K-2 and K-37)
Pusan

Airpower and the Science and Art of War

by Douglas MacArthur

T he first function of air power is to get command of the air. In modern warfare, air supremacy is the first absolute essential. The amount of enemy air opposition in this campaign was negligible. The essential targets were eliminated early and the air units were then able to devote their major emphasis on ground support. In the beginning of a war, all the air forces should be under air command in order to rid the skies of hostile air and when this is done the ground forces are entitled to ground support that is required in these days of intense firepower. Modern infantry cannot advance without close air support. It must have more of it.

Modern firepower which the enemy bring to bear with the burp guns is so heavy that even with artillery back of our lines hub-to-hub there would not be sufficient power for the ground elements to advance and this artillery power must be backed up with air power. It is not a question of the courage of the ground soldier, it is only a question of survival. Air support is the only effective answer. This necessitates the closest cooperation between air and ground command. In the first stage of the war and until air supremacy has been attained there must be the closest coordination between the air and the ground command. The ground commander must be in a position to call for air support as he needs it.

The American soldier has been reared from boyhood with the standard of living of the very highest and therefore, that American soldier on the field of battle has every right to expect, and does expect, a higher standard of living than all other soldiers. Therefore, he has a right to expect firepower of both artillery and air force in battle.

We differentiate between the science of war and the art of war. The principles are immutable. The art changes with each campaign and there is no such thing as a normal war. World War I was not normal. World War II was not normal. We will probably not see positioned warfare again, particularly since men may be moved one thousand miles over night. They may be transported and supplied by air, thus the coordination of joint ground-air is more than ever important. As Napoleon said, "the tactics of warfare should be rewritten every ten years." Considering the coordination of air and ground forces we must be ever looking to the future no matter how good it may have been in the present Korean campaign.

General of the Army Douglas MacArthur,
*November 22, 1950**

---

*As quoted by Lieutenant General George Stratemeyer (from *The Three Wars of Lt. Gen. George E. Stratemeyer*, edited by William T. Y'Blood, Air Force History and Museums Program).

Introduction

What Was MacArthur's Air Force?

D ouglas MacArthur is one of the towering figures of World War II, and indeed of the 20th century. In the pantheon of great American military leaders during World War II, he is at the apogee, along with Eisenhower, Nimitz, Marshall, and Patton.

What is often overlooked among his superlatives is that the second-largest air force in the US Army Air Forces (USAAF) was in his chain of command.

MacArthur commanded the South West Pacific Area (SWPA), a theater of World War II, until 1944, when he was made commander of all US Army and USAAF forces in the Pacific. MacArthur's air force, as described herein, was initially a SWPA constituent called Allied Air Forces, created in April 1942. It contained the USAAF Fifth Air Force and elements of the Royal Australian Air Force (RAAF). In 1944, the USAAF Far East Air Forces (FEAF) was created under MacArthur's theater command. It contained the USAAF Fifth Air Force, as well as the Seventh Air Force and the Thirteenth Air Force.

In 1945, the air forces of FEAF contained 216,616 personnel, or 26 percent of all overseas deployed USAAF airmen, as well as just over 4,000 combat aircraft.

During the postwar occupation of Japan, MacArthur held the title of Supreme Commander for the Allied Powers (SCAP), and within this chain of command was the postwar FEAF, comprising the Fifth, Eighth, Thirteenth, and Twentieth Air Forces. Under MacArthur's command during the Korean War, the FEAF contained more than 90,000 personnel and 1,800 aircraft.

Often overlooked, though still important historically, are that as Chief of Staff of the US Army between 1930 and 1935, MacArthur had the entire US Army Air Corps within his chain of command, and as Field Marshal of the Philippine Army between 1936 and 1941, he had the small Philippine Army Air Corps in his table of organization.

Within the large personnel counts, and perhaps the most important element of what comprised MacArthur's air forces, are the individuals whose heroism and command skills are the very texture of those air forces. At the tops of the chains of command were men whose names are household words wherever airpower is discussed – men such as George Kenney, Ennis Whitehead, Paul Wurtsmith, and Earle Partridge. There were others at the apogee of the command structure, from Ken Walker to Howard Ramey, who gave their lives in combat.

There were characters so unique that they seem fictitious. Take for example Paul Irvin "Pappy" Gunn, whose skill as a flightline engineering genius was so astounding that he amazed the people who had designed the aircraft in the first place – and who also filled a niche as a brilliant low-level attack pilot.

There were bomber pilots from Ed Larner to Don Hall, whose exploits seem like the impossible stuff of Hollywood fabrication. There were many great and heroic fighter aces, including Dick Bong and Tommy McGuire, who became the highest-scoring American aces of all time while in combat within MacArthur's chain of command. There were many, many more heroes, including all of those who took home Silver Stars and Distinguished Flying Crosses, not to mention Medals of Honor.

This is the story of the times and the unique circumstances within which all of this came to pass.

Prologue

MacArthur and Airpower

Neither ground nor sea forces can operate safely unless the air over them is controlled by our own air power.

Douglas MacArthur, 1925

Douglas MacArthur was born into the US Army. His father, Captain Arthur MacArthur, Jr, of Milwaukee had served with the 24th Wisconsin Volunteer Infantry Regiment during the Civil War, and earned the Medal of Honor at Missionary Ridge. When Douglas, his third son, was born on January 26, 1880, Arthur was posted to Little Rock Barracks in Arkansas. Four years later, Arthur was reassigned to Fort Selden in New Mexico, where he took part in the campaigns against Geronimo and the Chiricahua Apache. As a brevet brigadier general, he went on to serve as a brigade commander during the Spanish–American War.

Being in the West when it was still the "Wild West" made an impression on young Douglas. As he claimed in his memoirs, "I learned to ride and shoot even before I could read or write – indeed, almost before I could walk or talk."

A precocious child, Douglas worked hard and excelled in school. He also overcame a spinal condition to become a good athlete. After his father was assigned to Fort Sam Houston in San Antonio in 1893, he attended the West Texas Military Academy (now Texas Military

Institute), where he was the head of his class academically and the quarterback for the football team.

Though the MacArthurs, like military families then and now, were constantly on the move, they maintained their connection to Milwaukee. Douglas and his mother, Mary Pinkney "Pinkie" MacArthur, often spent time there when Arthur was on assignment. This would hardly be worth mentioning but for an important connection to the roots of Douglas MacArthur's association with airpower. Congressman John Lendrum Mitchell, also of Milwaukee, had served with Arthur MacArthur in the 24th Wisconsin and the two were friends.

John Mitchell had three children, a daughter and two sons, who were about Douglas's age. Douglas had a boyhood crush on Ruth Mitchell, who went on to be notable for, among other things, fighting alongside the Yugoslav partisans during World War II. The elder son – just a month older than Douglas – was William Lendrum "Billy" Mitchell, who became one of the US Army's first generation of pilots and an airpower visionary who was destined to be the central figure in American airpower doctrine during World War I and into the following decade.

Douglas's older brother, Arthur MacArthur III, entered the US Naval Academy, but Douglas remained in the family business, enrolling in the US Military Academy at West Point in 1899. As at the West Texas Military Academy, he participated in sports and excelled in his studies. In his final year, he was First Captain, the highest-ranking member of the Corps of Cadets, and he graduated at the head of the Class of 1903. Those graduating with the highest academic standing were traditionally commissioned into the Corps of Engineers, the branch of the US Army requiring the highest level of academic skill, so newly minted 2nd Lieutenant Douglas MacArthur became an engineer.

MacArthur's early military career presaged his career during World War II. His first engineering assignment was to the Philippines – where his father had served as governor-general while Douglas was at West Point – and in 1905 he went to Japan as an aide to his father, who was the American military attaché and an official observer of the Russo-Japanese War.

Military aviation played no role in MacArthur's early military career, but by the fall of 1906, when he was ordered to Washington, DC to attend the US Army Engineer School (then the Engineer School of Application), the US Army was in the process of acquiring an air force.

The service had dabbled in aeronautics during the Civil War, when the Balloon Corps of the Army of the Potomac conducted reconnaissance of Confederate positions in 1861–63, and the Signal Corps had begun acquiring balloons in 1892 with a long-term plan to incorporate them into their operations. Piloted, heavier-than-air flight was born with the Wright Brothers in 1903, the same year that MacArthur graduated from West Point. However, there was initially very little official interest within the US Army, and indeed among the general public, in airplanes. They may have been brilliant engineers, but the Wrights were poor promoters.

Inside the Signal Corps, though, among the men who managed the balloons, there were those who kept abreast of the work being done by the Wrights. It was Major George Squier who convinced Brigadier General James Allen, the Chief Signal Officer, to create the Aeronautical Division of the Signal Corps. This entity formally came into being on August 1, 1907. This was coincidentally the same day that Lieutenant Frank Lahm was being introduced to Wilbur and Orville Wright. Lahm was destined to be the division's second officer and the first to fly in an airplane. In September 1908 the Signal Corps bought its first heavier-than-air aircraft from the Wrights.

Douglas MacArthur left Washington in 1907 within a matter of days of the creation of the Aeronautical Division, probably unaware that it existed. However, by the time he returned in 1912 – to a post in the office of the Chief of Staff, Major General Leonard Wood – the division was a going concern. The Army bought a dozen airplanes in 1912 and was using them for observation duties during routine maneuvers. It had contracted with the Wright Brothers to train Army pilots and had set up a school at College Park, Maryland. Those learning to fly included Lieutenant Henry Harley "Hap" Arnold, who was to command the US Army Air Forces (USAAF) in World War II.

In September 1913, Captain MacArthur became the youngest of 38 members of the General Staff. It was here that he again crossed paths with Captain William Lendrum Mitchell, now of the Aeronautical Division, whom he had known as a boy in Milwaukee. Doug and Billy would meet again during World War I, and at the climax of Mitchell's career in 1925.

In January 1914, the Aeronautical Division activated its first squadron shortly before MacArthur left Washington to see combat action during the brief American intervention in the Mexican port city of Veracruz. The 1st Aero Squadron took no part in the 1914 Veracruz operation, but had its baptism of fire over Mexico two years later, when General John J. Pershing went south in his ill-fated pursuit of Pancho Villa after the bandit leader attacked Columbus, New Mexico.

MacArthur was back in Washington, DC on the staff of Secretary of War Newton Baker when Europe stumbled into World War I in August 1914. Promoted to major in 1916, he called himself Baker's "press censor," but his role was essentially that of the Army's first public affairs officer.

When the United States entered the war in April 1917, Pershing was named to lead American troops overseas, and National Guard units formed the nucleus of the American Expeditionary Force (AEF). The first division created was the 42nd Infantry Division, and MacArthur himself, now a colonel, was named as its chief of staff. Observing that the division was comprised of Guard units spread across the country like a rainbow, he dubbed it "the Rainbow Division," and the name stuck.

In the meantime, the Aeronautical Division had grown slowly, from a personnel strength of 51 in June 1912 to 311 four years later. Renamed as the Aviation Section of the Signal Corps in 1914, the Army's air arm had a head count of 1,218 in June 1917 as mobilization got underway. By the end of the war, it had grown to around 200,000. Yet the growth of the Aviation Section was merely a microcosm of the total US Army. From a strength of 133,111 in April 1917, the service had inducted 4,178,172 personnel by November 1918.

The immense capacity of the United States to quickly mobilize manpower was not matched by the ability of American industry to manufacture aircraft. Though heavier-than-air flight was born in the United States, it had been embraced and nurtured in Europe. The aviation industry in Britain, France, and Germany was far ahead of that of the United States both in total production and in technological refinement. The air forces of the European powers were qualitatively and quantitatively superior to the Aviation Section, as well as in development of tactical doctrine for the use of airpower.

When Douglas MacArthur reached the battlefront in France in October 1917, he arrived beneath a sky filled with British and French aircraft, and beneath a US Army chain of command dominated by senior officers who were "old cavalry soldiers" for whom aircraft were a generally irrelevant novelty. Indeed, MacArthur himself had no experience with aircraft at war. They had been used – albeit not very successfully – in the Mexican expedition of 1916, but not in that of 1914 in which MacArthur had taken part.

MacArthur found that American airmen were already overseas. Billy Mitchell, now a major, had arrived in April 1917 within a week of the American declaration of war, and had already set up an advance office for the air units of the AEF. Mitchell, who would go on to become the US Army's senior air commander in Europe, was already refining his ideas for the use of airpower in coordination with ground forces as part of a tactically integrated force. It was a revolutionary idea that would become a standard and effective operating procedure in World War II. Mitchell would also be the first tactician to plan and execute massive air attacks behind enemy lines, a doctrine that was followed successfully by the United States in World War II.

Meanwhile, in May 1918, the Aviation Section had been upgraded in prominence, having been moved out from the shadow of the Signal Corps as the US Army Air Service.

The mammoth battle of Saint-Mihiel, which took place near the town of the same name in northeastern France between September 12 and 15, 1918, marked a crossroads of American military history. It was the first major action in which the US First Army mobilized against the Germans as an integral organization. One of the 14 divisions comprising the First Army front was the 42nd "Rainbow" Division, now commanded by Brigadier General Charles Menoher, with Colonel Douglas MacArthur still serving as chief of staff.

Saint-Mihiel was also the largest deployment of Billy Mitchell's tactical air units – he commanded a force of 1,476 Allied aircraft – in coordination with the ground forces. Indeed, the order of battle paired aero squadrons with infantry divisions. The 42nd Infantry Division, attacking at the center of the First Army front, was paired with the 90th Aero Squadron.

The victory achieved by the First Army at Saint-Mihiel earned the Americans the respect of their allies, while Mitchell's successes in the air earned him high praise from General Pershing. Saint-Mihiel was the beginning of the end for Germany and for the war itself – a finale that was reached via the bloody Meuse–Argonne offensive on "the eleventh hour of the eleventh day of the eleventh month" of 1918.

While both MacArthur and Mitchell remained in Europe as part of the occupation force in Germany, the US Army went through a downsizing that was nearly as rapid as its mobilization. By 1920, the total personnel strength of the US Army as a whole, as well as that of the microcosm that was its Air Service, had dwindled to just 5 percent of its wartime peak. As with the aftermath of other wars, Americans were anxious to put thoughts of war behind them and embrace the expansive new decade that would come to be known as the "Roaring Twenties."

As MacArthur and Mitchell returned to the United States, each of them now promoted to the rank of brigadier general, their career paths diverged. Mitchell landed in Washington, DC at the center of power within an Army in flux, while MacArthur landed far from the middle of the action. His first postwar assignment was as superintendent of the US Military Academy at West Point. MacArthur sought to bring his alma mater into the 20th century, replacing the Civil War maps that the tactical classes studied with new ones from World War I. He even brought Billy Mitchell up to lecture to the cadets about airpower doctrine and practice. Many men who became USAAF combat commanders in World War II had heard Mitchell's lectures.

Mitchell, who became Chief of Training and Operations for the Air Service, had begun to ruffle official feathers with his outspoken advocacy of airpower within the scope of Army doctrine. When it came time to name the first postwar chief of the Air Service, Chief of Staff General Peyton March passed over the irksome Mitchell and picked Charles

Menoher, the wartime commander of the 42nd Infantry Division. Menoher, an artilleryman, not an airman, was a West Point classmate of General Pershing. Mitchell was awarded a consolation prize, serving as Menoher's assistant until 1926.

These would be turbulent years at headquarters, but for airpower advocates, they were years in which Mitchell continued to lay the groundwork for the future use of aircraft in offensive operations. Mitchell earned not only the ire of the Army establishment, but that of the US Navy as well. He asserted that his bombers could sink a battleship – this at a time when battleships were the very symbol of military might, and the first, last, and middle line of defense to protect American shores.

In 1921, Mitchell organized a series of demonstrations to show that aircraft were an effective weapon against warships. In July, Mitchell's bombers sank the captured German battleship *Ostfriesland* and two other warships, and in September, they sank the retired US Navy battleship USS *Alabama*. The US Navy was both embarrassed and enraged, and it demanded that the US Army declare officially that battleships would always be America's ultimate weapon. Attempts were made to keep the embarrassing results out of the newspapers, but to no avail. Menoher requested a change of assignment and was replaced by Brigadier General Mason Patrick, an engineering officer.

Douglas MacArthur remained distant from the fray. He left West Point in 1922 to return to the Philippines – which would figure prominently in his future career – after an absence of 18 years. Here, he assumed command of the Military District of Manila, and later of the Philippine Division as a major general. Based at Fort William McKinley, the Philippine Division was a component of the Philippine Department, which also contained the nucleus of the air arm that MacArthur would command at the beginning of World War II.

In December 1922, most Army Air Service assets in the Philippines – located mainly at Nichols Field near Manila and at Clark Field, 50 air miles to the northwest – were consolidated under the 4th Composite Group. It had been formed in 1911 as the 1st Observation Group, and became the 4th Composite in 1922. It operated various aircraft, mainly Boeing-built DH-4s, in a variety of roles.

MacArthur returned stateside in early 1925, briefly posted to Fort McPherson, Georgia as commander of the Fourth Corps Area, and later as head of the Third Corps Area out of Fort McHenry, Maryland.

Also in 1925, Billy Mitchell's term as assistant chief of the Air Service expired, and he was reassigned to a ground forces command in Texas, a post which his supporters saw as a humiliating exile. Mitchell did not go away quietly. He continued to criticize both Army and Navy, and to speak out about the importance of airpower, even when ordered not to. He even made the statement, considered preposterous at the time, that the US Navy's great base at Pearl Harbor could be attacked from the *air*.

When the US Navy's rigid airship *Shenandoah* crashed in a storm in September 1925, Mitchell publicly charged the senior leadership of both services with "almost treasonable administration of national defense." On the direct orders of President Calvin Coolidge, Mitchell was summoned to Washington to face a court martial on charges of "conduct prejudicial to good order and military discipline."

With Major General Robert Lee Howze presiding, a panel of officers sat down in November to hear testimony and to pass judgment. The youngest among them was 45-year-old Major General Douglas MacArthur, who wrote that having to sit in judgment of Mitchell was "one of the most distasteful orders I ever received."

Popular opinion supported the colorful Mitchell, and the media, which heavily covered the court martial, portrayed the proceedings as an unfair attack on a popular hero.

Mitchell's defense team cited Mitchell's freedom of speech, and insisted that his criticism of shortcomings in procedures and practices was true. However, the court ruled that whether it was true or false was irrelevant.

After a seven-week trial, the officers cast their secret ballots, of which two thirds were required for a verdict. Mitchell was convicted. No one outside the deliberation room would know who voted how. MacArthur later wrote:

When the verdict was reached, many believed I had betrayed my friend, and certain rabid and irresponsible columnists even assailed me for joining "in the persecution of Mitchell." Nothing could be further from the truth. I did what I could on his behalf and I helped save him from dismissal. That he was wrong in the violence of his language is self-evident; that he was right in his thesis [regarding airpower] is equally true and incontrovertible.

Suspended without pay but not discharged dishonorably, Mitchell resigned from the service. He died in 1936 before he could witness the vindication of his airpower theories in World War II.

Nevertheless, the Mitchell trial and the publicity devoted to it had given a forum to airpower advocates, and the message was heard. In July 1926, six months after Mitchell resigned, the US Army upgraded the status of its Air Service, which now became the US Army Air Corps.

MacArthur remained in Baltimore in command of the Third Corps Area until 1928, when he was briefly placed on detached service in order to head the US Olympic Committee during the Games of the IX Olympiad in Amsterdam. His team led the field in both gold medals and the total medal count.

After another short stint in the Philippines as head of the US Army's Philippine Department, MacArthur was summoned to Washington in November 1930 by President Herbert Hoover, who promoted him to brevet four-star rank and named him to succeed General Charles Summerall as Chief of Staff of the US Army. He was in the post for five years, a four-year term plus a one-year extension. During that time, MacArthur would earn high marks from both the media and the rank-and-file of the Army for his reorganization and modernization efforts, and an indelible black mark for his using tanks and troops in a heavy-handed suppression of the "Bonus Marchers." The latter were a group of around 17,000 World War I veterans, plus their families, who came to Washington in 1932 in the depths of the Great Depression, camped on the National Mall, and demanded payment of bonuses that they had been promised, but which were not payable for more than a decade.

With regard to airpower, MacArthur was now in a position to at least promote significant change – even if his tenure coincided with the trough of the Great Depression, when the government's purse strings were drawn tight across a depleted purse.

"I stormed, begged, ranted, and roared," he wrote colorfully in his memoirs. "I almost licked the boots of certain gentlemen to get funds for motorization and mechanization and air power ... I called for increased speed, increased fire power, fast machines, airplanes."

As he said at the time, echoing the Mitchell doctrine, "We will be dependent on our air force to defend our coastlines, for attack against hostile ground forces, for bombardment of sensitive points in the enemy's supply organization."

This translated into only modest growth for the Air Corps, where the head count increased from 13,531 to 16,247 on MacArthur's watch. During those five years, the Air Corps began acquiring enclosed cockpit monoplane bombers, such as the Martin B-10. The four-engine Boeing B-17 Flying Fortress, destined to be one of the defining warplanes of World War II, made its debut flight two months before MacArthur left his post as Chief of Staff.

During MacArthur's final year, he also created the short-lived General Headquarters Air Force (GHQAF), an organization that would control operational combat units and answer directly to the Army Chief of Staff. This was seen as a positive step by many airpower advocates, but rather than streamlining air operations, GHQAF complicated them because it existed in parallel with the Army Air Corps, with neither side answering to the other. The Air Corps retained responsibility for training, doctrine, and aircraft development.

The pendulum of airpower advocacy that had swung with the proponents under MacArthur would reverse course under his successor. General Malin Craig was part of that generation of "old cavalry soldiers" who had little use for airpower except in direct support of troops on the ground. On October 24, 1938, Craig, a former Chief of Cavalry, famously complained to Lewis Douglas, Director of the Bureau of the Budget, that the "defense of the country ... rests with ground troops." He went on to tell Douglas that the money was better spent on weapons other than airplanes, which had a rapid rate of obsolescence.

As he had been outside Washington, DC during the Army reorganization in the aftermath of World War I, MacArthur was far distant from the machinations that swirled through the service and the nation's capital in the late 1930s and the 1940s. Indeed, he was *very* far distant – 11,000 miles distant. In the fall of 1935, he stepped aboard the SS *President Hoover* in San Francisco, bound for Manila. Except for a brief visit in 1937, MacArthur would not be back in the United States for 16 years. Involving events that lay beyond his wildest imagination, they would be the most momentous years of his career.

I

The Field Marshal's Air Force

The Philippine Archipelago comprises a dozen major islands and more than 7,600 lesser ones, with the largest, Luzon, accounting for 12 percent of its area and containing over half the Philippine population. The Philippines came into the possession of the United States in 1898, ceded by Spain in the wake of the Spanish–American War. In 1935, under the 1934 Tydings-McDuffie Act – aka "the Philippines Independence Act" – the United States granted commonwealth status to the Philippines, stipulating a transition period aimed at full independence in July 1946. As a first step, the Philippine Constitution was drafted in Manila in 1935. To MacArthur's credit, on a visit to Los Angeles in 1937, he famously commented to reporters that he thought the Philippines should be independent by 1938.

A new constitution was adopted, calling for the election of a Filipino president and the replacement of the American governor-general with a high commissioner. Elected as the first president under the Commonwealth was Manuel Quezon, a one-time revolutionary who had surrendered while Arthur MacArthur was governor-general, and who had later served in the colonial-era legislature. Douglas MacArthur had first met Quezon in 1903, and the two men had become friends.

In 1934, based on MacArthur's past experience in the archipelago and his friendship with Quezon, President Franklin Roosevelt offered the post of high commissioner to MacArthur when his time as Chief of Staff was over. MacArthur liked the idea, but two problems arose to scuttle this plan. First, the current governor-general, Frank Murphy, wanted to stay on in the Philippines, and lobbied hard for the job and against MacArthur. Secondly, MacArthur could not accept the civilian post without resigning from the US Army – which he did not want to do.

Roosevelt saw an opportunity. In the meantime, Quezon had come to the United States to enlist American support in building up Philippine defenses. Roosevelt decided that Murphy would remain, and that MacArthur's next assignment would be a two-year stint as "Military Advisor to the Commonwealth Government." Plans were already being made by the end of 1934, but MacArthur's official orders were issued by the War Plans Division of the General Staff on September 18, 1935, less than two weeks before his extended term as Chief of Staff concluded.

In Manila for Manuel Quezon's presidential inauguration on November 15, 1935, MacArthur and his two aides, Major James Ord and Major Dwight Eisenhower, went to work. With a timetable aimed at 1946, MacArthur developed a master plan for the Armed Forces of the Philippines, an entity that officially came into being on December 21, 1935 – having grown out of the existing Philippine Constabulary, which remained part of the Philippine Commonwealth Army until 1938. The headquarters was at Camp Murphy – named for the high commissioner and renamed Camp Aguinaldo in 1965 – on the outskirts of Manila.

MacArthur conceived of the Philippine Commonwealth Army as a "citizen soldier" force based on the conscription model developed by Switzerland, with a goal of an army of 40 divisions, or 400,000 men. The Offshore Patrol (OSP) component of the Commonwealth Army, constituting the commonwealth's "navy," was to be based around shallow draft torpedo boats that could operate effectively in and around the rugged coastlines of the myriad islands. Only two had been delivered when World War II began.

Also within the Commonwealth Army, the Philippine Army Air Corps (PAAC) was created with an ambitious plan of having 250 aircraft, including 100 bombers, by 1946. In fact, when World War II started, the service would have about 50 trainers and fewer than 20 combat aircraft, all of them outdated.

As they had for a quarter century, the Americans continued to assume the lead role in the defense of the Philippines. The US Army chain of command was headed by its Philippine Department, which had been formed in 1911 and which MacArthur himself had commanded back in 1928–30. The core combat unit of the Department was the US Army's Philippine Division, which existed in parallel with the Philippine Commonwealth Army. Three quarters of the Division's personnel were Filipinos in American service. They were members of the Philippine Scouts, a US Army organization, and *not* part of the Philippine Commonwealth Army. The Philippine Department's air arm, based around the 4th Composite Wing, had double the number of aircraft that the PAAC had, but they too were staring obsolescence in the eye.

Meanwhile, the US Navy's small contribution to Philippine defense was its Asiatic Fleet, commanded by Admiral Thomas Hart (as of 1939) and based at Cavite on Luzon. At a time when battleships were the yardstick by which naval force was measured, the US Atlantic Fleet and Pacific Fleet each boasted many of the large warships, while Hart's Asiatic Fleet was comprised of two cruisers – three by 1941 – and various smaller ships.

Japan, with its own large army and navy, and its aggressive posture, was already seen as the major potential threat. This was based on such actions as Japan's adding Korea to its empire in 1910 and its occupation of Manchuria in 1931. Though Japan's full-blown invasion of China would not come until 1937, the Japanese already had troops stationed inside China. Meanwhile, as MacArthur quoted in his memoirs, an internal memo from his staff reported that "the Philippines are overrun with Japanese political spies – businessmen, sidewalk photographers and bicycle salesmen in every small town and hamlet. One is sure to see them." It was not mere paranoia; the Imperial Japanese Army *did* have an ongoing intelligence-gathering operation in the Philippines.

With regard to defense – and possible war – against Japan, the United States operated under the top-secret War Plan Orange (WPO), drafted in 1924 and periodically updated. Under WPO, the Philippines were expected to defend themselves, and American forces would arrive to reinforce the archipelago only when the West Coast and Hawaii were deemed secure. Preparing the Philippines to defend themselves was the role given to MacArthur and his tiny staff.

In his 1967 memoir, *At Ease*, Dwight Eisenhower clarified that from his perspective, the "principal enemy [for the Philippines] was in the late 1930s, not so much Japan, [but] money or its lack ... Ours was a hopeless venture, in a sense. The Philippine government simply could not afford to build real security from attack." Quezon slashed the budget that Eisenhower and the staff recommended by two thirds. In the meantime, though, Quezon looked to the United States for the materiel and the support that his armed forces needed, and he saw that keeping MacArthur happy was the essential element in this.

Part of that happiness came in the form of MacArthur's paycheck. His brevet four-star rank had been terminated when he stepped down as Chief of Staff, and much to MacArthur's dismay, he reverted to his two-star permanent rank with a $7,500 annual Army salary. This would be dwarfed by the stipend he would receive from the Philippine government. According to official documents in the files of the MacArthur Memorial Archives, the Philippines agreed to pay him $18,000 a year, plus a $15,000 personal allowance, and give him the use of the large, air-conditioned penthouse at the posh Manila Hotel.

Quezon even went so far as to insist that MacArthur assume a rank unprecedented for an American officer. On August 24, 1936, in a ceremony at Malacañan Palace, Quezon conferred the title of Field Marshal of the Philippine Army, while Mrs Quezon handed MacArthur a gold baton.

According to an oral history interview in the files of the MacArthur Memorial Archives, Eisenhower said that he tried to talk MacArthur out of accepting this position because it was "pompous and rather ridiculous to be the Field Marshal of a virtually nonexisting army." It had long been assumed that the field marshal idea had been Quezon's, but Eisenhower insisted that it originated with MacArthur. Eisenhower himself was offered a post in the Philippine government, which he declined.

Technically, MacArthur did not now hold rank in the armies of two countries because the Philippines were a commonwealth of the United States. The US Army considered the Philippine Commonwealth Army to be the equivalent of the National Guard organization of one of the states.

Meanwhile, US Army Chief of Staff Malin Craig had made it known that MacArthur would be ordered back to the States when his two-year assignment concluded in 1937. MacArthur liked it in the Philippines and intended to stay on. He announced on September 16, 1936 that he planned to resign from active duty effective at the end of the year. He had promised the Philippine president that he would stay through the end of Quezon's six-year term.

To put it mildly, MacArthur was noted – and notorious – for his flair for the dramatic, but beyond the pomp, ceremony, and gold braid, he took his new job seriously. He worked hard in his efforts to organize the Philippine Commonwealth Army, though problems manifested themselves quickly. When the first 220,000 conscripts arrived for the Philippine Commonwealth Army in early 1937, MacArthur discovered – though he should have anticipated – that they spoke eight separate languages and nearly a dozen times that many dialects. Of these, at least one out of five could not read or write any language. Then, too, there was the fact that the new commonwealth was strapped for cash. MacArthur's staff came up with a $25 million defense budget that Quezon and his field marshal had to slash to just $8 million.

In the spring of 1937, Quezon and his field marshal made a brief visit to the United States, MacArthur's only one during 16 years of living abroad. On the last day of April in New York, he took time out for a city hall wedding at the Manhattan Municipal Building, marrying his girlfriend, Jean Marie Faircloth, a Tennessee socialite whom he had met on the SS *President Hoover* bound for Manila in 1935. He was 57; she was 39. Their only child, Arthur MacArthur IV, was born ten months later in Manila.

Douglas MacArthur spent much of his time in the States lobbying for armaments. As hard as he worked to build his army, MacArthur worked just as hard lobbying distant Washington, DC for help. In *At Ease*, Eisenhower wrote that because the US Army itself was on such a shoestring in the late 1930s, there was little that could be done "for the Philippines without cutting the ground from under US preparedness."

Even if the resources had been available, there was little willingness in Washington to aid MacArthur's faraway fiefdom. With the United States still mired in the Great Depression and domestic issues piled high in the inboxes of both Capitol Hill and the White House, there were nearer fish to fry. Many in the nation's capital – from Maryland Senator Millard Tydings, coauthor of the act conferring commonwealth status to the Philippines, to Interior Secretary Harold Ickes – were anxious to withdraw *all* support from the Philippines. Malin Craig thought that America's defensive perimeter should extend no farther west than Hawaii. These positions were all contradictory to the Philippines Independence Act, which called for the United States to defend the archipelago until 1946. However, under the ambiguities of War Plan Orange, defending the commonwealth had low priority.

MacArthur and his bride returned to wedded bliss in their penthouse, but the groom had little to show for the business trip aspect of the sojourn.

In July 1937, shortly after they landed back in Manila, the Marco Polo Bridge Incident outside Beijing set off the full-blown Japanese invasion of China. By the end of the year, Beijing, Shanghai, and most Chinese ports were in Japanese hands, the Rape of Nanking had occurred, and a dark shroud of crisis descended across the Far East. In the Philippines, Quezon, MacArthur, and those around them were startled and concerned by the ease with which the Japanese overran the Nationalist Army of Chiang Kai-shek. It had been assumed that it would be more effective against the invaders.

Within a year, Hitler had annexed Czechoslovakia's Sudetenland – over Czech protestations, but with the acquiescence of Britain and France – and the world seemed to be edging toward war. By early 1939, Hitler had annexed *all* of Czechoslovakia with mere chastisement from Britain and France. Everyone from editorial writers to people on the street could see war clouds gathering over Europe as the Japanese continued their push against Chiang Kai-shek.

For the Philippine Commonwealth Army, things were progressing slowly. Construction of army camps throughout the archipelago, begun in 1936, continued, but morale issues dogged the troops. Filipino conscripts were paid $7 a month at a time when their counterparts in the US Army were paid $30 – although the cost of living was substantially less. According to 1939 memoranda between MacArthur and Quezon in the files of the MacArthur Memorial Archives, draft registrations had fallen off precipitously, and the Philippine Commonwealth Army had dwindled to just 3,697 men and 468 officers. Two years later, in Quezon's message to the Philippine National Assembly, quoted in the February 1, 1941 issue of *The Philippines Herald*, he put the respective numbers down slightly at 3,665 and 466. The number of Filipinos in the US Army's Philippine Scouts was twice this.

Within the Philippine Commonwealth Army, the Field Marshal's air force was slowly taking shape. A flight school, Zablan Field, was established at Camp Murphy and training began. Its namesake was Porfirio Zablan, a student pilot killed in a crash.

According to Eldon Nemenzo and Guillermo Molina in their history of the Philippine Army Air Corps, the first class began on May 11, 1936 with US Army Air Corps lieutenants William Lee and Hugh Parker as flight instructors. Lieutenant Colonel Dwight D. Eisenhower was one of their students. Lieutenant Colonel James Ord, meanwhile, was killed as a passenger in a plane crash in January 1938 at Camp John Hay, near Baguio, 125 air miles north of Manila.

By 1940, the number of trained Filipino pilots in the PAAC finally topped 100, and the number of training aircraft had grown from just three when the service was born to around 50. Pilot training had a long learning curve. There was a positive spin put on the process in 1937 in Quezon's *Second Annual Report* to Roosevelt and the US Congress, which noted:

> … the first class of pilots trained exclusively at the Philippine Army Aviation School was graduated at Camp Murphy [after a year and a half]. Additional planes were acquired, the flying and auxiliary facilities were improved, and assistant flying instructors were developed from among Filipino pilots. This institution is now ready to begin functioning at scheduled capacity. Air Corps instruction continues to emphasize quality above quantity, but experience to date furnishes ample evidence that the adopted program will assure the availability, at the required time and in required numbers, of Filipino pilots of real aptitude and skill.

The "additional planes acquired" were still modest in number by 1940. The 50 training aircraft included mainly Stearman Model 75 and 76 Kaydet primary trainers, which also served in large numbers with the US Army Air Corps as PT-13s and PT-17s, and in the US Navy under the N2S designation. The PAAC also had a handful of observation planes and a pair of Beechcraft Model 18 light transports.

At the time, the PAAC was the *second*-largest air force in the Philippines, the largest being that of the US Army Philippine Department – which was outside MacArthur's chain of command. As they had been since the 1920s, the operational air assets of the Philippine Department were mainly concentrated in the 4th Composite Group, which contained the 2nd Observation Squadron, the 3rd Pursuit Squadron, and the 28th Bomb Squadron. Operations were complicated by personal animosity between Colonel Harrison Richards, the Department's senior air officer, and Colonel Lawrence Churchill, the commander of the 4th.

Being at a nearly forgotten extremity of the logistical chain, the 4th operated a collection of cast offs from the stateside Air Corps, the largest concentration of which were 28 open-cockpit Boeing P-26A Peashooter fighters. When they had entered service with the US Army Air Corps in 1936, P-26s were the service's first operational all-metal monoplane fighters, but they were soon overtaken by more advanced types. By 1940, the Air Corps back in the States had long since moved on to such aircraft as the Curtiss P-36 Hawk. Richards also had 17 Martin B-10B twin-engine monoplane bombers. The B-10, which reached the squadrons of the US Army Air Corps in 1934, was quite advanced for its day, but by 1940 it was essentially obsolete.

The PAAC, like the 4th Composite Group, survived on hand-me-down equipment – much of it handed down from the 4th. The centerpiece of their tactical effectiveness was a dozen Peashooters. The PAAC also had a couple of Boeing P-12E open-cockpit biplane fighters. Standard equipment for the US Army Air Corps in the early 1930s, these aircraft, with their technological roots in World War I, were now clearly obsolete. On the bomber side of the PAAC combat force, the same could be said of their lone Keystone B-3A twin-engine biplane that had served with the Americans a decade earlier.

The PAAC also received three cast-off Martin B-10Bs. It should be noted that, also in the Far East, the Military Aviation of the Royal Netherlands East Indies Army (Militaire Luchtvaart van het Koninklijk Nederlands-Indisch Leger, ML-KNIL) operated 80 Martin Models

139 and 166 bombers, the export equivalents of the B-10, and would use these in combat during World War II.

It took the war in Europe, rather than the Japanese onslaught in China, to begin the process of American military engagement in the Philippines. The German invasion of Poland on September 1, 1939 brought the declarations of war from Britain and France that marked the start of World War II. The signing of the Tripartite Pact between Italy, Germany, and Japan a year later on September 27, 1940 brought into being the Rome–Berlin–Tokyo Axis, and brought into focus the shape and scale of the enemy that the United States would face if or when it entered World War II.

By the end of 1940, the Roosevelt Administration had begun a military and industrial expansion under the heading of "National Defense." A peacetime draft had been initiated, and the President himself had called for a greatly expanded US Army Air Corps. A trickle of American troops were now also being sent to bolster the Philippine Division, and add to the defense of the archipelago.

In her April 1941 article, "Preparedness in the Philippines," published in the journal *Far Eastern Survey*, Catherine Porter wrote:

> … the early months of 1941 have seen much unusual activity in the Philippines. American military forces in the islands have been steadily augmented; American cruisers have been making large deliveries of airplane parts and munitions; wives and children of United States Army and Navy men have been leaving by every transport. In January the entire island of Luzon, largest and most important in the archipelago, was the scene of large-scale maneuvers of United States Army troops, which were considered unusually significant.

At the end of March a large number of Filipino reserves were undergoing active duty training under the direction of the Philippine Commonwealth Army. The New York *Herald Tribune* wrote that the word "mobilization" was not used lest the term "unduly excite" the civilian population. In the first week of April the annual registration of men of 20 years of age was held. Catherine Porter noted that "it was estimated that some 100,000 Filipinos would register from whom the yearly class of trainees for the reserve forces would be drawn."

Things were moving toward climactic changes. In his February 1941 message to the National Assembly, Quezon had said:

... the Government of the United States has embarked upon a program of national defense which, we earnestly hope, includes the Philippines; for the defense of our country remains primarily the responsibility of the United States. This is as it should be, because so long as we are under the American flag it rests exclusively with the United States, and not with us, to determine whether we shall be at peace or at war.

2

Into the Crosshairs of Calamity

On May 21, 1941, Major General George Grunert, head of the US Army's Philippine Department, wired his boss to request permission to work directly with Field Marshal Douglas MacArthur, the commander of the Philippine Commonwealth Army. Grunert's boss, General George Marshall, who had succeeded Malin Craig as Chief of Staff of the US Army in 1939, assented, writing on May 29 that "MacArthur's support will be invaluable to you in the accomplishment of the difficult task with which you are confronted." This exchange illustrates how poorly coordinated the US Army and the Philippine Commonwealth Army had been prior to this time.

MacArthur, though, was one step ahead of Grunert. He had already written to Marshall proposing that all US Army and Philippine Commonwealth Army activities in the Far East be unified into a single command – which MacArthur, of course, suggested should be headed by himself.

Marshall agreed with him. On July 26, the US Army Forces in the Far East (USAFFE) command was created and Douglas MacArthur was recalled into active duty with the US Army. He traded his field marshal's baton for the two stars of his former permanent rank, though the following day, he was authorized a third star as a lieutenant general. At the time, similar commands – such as Hawaii and the four geographic regions within the continental United States – were three-star commands.

As his chief of staff, MacArthur picked Brigadier General Richard Sutherland, who had been on his staff since 1938, and who served as a sort of gate guard controlling access to MacArthur from his subordinates. MacArthur and his inner circle then turned to preparing the USAFFE for war against Japan, operating under the assumption that the Japanese would attack the Philippine and/or American interests in the Pacific by or about April 1942.

By executive order in July 1941, President Roosevelt called for the Philippine Commonwealth Army to be absorbed into US Army service under USAFFE and MacArthur's command. Roosevelt also allocated $10 million from his emergency fund to train and equip about 75,000 Filipino recruits for the Philippine Commonwealth Army – which had a personnel strength of just 4,131 in February 1941. It was the sort of rapid expansion that MacArthur had attempted without success five years earlier. In the coming months, MacArthur would mobilize ten Philippine Commonwealth Army divisions.

"We began an eleventh-hour struggle to build up enough force to repel an enemy," MacArthur wrote in his memoirs. "The ten-year period so essential for the successful completion of my basic plan was evidently going to be cut in half. Too late, Washington had come to realize the danger. Men and munitions were finally being shipped to the Pacific, but the crucial question was, would they arrive in time and in sufficient strength?"

By the summer of 1941, the Philippine Department, the US Army component within USAFFE, was comprised of 22,532 troops. Of these, 11,972 (up from 6,500 at the start of 1941) were ethnic Filipino members of the Philippine Scouts. The Philippine *Division*, essentially the only US Army field combat organization in the USAFFE, had 10,473 officers and men, three quarters of whom were Philippine Scouts. Other US Army personnel included 5,360 members of the Coast Artillery Corps. Through November, large quantities of supplies, including infantry arms, artillery, and ammunition, reached MacArthur, along with two tank battalions.

The reinforcement of the Philippines was executed under War Plan Rainbow 5, which was introduced in May 1941. It superseded earlier plans, including War Plan Orange, but still left Philippine defense a low priority. Indeed, Rainbow 5 assumed that the United States would enter World War II fighting both Germany and Japan, and that defeating Germany would be the first priority, while the reaction to Japan would be merely a holding action until that was accomplished. If war came, the Philippines would essentially be on their own until the US Navy stabilized its position in the eastern Pacific.

In May 1941, the air assets of the Department were designated as the Philippine Department Air Force (PDAF) and Brigadier General Henry Clagett arrived as the new senior American air officer in the Philippines. By July, this organization had 2,407 officers and men, most assigned to the 4th Composite Group. Nearly 200 additional pilots were added through November 1941, by which time the total head count would be 5,609.

As the Philippine Commonwealth Army was inducted into the USAFFE, the Philippine Army Air Corps (PAAC) component now became part of the command structure of the PDAF. In turn, the PDAF was renamed as Air Force, USAFFE (AFUSAFFE) from August to November 1941, when it became the Far East Air Force (FEAF). Within the FEAF command structure, the V Bomber Command was created to contain FEAF bomber assets, while fighters were to be under the new V Interceptor Command. Initially, each of these commands contained just a single group, but they were formed with future expansion in mind.

In the meantime, on June 20, 1941, General Marshall had authorized the US Army Air Corps to be reorganized as the autonomous US Army Air Forces (USAAF), which would greatly streamline air operations in the coming years. In July 1941, the USAAF chief, Major General Henry Harley "Hap" Arnold, called for a major buildup of air assets in the Philippines. Unfortunately, the bombers that he allocated were still in the pipeline and hadn't been built.

By the summer, the 4th Composite Group, which had long been the core of the PDAF/AFUSAFFE, was being augmented with other units now arriving from the United States. The 17th Pursuit Squadron was detached from the 1st Pursuit Group at Selfridge Field, Michigan, and the 20th Pursuit Squadron was taken from the 35th Pursuit Group at Hamilton Field, California to be reassigned to the Philippines. However, the aircrews initially reached Nichols Field without their aircraft and had to share Peashooters with the pilots of the 3rd Pursuit Squadron of the 4th Composite.

As the airmen in the Philippines had been making do for decades with what they could scrounge, they continued to scrounge. A shipment of nine North American Aviation NA-69s, the strike aircraft variant of the famous AT-6 Texan trainer, which had been ordered by the government of Thailand, passed through the Philippines – and was commandeered by the 17th. They were redesignated in the field as A-27s, this being the USAAF designation for the type.

President Roosevelt also got creative in his effort to help his airmen in the archipelago. In October, he signed an executive order allowing for a shipment of 40 Seversky P-35As that had been built for the Swedish Air Force to be diverted to the Philippines. They weren't exactly state of the art, but they were better than Peashooters. They reached the Philippines with Swedish insignia and manuals that required translation.

In the meantime, the FEAF had started to receive shipments of Curtiss P-40 Warhawks, the standard frontline fighters in the USAAF. In July, P-40B models arrived, and by November, crates filled with the more advanced P-40E variant were reaching the FEAF.

Boeing B-17 Flying Fortress heavy bombers, meanwhile, did not need to be shipped. They could be flown out to the Philippines, albeit with refueling stops. Nine of them, assigned to the 14th Bomb Squadron of the 11th Bomb Group at Hickam Field in Hawaii, were the first to arrive, reaching Clark Field in September. The 19th Bomb Group at March Field, California soon arrived with two squadrons, raising the number of Flying Fortresses in the FEAF to 35, all of them early model B-17C and B-17D variants. Clark was the only airfield on Luzon with a runway long enough for B-17 operations. Del Monte Field – part of a pineapple plantation owned by the American fruit company of the same name – 450 miles away on the southern island of Mindanao, was also available, and some B-17 operations had been conducted there.

On November 1, the 4th Composite Group was disbanded, with its 3rd, 17th, and 20th Pursuit Squadrons going to the recently formed 24th Pursuit Group at Clark Field. The 28th Bomb Squadron was transferred from the 4th to the 19th Bomb Group, and the 4th Composite Group's last squadron, the 2nd Observation Squadron, was placed under the control of FEAF headquarters.

The next wave of reinforcements, including the 21st and 34th Pursuit Squadrons of the 35th Pursuit Group, reached the FEAF in late November, but they arrived without their aircraft and with only half their pilots. The first two dozen of 50 P-40Es that had been promised finally arrived at the end of the month. Another 20 arrived by December 6.

By the first week of December, MacArthur's FEAF had sufficient operational Warhawks to equip four of the five squadrons of the 24th Pursuit Group with 18 each, with between 18 and 35 in reserve. The fighters were all based at airfields on Luzon that were within an 80-mile radius of Manila. Nichols Field, with the only paved runways in the Philippines, was home to the 17th and 21st Pursuit Squadrons. Clark Field, with the FEAF's longest runway, hosted the 20th Pursuit Squadron. Iba Field was home to the Warhawks of the 3rd Pursuit Squadron, while the 34th Pursuit Squadron at Del Carmen Field operated the "Swedish" P-35As. Other, more primitive, airfields existed as dispersal locations, but their facilities were less well developed. Tuguegarao Field in northern Luzon, for example, served the USAFFE summer headquarters at Baguio, but had no combat units assigned.

Also available to FEAF fighter strength was the PAAC 6th Squadron, flying a dozen Peashooters.

In addition to the 35 B-17s at Clark, other FEAF air assets included the nine North American A-27s, several B-10Bs, 18 Douglas B-18As that were configured as transports, a few Curtiss O-52 observation planes, and around 60 miscellaneous aircraft inherited from PAAC, including about 42 Stearman trainers.

On November 3, Major General Lewis Hyde Brereton flew into Manila by Pan American Clipper to replace the aging Henry Clagett, who was suffering from recurring bouts of malaria and a drinking problem. Formerly the commander of the Third Air Force in the Southeast United States, Brereton had been a flyer in World War I, and had been a subpoenaed defense witness at Billy Mitchell's court martial. He was also MacArthur's choice of the air officers that Washington had offered as potential commanders for the FEAF.

Brereton initiated daily B-17 reconnaissance flights over the open water north of Luzon to look for potential Japanese naval movements out of their bases on Formosa (now Taiwan), just 200 miles away. To guard against surprise air attack, Brereton ordered his Warhawks to be armed and fueled, with pilots ready to take off on 30 minutes' warning if Japanese aircraft were reported to be incoming.

"Warning" meant a cumbersome dependency upon spotters located along the northern Luzon coastline watching for aircraft inbound from Formosa. They were linked tenuously via telephone and telegraph by way of post offices to the FEAF air warning center.

Just a year earlier, radar had been a decisive factor in the victory by the Royal Air Force over the Luftwaffe in the Battle of Britain, but this technology was still in its infancy. The state-of-the-art American systems were the mobile Signal Corps Radar Model SCR-270 and its fixed location analog, the SCR-271. They were capable of detecting aircraft at a range of 100 miles if they were at 20,000 feet. However, if aircraft came in "under the radar" at 1,000 feet, they were detectable at a range of just 20 miles.

These systems had been declared operational in the summer of 1941, but relatively few had been deployed and the procedures for their use were not formalized. The SCR-270s installed in Hawaii were operated only for a few hours each day, and direct phone lines to the operator's station were an afterthought. On the West Coast of the United States, SCR-270s were located at only ten sites, and were not yet operating. In the Philippines, several of both types had been delivered, but only two SCR-270s were up and running by early December.

As MacArthur concentrated his air forces in Luzon, he did so with his USAFFE ground forces. Under the command of Major General Jonathan Wainwright, the North Luzon Force contained four Philippine Commonwealth Army divisions, as well as Philippine Scout units, including field artillery batteries and the 26th Cavalry Regiment. The South Luzon Force under Brigadier General George Parker contained two Philippine Commonwealth Army divisions, while Brigadier General William Sharp commanded three Philippine Commonwealth Army divisions in Mindanao and the southern Philippines. The Philippine Division, under Wainwright's command, remained in reserve.

All the preparation, and the planning for a massive increase in both land and airpower in early 1942, came to an abrupt end on December 8, 1941. Across the International Dateline in Hawaii and the mainland United States, it was still December 7, the date which President Roosevelt later said would "live in infamy."

At 03:40hrs Manila time that morning, Douglas MacArthur received a phone call from Richard Sutherland at his penthouse. He was informed that at Naval Station Pearl Harbor in Hawaii, the Japanese had struck the first blow of World War II in the Pacific.

Elsewhere in the Pacific and the Far East, the Japanese made simultaneous air, sea, and/or ground assaults at Guam, Hong Kong, Malaya, Singapore, Thailand, and Wake Island. Within days, the loss of Guam and Wake would cut the aerial supply line to the Philippines, but by then this would be the least of MacArthur's worries. As part of the breathtakingly large number of coordinated attacks across the vast region, the Japanese set their sights on the Philippines.

Sutherland had also contacted Brereton, and the two met at USAFFE headquarters at about 05.00hrs. "I told Sutherland I wished to mount all available B-17s at Clark Field for missions previously assigned," Brereton recalled in his published diaries, "and to prepare the B-17s at Del Monte for movement, refueling and bomb loading at Clark Field for operations against the enemy on Formosa. General Sutherland agreed with my plans and said to go ahead with preparations; in the meantime he would obtain General MacArthur's authority for the daylight attacks."

"All available B-17s" at Clark numbered 19. Another 11 were at Del Monte Field on Mindanao and another five were en route to that base.

Pending word from MacArthur, Brereton understood that he was "to prepare our heavy bombers for action but not to undertake any offensive action until ordered. In the meantime, in preparation for this, Brereton ordered Lieutenant Colonel Eugene Eubank, head of his V Bomber Command, to "mount an operation against targets in Takao Harbor, Formosa, first objective enemy transports and warships, and to prepare three planes for a reconnaissance of airfields on Formosa."

Brereton wrote later, in the notes to his published diaries, that "neither General MacArthur nor General Sutherland ever told me why authority was withheld to attack Formosa after the Japanese had attacked Pearl Harbor. I always have felt that General MacArthur may possibly have been under orders from Washington not to attack unless attacked."

However, MacArthur recalled it differently. In his 1964 memoirs – paraphrasing a 1946 press release from his office – MacArthur wrote:

[Sometime that morning] Brereton suggested to General Sutherland a foray against Formosa. I know nothing of any interview with Sutherland, and Brereton never at any time recommended or suggested an attack on Formosa to me. My first knowledge of it was in a newspaper dispatch months later. Such a suggestion to the Chief of Staff must have been of a most nebulous and superficial character, as there was no record of it at headquarters. The proposal, if intended seriously, should certainly have been made to me in person.

Nevertheless, as historian Louis Morton points out, an examination of the records confirms that a strike on Formosa *was* authorized at 10:14hrs, and that Brereton ordered Eubank to prepare for such a mission later on December 8. Morton also noted that in a December 8 radiogram to Major General Emory Adams, the Adjutant General at the War Department, MacArthur promised "a heavy bomber counterattack tomorrow morning [December 9] on enemy airdromes in southern Formosa." This never materialized.

Brereton had earlier received a phone call from his other boss, USAAF chief Hap Arnold, ordering him to get his aircraft aloft to avoid being caught on the ground in an air raid.

Brereton had already ordered Lieutenant Colonel Harold George of the V Interceptor Command, at his command center at Nielsen Field, to send the 18th and 20th Pursuit Squadrons at Nichols and Clark aloft to investigate reports of inbound Japanese aircraft, and his B-17s to patrol the coastline. As Brereton recalled, by 09:00hrs "when no word was received of any contact with the enemy," he ordered the interceptors to fly fighter cover for the airfields. However, as the interceptors landed back at Clark, news was already coming in that Baguio and Tuguegarao Field were under attack.

In a rare moment of cooperation, the Japanese were sending two rival air forces to attack Luzon that day. As within the United States armed forces, both the Imperial Japanese Army (IJA) and Imperial Japanese Navy (IJN) maintained separate air arms with distinct aircraft types and organization, and with little or no coordination. For Luzon, both air forces were in action, launching about two hours apart. Arriving first, at around 09:25hrs, the 5th Hikoshidan (Air Division) of the Imperial Japanese Army Air Force (IJAAF) attacked targets north of the 16th Parallel, such as Baguio. The strike force of nearly 100 aircraft included Mitsubishi Ki-21 twin-engine heavy bombers escorted by Nakajima Ki-27 (Type 97) fighters.

At 09:30hrs, as the IJA was attacking, the 11th Kokukantai (Air Fleet) of the Imperial Japanese Navy Air Force (IJNAF) took off from Formosa, heading toward the main FEAF airfields.

Brereton had ordered Eubank to recall the B-17s to Clark to refuel for the Formosa mission that was finally authorized at 10:14hrs and planned for late afternoon. At 10:45hrs, bomb loading began for the B-17s on the ground, while two remained aloft on patrol.

Around 11:30hrs the FEAF air warning center at Nielsen Field was deluged with radar reports and sightings of Japanese aircraft over Luzon. Unfortunately, a message teletyped from Nielsen to Clark did not go through.

The first attack on Clark came at 12:35hrs with 26 IJNAF Mitsubishi G3M and 27 Mitsubishi G4M twin-engine bombers coming over at 20,000 feet. Immediately thereafter, 34 Mitsubishi A6M Zero fighters made a strafing attack against the field. Only seven minutes later, another 53 G4Ms attacked Iba Field from high altitude, with 51 Zeros following them at low level. Some of the FEAF interceptors had managed to take off, but they had difficulty reaching the bombers at high altitude.

The IJNAF strike force devastated the FEAF, which, by fluke of circumstance, was mostly on the ground. An hour earlier or later would have made all the difference. Of the 17 B-17s on the ground, a dozen were destroyed and four were damaged. They had been in a neat line along the ramp.

Of the P-40 interceptors at Clark, 34 were destroyed on the ground or shot down. The 3rd Pursuit Squadron returned to Iba low on fuel in the midst of the attack. Only two Warhawks survived this battle. Total fighter losses that day included at least 53 P-40s and three P-35s. Two dozen or so other aircraft, including B-10Bs and B-18As, were lost. Only seven Zeros were shot down, and the Japanese lost no bombers.

Half of the FEAF fighting strength was erased in less than two hours. Hap Arnold phoned Brereton to ask "how in the hell" this could have happened. According to Louis Morton, the "how" answer remains a mystery, complicated by records that would be lost forever, and by incomplete memories of participants with much to forget.

The mauling continued. On December 9, a Japanese attack on Nichols Field destroyed several aircraft and much of the base infrastructure. On December 10, more than 80 Japanese bombers struck the US Navy's main Asiatic Fleet facility at Cavite, igniting enormous fires, and fuel burned. Most of the larger ships had already escaped and were steaming south.

In the meantime, 13 of the B-17s at Del Monte returned to Clark to engage in strikes against Japanese naval vessels supporting the ground invasion of the Philippines. On December 10, Captain Colin P. Kelly, a B-17 pilot with the 14th Bomb Squadron, became one of America's first heroes of World War II. Ordering his crew to bail out to save themselves, Kelly undertook a dangerous attack on the IJN cruiser *Natori* that cost him his life. When the news was relayed to the United States, the story was that Kelly singlehandedly sank the battleship *Haruna*. In fact, his bombs barely damaged the *Natori*.

On December 13, the FEAF could boast another prominent hero as Lieutenant Boyd "Buzz" Wagner of the 17th Pursuit Squadron shot down four IJNAF Zeros in a single mission. He downed a fifth on December 16, making him the first FEAF ace. Not to be overlooked is the fact that some of the Filipino fighter pilots of the PAAC, in their antiquated P-26s, managed to score aerial victories over the Japanese. Lieutenant Jesus Villamor shot down two enemy aircraft.

When it comes to heroic pilots, one who was now coming to prominence was a man named Paul Irwin Gunn. He had served as a naval aviator for more than a decade before retiring from the US Navy in 1939, and had flown with Inter-Island Airways (a predecessor of Hawaiian Airlines) before relocating to the Philippines. When Philippine Airlines was founded in February 1941, he was its first pilot. Ten months later, Lewis Brereton commandeered the airline's three Beechcraft transports, and commissioned Gunn as a USAAF captain to manage them.

Major Japanese air attacks, stymied only by weather, continued on an almost daily basis. Nichols, Clark, and Cavite were hit again and again. By December 13, only 22 P-40 Warhawks and five P-35s survived in flyable condition. Most of the US Navy's Consolidated PBY Catalina flying boats at Cavite had also been destroyed. Just 16 B-17s remained, most of them in compromised condition, and they were wearing out rapidly as they were being shuttled between Clark and Del Monte to keep them from being destroyed. There were no spare engines in the Philippines and aircraft were kept in service only by cannibalizing parts from other aircraft. On December 17, having won MacArthur's approval, Brereton withdrew ten of the 19th Bomb Group B-17s to Darwin, Australia, 1,500 miles to the south.

In the meantime, Paul Gunn had already been flying evacuation missions from Manila to Mindanao, and from Mindanao to Australia in his Beech 18s. Indeed, he flew Philippine President Quezon to Mindanao. Unfortunately, he was never able to fly his own family to safety.

Time was running out. The Japanese began their initial amphibious landings in northern Luzon on December 10 and at Lamon Bay in southern Luzon on December 18. In the south, the Japanese landed at Davao on Mindanao on December 20. The major landing by the bulk of the IJA 14th Army under Lieutenant General Masaharu Homma at Lingayen Gulf on Luzon came on December 22. The 14th Army moved quickly, rolling over MacArthur's USAFFE forces in a series of one-sided battles.

The noose was tightening around Manila. MacArthur was adjusting to the strategic reality. The previous week, he had been elevated in rank – a permanent fourth star – but the area of his command was shriveling by the hour and his troops were reeling. By December 24, he had made the decision to move his headquarters to the island fortress of Corregidor in Manila Bay and to withdraw all of his forces into the 600-square-mile Bataan Peninsula. Here, they would hold out as long as possible for reinforcements from the United States, which under Rainbow 5 MacArthur knew were unlikely.

The United States had also been at war with Germany since December 11 and even as MacArthur was setting up housekeeping on "the Rock," as Corregidor was known, British Prime Minister Winston Churchill was in Washington, DC for the Arcadia Conference. At this meeting, he and Roosevelt, along with their combined chiefs of staff, were confirming the grand strategy of the Anglo-American Allies – defeat Germany first, and merely stop and hold Japan as soon as possible with no counterattack in the foreseeable future.

Manila fell on January 2, 1942, and the battle for Bataan began five days later.

In the air, a few of the Darwin-based B-17s were able to strike the Japanese beachheads at Davao several times through Christmas Eve, but it was too little too late. By then, Brereton had closed his headquarters at Fort McKinley and headed south to Batchelor Field in Darwin to officially relocate the FEAF headquarters there.

Harold George of the V Interceptor Command took control of the surviving FEAF assets in the Philippines – nine surviving P-40s. He then moved his command into the Bataan Peninsula, where five dirt landing fields were now being scratched out of level terrain. Because there were so few aircraft left, most of the FEAF ground echelon men joined infantry units.

On Christmas Day, MacArthur wired Emory Adams in Washington to tell him that "Operations heavy bombardment no longer possible from bases here. B-17s have been moved to Australia and Dutch East Indies bases. Brereton, with skeleton staff departed on the 24th." Ironically, Lewis Brereton of the USAAF left the Philippines flying aboard a US Navy PBY Catalina.

The story of the US Army, its Philippine Scouts, and the Philippine Commonwealth Army in Bataan is both legendary and tragic. Fighting the Japanese 14th Army tenaciously for every inch of ground, they held out on the rugged peninsula for three months, much longer than they or the Japanese expected.

The FEAF fighters on Bataan were used mainly to attack Japanese forces engaged on the peninsula, but on the night of January 26, they conducted strafing attacks against Nielson and Nichols Fields – now in Japanese hands – doing considerable damage. By February, only five of Harold George's P-40s on Bataan remained. While these were used mainly for ground attack missions, in a spectacular final aerial battle on February 9 the Americans downed four Japanese aircraft. By March, only one P-40E and a hybrid cobbled together from P-40B and P-40E parts survived.

Meanwhile, four P-40s survived on Mindanao, including three that were shipped in unassembled by a blockade runner and put into service by April 2. There were also two P-35s that had escaped from Bataan, but these flew back to Bataan on April 4 to successfully rescue three fighter pilots. The last two Bataan Warhawks flew south on April 8, but both crashed while attempting to land. Only one P-35 and two P-40Es survived to be captured by the Japanese on May 12.

FEAF had lost 108 P-40s and 25 P-35s. Only 19 percent were lost in aerial combat, while American pilots shot down 35 Japanese aircraft, and the Filipinos of the PAAC shot down four with their obsolete P-26 Peashooters.

Understanding that the outlook for the Philippine garrison was hopeless, President Roosevelt ordered MacArthur to evacuate to Australia to regroup and to command American forces in the coming actions of the Pacific war.

MacArthur departed surreptitiously from Corregidor on the night of March 11/12. A flotilla of four PT Boats carried him and his family, along with Harold George, Richard Sutherland, and members of his inner circle to Mindanao, where they would be picked up by B-17s and flown to Australia. President Quezon had been evacuated by submarine on February 20, but MacArthur preferred to travel above the waves.

On April 9, as 60,000 Filipino and 15,000 American prisoners of war surrendered and began the horrific Bataan Death March, around 13,000 Allied troops still remained on Corregidor under the command of Jonathan Wainwright, who had now been promoted to lieutenant general. These troops held out for nearly a month until the Japanese landed on the island with overwhelming force on May 5. The following day, Wainwright surrendered Corregidor. Under threat from Homma, who asserted that he would start murdering prisoners of war if he refused, Wainwright went on the radio to demand the surrender of all American troops in the Philippines, including those on Mindanao who had not yet been defeated. The defense of the Philippines was over by the end of the month.

In the wake of the greatest defeat suffered by the US Army since the Civil War, MacArthur picked up the broken pieces of what had been his USAFFE and began to look to the future.

For the FEAF, that new chapter had already begun.

3

For Whatever Came Next

The Far East Air Force, its strength cut in half by Japanese airpower in the first 48 hours of the war – and by 72 percent inside a month – would next be halved geographically by the circumstances of the war. As the handful of remaining fighter aircraft disappeared into camouflaged revetments adjacent to primitive airstrips in Bataan and Mindanao, FEAF bombers headed south to become the nucleus of whatever – it was not entirely certain at the time – was to come next.

With this dividing of forces, Douglas MacArthur and his first wartime air officer, Major General Lewis Brereton, went their separate ways. In December 1941, as MacArthur had set up shop at the fortress of Corregidor, Brereton had gone south.

Under MacArthur's orders, Brereton, along with Lieutenant Colonel Eugene Eubank of the FEAF V Bomber Command, left the Philippines on December 24, 1941, bound for Australia. MacArthur's orders read like wishful thinking. He was to "organize advanced operating bases" from which the FEAF could "support the defense of the Philippines" by the US Army Forces in the Far East – an organization that was even then withdrawing into Bataan for what MacArthur knew was a hopeless last stand.

More realistically, MacArthur told Brereton to "cooperate with the US Navy and with the air and naval forces of Australia and the Netherlands Indies [now Indonesia]." At the time, neither of them could have imagined that, while MacArthur was embroiled in Bataan, Brereton and his FEAF would be spending most of their time over those Netherlands Indies.

The Netherlands had been occupied for a year and a half by the Germans, but the government had not surrendered and was in exile in Britain, while its largest colony – with a land area more than 50 times that of the mother country – along with Dutch military assets there, remained outside Axis control.

The Royal Netherlands Navy (Koninklijk Marine) fleet in the Indies was unaffected by the defeat in Europe. The Royal Netherlands East Indies Army (Koninklijk Nederlands Indisch Leger, KNIL) and the Military Aviation of the Royal Netherlands East Indies Army (Militaire Luchtvaart van het Koninklijk Nederlands-Indisch Leger, ML-KNIL) also remained intact and ready to face the Japanese. Indeed, the Dutch fleet in the Dutch East Indies was on par with Australian naval forces in the area and the American Asiatic Fleet – and their air force was larger than Brereton's FEAF. Moreover, after its withdrawal from the Philippines, the US Navy Asiatic Fleet was now based in the Indies.

It was on the island of Java, the center of administration for the Indies, that Brereton and Eubank made their first stop. Here, they met with Lieutenant General Hein ter Poorten, commander of the KNIL, Major General Henrik Ludolph Van Oyen of the ML-KNIL, and Admiral William Glassford, the US Asiatic Fleet task force commander, who welcomed them aboard his flagship, the USS *Houston*, anchored at the Java port of Surabaya (then Soerabaja).

Before Brereton moved on to Australia on December 29, he agreed to forward deploy the 19th Bomb Group B-17s to Malang, near Surabaya, where they could be used to defend the Dutch East Indies, as well as to fly missions into the Philippines in support of MacArthur. The first such mission, staging through Samarinda on Borneo, would be flown against Japanese shipping in the harbor at Davao on Mindanao on January 5.

When he reached Batchelor Field in Darwin, which was to be the interim FEAF headquarters, Brereton found that only nine of his heavy bombers were operational, with three in the shop and two more that needed to be sent to Melbourne for major depot overhauls.

On New Year's Eve, Brereton pressed on to Townsville, 1,200 miles to the east, and then to Brisbane, 700 miles farther down the coast. Here, as MacArthur had ordered him to do, he made contact with Major General George Brett, a USAAF officer who had just flown in from the Middle East by way of Chungking and Rangoon, to set up the US

Forces in Australia (USFIA), a short-lived, mainly logistical, umbrella command for the trickle of American materiel that had started to arrive down under. Brett was, Brereton recalled in his diary, "disappointed to learn that his command did not include the [FEAF], which was specifically exempted by instructions from the War Department." Nevertheless, the two formed a cordial working relationship.

In Brisbane, Brereton also found that the size of his modest air force had more than doubled – at least on paper. He caught up with Major John Davies and the 27th Bomb Group (Light) – aka "27th Dive Bomb Group." Davies, along with some aircrewmen and the ground echelon, had arrived in Manila in November, but when their aircraft had not yet arrived by the time of the December 8 disaster, the pilots were flown to Brisbane. Their complement of Douglas A-24 Dauntless (aka "Banshee") dive bombers was rerouted, and by late December, they were being unloaded and uncrated in Brisbane.

The excitement, however, quickly faded, as Brereton noted in his diary for January 2, 1942:

> … in addition to the 52 A-24s in the convoy, there were 18 P-40s – and we desperately needed every plane. Inspection showed that they had been loaded carelessly. Some of them actually still had the Louisiana mud on undercarriage and fuselage, reminders of the maneuvers in which they had participated last year. There were no machine-gun mounts for the rear .30 caliber guns, and no trigger motors for the forward firing guns. This latter oversight was known in the States and trigger motors were dispatched, but the B-17s bringing them were caught at Hawaii and ordered to remain there until further orders. The A-24s had no self-sealing gas tanks. Since it was a dive-bomb group, lack of protected tanks presented a grave hazard. As for the P-40s, no Prestone – essential for their air-cooled motors.

Such was the logistical state of affairs for MacArthur's and Brereton's FEAF as 1942 began – but there were other troubles to contend with.

When Brereton flew down to Melbourne – then the seat of government – to confer with Sir Charles Burnett, Chief of the Australian Air Staff, and General Sturdie, Chief of the Australian General Staff, he found that "heavy political and military pressure was brought to bear on me to adapt our plans to the defense of Australia."

As Brereton recalled, Australian authorities had made grandiose promises of "the establishment of assembly and repair shops at Brisbane; a construction, assembly, and forwarding plant for fighters at Townsville; and the construction of a maintenance and general repair depot at Melbourne for heavy bombers."

Throughout December, as MacArthur and Brereton were focused on the Philippines, a much broader panorama of Japanese offensive operations was unfolding all across Southeast Asia. As the IJA 14th Army closed in on Manila, its 25th Army was pressing south through Malaya toward Singapore and its 15th had swept through Thailand and into Burma. Its 16th Army would soon undertake action against the Dutch East Indies. The formidable Imperial Japanese Navy, meanwhile, was threatening Allied naval forces across the region.

The initial Japanese landings were aimed at capturing Sarawak, Brunei, and North Borneo, the British protectorates across the north side of Borneo. The Dutch, who controlled the southern two thirds of the 287,000-square-mile island, expected the other shoe to drop soon. For the Japanese, the big prize on oil-rich Borneo was the great petroleum refinery complex at Balikpapan – arguably the biggest in all the Dutch East Indies.

Even as Brereton had been eating his Christmas dinner in Surabaya, the Arcadia Conference was ongoing in Washington, DC and shaping the global strategic plan. Franklin Roosevelt and Winston Churchill may have adopted the "Germany First" approach to prosecuting the war, giving second priority to the Far East, but the latter was not forgotten in the grand strategy. At Arcadia, the Allied leaders agreed to the formation of an Allied joint command for the distant theater.

It had been decided that the American–British–Dutch–Australian Command (ABDA or ABDACOM) would be officially activated on January 15, 1942 with the mission of stopping the Japanese southward advance. It would be commanded by British General (later Field Marshal) Archibald Percival Wavell, who also headed the British India Command, with General ter Poorten commanding ABDA ground forces and Admiral Thomas Hart, commander of the US Asiatic Fleet, commanding ABDA naval forces – though the ABDA naval strike force was commanded by Dutch Rear Admiral Karel Doorman. The unified ABDA air contingent was headed by Air Marshal Richard Peirse of Britain's Royal Air Force who was flying in from London.

MacArthur was conspicuously absent from the table of organization. ABDA was essentially irrelevant for him. No ABDA army or air force was coming to his aid. Even Hart's Asiatic Fleet had abandoned Philippine waters.

MacArthur had explicitly given Brereton the mission "to keep open the lines of communication to the Philippine Islands [and] to support the defense of the Philippines." However, as Brereton had seen in Java, and discovered in Australia, "everyone in the Pacific except the Americans had written off the Philippines."

As Brereton told the Australians in Melbourne, and his diary on January 8, "action in the Malay Peninsula or the Singapore area was not within the sphere of action [for the FEAF]." Nevertheless, the ABDA chain of command named Brett as Wavell's deputy, and Brereton was ordered by the US War Department to "report to General Wavell for instructions and operate under his strategic control."

During the ensuing six weeks, Brereton went through a series of changes to his role and his assignment. He was designated to serve both as Peirse's deputy and as commander of all American air forces in the ABDA area, and it was suggested that he might assume the role of commander of all United States ground and air forces as Brett focused on his position as Wavell's deputy. Ultimately, he remained simply as the American air commander for the ABDA area, subservient to Wavell's command. Meanwhile, tactical necessity dictated that Brereton's FEAF, or at least that part of it outside the Philippines, was now under ABDA control.

On January 9, wearing his hat as commander of American air forces in the ABDA area, Brereton returned to Java along with Brett and Eubank. They met Wavell in Batavia, the colonial capital, and began the complicated planning for melding armed forces and intelligence services from four countries into a single workable command. It was high time, in that on January 11, the Japanese began their attack on the Dutch East Indies with landings on oil-rich Tarakan Island, just off the Borneo coast. Brereton dispatched seven Malang-based B-17s to attack the landing force, but four were turned back by bad weather.

With the official activation of ABDA on January 15, Brereton closed the FEAF headquarters at Darwin, relocating his staff to ABDA in Java and transferring control of the FEAF airfields at Darwin and Batchelor Field to ABDA control. He then departed for Melbourne to head off a burgeoning crisis. The Australian government, he observed, was "frightened by the rush of the Japanese southward, [and] was bringing heavy pressure to bear to divert American air and ground troops and equipment to the defense of Australia."

Despite this apparent urgency, Brereton discovered in Melbourne that of the promised assembly and repair shops at Brisbane, Townsville, and Melbourne, nothing "had progressed beyond the planning stage."

Exacting further promises, Brereton returned to Java, where his bombers were at work. Now under ABDA control, the focus of attention for the 19th Bomb Group B-17s had shifted westward from the Philippines to targets in the Dutch East Indies. Through the month of January, staging through Palembang on Sumatra, they attacked Japanese positions in northern Malaya.

By the middle of January, they were joined by the first of a trickle of heavy bombers belonging to the 7th Bomb Group. This group had originally been sent to join FEAF on December 6, 1941, and they had just completed the first leg of their flight, from California to Hawaii, when they found themselves attempting to land at Hickam Field in Hawaii in the midst of the Japanese attack on Pearl Harbor. The 7th ground echelon, at sea at the time, was diverted to Australia to wait for the aircraft, which did not proceed past Hawaii, and never did reach the Philippines. Now, they were finally arriving in the Far East, though not under the circumstances they had originally expected. Gradually, a few aircraft at a time, they added 37 of the new B-17E variant of the Flying Fortress, and some Consolidated LB-30 Liberators – the export variant of the B-24 – also arrived. Many of the aircraft were arriving by way of Africa and India, taking the long way around the world.

According to USAAF records, from January 22 through February 3, there were 15 separate FEAF heavy bomber missions flown against Japanese shipping in the Macassar Strait between Borneo and Celebes (now Sulawesi). Of these, four aborted because of bad weather, and only five managed to inflict any damage. On January 28, missions were flown against Kuala Lumpur, the capital of Malaya, which had fallen to the Japanese more than two weeks earlier.

In his diary for January 29, Brereton noted "there was good news at ABDACOM headquarters. A daring naval-air attack on a large enemy convoy off Tarakan in the northern part of the Macassar Strait on 23–30 January delayed the enemy advance southward for at least a week. This combined cruiser and submarine attack was supported by one squadron of Dutch [B-10 variant] medium bombers operating from Samarinda and by American B-17s and LB-30s from Malang."

The 91st Squadron of the 27th Dive Bomb Group arrived at Malang on February 12 with 11 A-24s. On February 19, when an air raid alarm was sounded, several A-24s happened to be loaded with bombs. Two pilots, Lieutenant Harry Galusha and Lieutenant Julius "Zeke" Summers, took off to avoid being hit. Once airborne, Galusha was heard asking, "How about going down and looking for some Japanese?"

They passed through some low clouds and saw a Japanese cruiser and a troopship in the harbor at Bali. As Brereton recalled, "reconnaissance planes reported later that of the six ships bombed by the A-24s, two were sunk, one cruiser was observed pulling a crippled destroyer, and a destroyer was seen pulling a crippled cruiser." Both pilots were awarded the Silver Star.

Brereton wrote that "the men of the [FEAF] Bomber Command were battling against every conceivable obstacle: bad weather, enemy attacks, lack of equipment and personnel, superiority of enemy numbers. But somehow they kept getting their planes off and hitting back."

But the air war cut the other way as well. On both February 3 and 4, Japanese bombers, around two dozen each time, struck Surabaya, and nearly that many hit Malang. A larger force returned on February 5. Having lost several bombers and most of his fighters, Brereton complained in his diary that "there was no antiaircraft on the Dutch airfields, and the air warning service was totally inadequate." He added that "the losses in the 3 February attack, practically wiped out the US fighter force defending Surabaya."

The heavy bomber force, which could barely launch a half dozen aircraft on each of its own missions, suffered losses each time. Between operational losses and almost daily Japanese air raids, attrition was taking a severe toll.

In the meantime, the ABDA naval contingent, including four cruisers and seven destroyers, suffered the humiliation of being attacked and forced to retreat from the Macassar Strait by five dozen IJNAF land-based bombers.

At an ABDA commanders' meeting on February 8, Brereton "stated for the record, that in view of our inability to reinforce the American Air Forces, and because of losses being suffered, the Bomber Command would be ineffective by the end of March." He added that when he proposed "the withdrawal of the remnants of the Far East Air Force, either to Burma or to Australia ... I was criticized by General Wavell and General Brett for what appeared to them to be a somewhat unwarranted and pessimistic attitude."

Brereton wrote that his men were making "a fine effort, but we can't last long without help as the Japanese are coming at us from three directions: west, north, and east."

Indeed, the Japanese onslaught was overpowering and essentially invincible. Though it had seemed like a good idea at the time, ABDA was so desperately outgunned that it would soon prove itself to be a futile exercise in wishful thinking.

British defenses in Malaya, which planners imagined could hold out for a year, were overcome in seven weeks. The last British troops retreated from the Malay Peninsula on the last day of January. Singapore, the great "Gibraltar of the East," deemed an invincible fortress, fell in one week, surrendering on February 15.

In the Dutch East Indies, the Japanese captured Balikpapan with its great petrochemical complex and adjacent oil fields on January 24, thus ensuring the resources that the Japanese war machine needed for its great offensive. By the time that Singapore fell, all of Borneo and Celebes was under Japanese control.

Java, the jewel in the Dutch colonial crown, was the last remaining Allied stronghold, but it was only a matter of time.

As late as February 16, Brereton wrote that "Java is of value to support naval operations in China seas and recapture Borneo, Celebes, and eventually the Philippines," but he added that efforts should not be made "to reinforce Java which might compromise defense of Burma and Australia. The situation was pretty hopeless, but we kept hitting back at the enemy."

On February 18, he reflected:

... fatigue and combat weariness had worn the men to their last ounce of resistance. Pilots returned from attack crying with rage and frustration when a crew member was killed or when weather or mechanical failures prevented successful completion of the mission. A flight commander, a fine leader, committed suicide. Boys were on the verge of mental and physical collapse. I felt that I had every reason to be thankful that I would not be called upon to ask much more of them.

The following day, Brereton received authorization to commandeer all available air transport on Java in order to evacuate Australian and American civilians. February 19 was also the day that Australia itself came under attack. Nearly 250 Japanese aircraft, coming in two waves, struck the port at Darwin as well as Batchelor Field. More than 200 people were killed, and 30 aircraft – including a number of P-40s – were destroyed. In the harbor, 11 ships of various size – including the destroyer USS *Peary* – were sunk. The onslaught, referred to as "Australia's Pearl Harbor," generated a mood of both fear and determination in the country.

At sea, the ABDA naval strike force was heavily defeated in the course of the battle of the Java Sea on February 27 and the battle of the Sunda Strait 24 hours later – and essentially erased in the second battle of the Java Sea on March 1. All the Allied cruisers and most of their destroyers had been lost. The Imperial Japanese Navy had achieved a decisive victory as the Imperial Japanese Army swept through ABDA ground forces like a hot samurai sword through butter.

ABDA ceased to exist on February 25, and its headquarters on Java closed on February 28. On February 24, both Wavell and Peirse flew back to Delhi, where Wavell resumed his post as Commander in Chief, India, and Peirse took command of Royal Air Force units in India. The US Navy's Asiatic Fleet had preceded ABDA in ceasing to exist as an administrative unit on February 5. Admiral Hart was relieved of duty by February 16 and summoned back to Washington for "health reasons." Admiral Doorman, commanding the ABDA naval strike force, died heroically in the battle of the Java Sea.

On February 20, Brereton had told Wavell that he was cabling the War Department to say that "it was against the best interests of the United States to maintain the American Air Forces on Java or attempt any further air operations." He accepted this "with the proviso that we would remain in place long enough to cover the evacuation of those combat elements which would leave the island."

On February 22 – the same day that he ordered MacArthur to leave the Philippines – Chief of Staff General George Marshall gave Brereton the authority to evacuate Java and the broadest possible latitude in deciding his next course of action. Wrote Marshall, "Your own headquarters will be withdrawn in such a manner, at such a time, and to such a place within or without the ABDA area as you may decide, for its timely withdrawal is important … When you withdraw, report to whom you have transferred command of Java."

When George Brett departed on February 24 for Australia, he recommended that Brereton join Wavell and head west to India. Wavell, meanwhile, "expressed the hope that [Brereton] would assume command of the [American] Air Forces in India and Burma." Having been given by Marshall the freedom to decide where next to go, Brereton decided to join Wavell as he returned to India.

Less than a week later, on March 1, Java was invaded in force by the Japanese 16th Army. Batavia, the center of Dutch rule, was occupied on March 5. Surabaya and most of Java had surrendered by March 10.

Lieutenant General ter Poorten, who commanded the KNIL before and during the existence of ABDA, had continued in that role. When Java surrendered, so did he, destined to spend the duration of the war in custody. He, along with Lieutenant General Jonathan Wainwright, who surrendered the Philippines, and Lieutenant General Arthur Percival, who surrendered Singapore, were kept in a series of progressively more inhospitable prisons. These three officers were the highest-ranking Allied prisoners captured during World War II.

Two months to the day after he left the Philippines under orders from General Douglas MacArthur, Lewis Brereton departed the region entirely, riding the coattails – briefly as it turned out – of General Wavell to India. In those two months, many elements of the elaborate Allied command structures, from ABDA to USFIA, had come and gone, and Allied leaders were left pondering how to structure what was left.

4

A Shoestring Air Force

W hen Major General George Brett returned to Australia as ABDA was imploding and Java falling, one of his first tasks was to make arrangements for the aerial evacuation of General Douglas MacArthur from Mindanao.

He took possession of several B-17Es that had originated with the USAAF 7th Bomb Group, but which had been commandeered – along with their USAAF crews – by the US Navy for their hastily assembled and short-lived Southern Bomber Command.

On March 17, 1942, Brett dispatched two of these Flying Fortresses, now officially transferred back to the USAAF and assigned to the 19th Bomb Group, from Batchelor Field. They reached Del Monte Field on Mindanao around midnight, where MacArthur had been waiting impatiently for four days, and loaded their passengers. This was despite concerns expressed by the general about the serviceability of these battle-worn aircraft. MacArthur, his wife and son, his aide Richard Sutherland, and about a dozen others, flew in the aircraft nicknamed *San Antonio Rose II*, piloted by Lieutenant Frank Bostrom. After a five-hour flight, through heavy turbulence and skies filled with Japanese interceptors searching for Allied bombers, they were greeted by Brett in Darwin.

The news traveled quickly. The headline in the March 18 *New York Times* read "MacArthur in Australia as Allied Commander. Move Hailed as Foreshadowing Turn of the Tide." The notion of MacArthur as the Allied commander in the Pacific was already enshrined in the currency of popular culture, though not quite yet in fact.

MacArthur and his party were then taken via Australian National Airways DC-3s to Alice Springs in the middle of Australia. MacArthur's wife – some sources, including his biographer William Manchester, say it was MacArthur himself – declined to board another aircraft, so while most of the group flew on, the general and his family traveled by rail. This would make for a dramatic entrance when their train reached Melbourne on March 21.

According to MacArthur's memoirs, when he deplaned at Batchelor Field, he told a gathering of reporters that "I came through and I shall return." Manchester wrote that he coined the phrase for a hand-written speech he delivered at the train station in Adelaide on March 20 in which he said:

> The President of the United States ordered me to break through the Japanese lines and proceed from Corregidor to Australia for the purpose, as I understand it, of organizing the American offensive against Japan, a primary objective of which is the relief of the Philippines. I came through and I shall return.

He apparently repeated this sentiment often that week, and the media repeated it often over the next several years.

Though he had come through and was celebrated in some quarters, he would also receive disapproving criticism from other quarters for leaving his command at its darkest hour. Nevertheless, the maxim "I shall return" drowned out much of the negativity. It resonated with the American people and with the Filipinos – and it became an effective Allied battle cry. To focus the MacArthur commentary on the positive, Chief of Staff General George Marshall recommended that Roosevelt authorize MacArthur for the Medal of Honor for his defense of the Philippines. It was awarded on April 1, but the citation was read at a dinner given by Australian Prime Minister John Curtin on March 26.

During the month between MacArthur's orders to leave Corregidor and his arrival in Melbourne, the Joint Chiefs of Staff in Washington had been debating the shape of the entity that MacArthur would now command. On the Army side, Marshall had gone so far as to request Brett to ask Curtin to specifically and officially request MacArthur as the theater commander. On the Navy side, Admiral Ernest King,

Commander in Chief of the US Fleet, saw the Pacific as the responsibility of the US Navy and did not want an Army man in charge.

A compromise was reached, and on March 24, the Pacific Theater was officially subdivided into operational "Areas": the South West Pacific Area (SWPA), with all Allied forces under US Army command, and the rest, which became the Pacific Ocean Areas (POA), with all forces under US Navy Command.

When the leadership assignments were officially announced on April 18, MacArthur became the Supreme Commander of the SWPA. This included Australia, the Philippines, New Guinea, the Dutch East Indies, Borneo, and all of the former ABDA areas, except Sumatra and Burma, which were assigned to General Percival Wavell as Commander in Chief, India – later as commander of the South East Asia Command (SEAC). Wavell also retained jurisdiction over Malaya and Singapore, but that was moot. The Japanese controlled these, and they would do so through the last day of the war.

Brett became MacArthur's deputy commander, while also wearing the hat of Commander of Allied Air Forces, SWPA. As this put him in command of both American and Australian air units, Brett's own second in command was Air Vice Marshal William Bostock of the Royal Australian Air Force (RAAF). Brett's earlier command, the US Forces in Australia (USFIA), was reorganized as the Services of Supply, SWPA.

Also under MacArthur as the SWPA theater commander were the Allied Land Forces, which were led by Australian General Sir Thomas Blamey, who had commanded Australian Imperial Force (AIF) in the Middle East until being brought home in March 1942 to organize the defense of Australia.

In the POA, the US Navy would have principal jurisdiction, with amphibious operations in the POA against Japan's island strongholds conducted by the US Marine Corps (USMC). Commanded by Admiral Chester Nimitz, Commander in Chief of the US Pacific Fleet (CINCPAC), the POA was comprised of the ocean and its islands – from China to the West Coast of the United States and north of the South Pacific Area. The POA was further subdivided into the North Pacific Area (NORPAC), the South Pacific Area (SOPAC), and the Central Pacific Area (CENPAC), which included Hawaii. Nimitz kept CENPAC, his largest area, under his direct command. SOPAC, where many of the early battles in the region – Guadalcanal, for instance – were fought, was commanded by Vice Admiral Robert Ghormley through October 1942, and by Vice Admiral William "Bull" Halsey thereafter. US Army units in SOPAC were commanded by Major General Millard Fillmore "Miff" Harmon of the USAAF, and were outside MacArthur's chain of command.

Nimitz controlled a much larger total area, though MacArthur's SWPA had a vastly larger *land* area. Neither MacArthur nor Nimitz appreciated the other, nor the division of responsibilities, both feeling that he should be the supreme commander of everything. Though they agreed to cooperate, a turf war between the two was ongoing throughout much of World War II.

In the meantime, the USAAF had reorganized and numerically redesignated its various subsidiary air forces. The first four numbered air forces were in the four geographic quadrants of the United States. What had been MacArthur and Brereton's Far East Air Force became the Fifth Air Force in the SWPA. The Sixth and Eleventh were existing and future air assets in the Panama Canal Zone and Alaska, respectively. The Seventh was the former Hawaiian Department Air Force. The Eighth Air Force was created to manage the strategic air offensive against Germany from bases in England, and it would become the largest and best known of USAAF wartime air forces. The Ninth and Twelfth were formed in the Mediterranean Theater, though the Ninth later moved to northern Europe. The Tenth was formed in India and was Lewis Brereton's first command after departing from Java. In 1943, the Thirteenth would be formed in SOPAC, the Fourteenth in China, and the Fifteenth as a strategic air force in the Mediterranean. There were no Sixteenth through Nineteenth until after the war. The Twentieth was later created specifically to operate B-29 Superfortresses against Japan and is the subject of Chapter 18.

As inherited by MacArthur's SWPA command in March 1942, the Fifth Air Force had no commander as such, and was directly under George Brett in his role as air commander for the SWPA. Initially, the Fifth Air Force consisted mainly of what was left of the 19th Bomb Group after its withdrawal from Java. The 7th Bomb Group, which had been part of the FEAF under ABDA, had gone to India to join the Tenth Air Force. The 27th Dive Bomb Group, decimated in Java, was disbanded to be reconstituted stateside for the North African Theater.

Lieutenant Colonel John Davies, who had commanded the 27th during its brief time in combat, remained in Australia along with about two dozen of his pilots. Also now in Australia was Captain Paul Gunn, the former Philippine Airlines pilot who had been flying transport missions for Brereton since December, and who was still flying spare parts and supplies between Darwin and Mindanao. Davies and Gunn became good friends, and soon they were collaborating on a project.

The advance echelon of 3rd Bomb Group had just arrived in Australia from the States, and by the third week of March so too had the first North American Aviation B-25 Mitchell medium bombers to reach the theater. When they were shipped, the B-25s had been intended for the Military Aviation of the Royal Netherlands East Indies Army (ML-KNIL), but after Java fell, that organization no longer existed. With a bit of bureaucratic wrangling, they were taken over by the 3rd. The 3rd had no aircrews assigned, so Davies, Gunn, and the men of the 27th took charge.

Gunn had already become something of a folk hero for flying numerous missions in an unarmed Beach 18 to such dangerous locations as Mindanao, Java during the Japanese assault, and even beleaguered Bataan. Now given the nickname "Pappy," because among the Allied pilots, most of them in their early 20s, he was a venerable 42, Gunn was now a legend for scrounging bombsights and weapons for the B-25s. He is especially remembered for retrofitting the bombers with extra machine guns salvaged from damaged aircraft to turn them into potent strafing machines.

Gradually other USAAF bomber units were filtering into Australia. Commanded by Lieutenant Colonel Millard Haskin, the 22nd Bomb Group showed up at Amberley Field, near Brisbane, at the end of March with their four squadrons of Martin B-26 Marauder medium bombers. They were the first combat-ready group to cross the Pacific as a unit. They soon took up residence at bases around Townsville, about 700 miles north of Brisbane, which was becoming a hub of USAAF operations.

All of this was happening at an auspicious moment. Though overshadowed by other events, the fight in the Philippines still raged. Indeed, the beleaguered Bataan garrison would hold out until April 9, and American and Filipino troops were still fighting on Mindanao in early May. Against this backdrop, MacArthur ordered Sutherland to instruct Brett to resume launching air strikes against Japanese targets in the Philippines. These had been discontinued in January because of the distances involved, and the precedence that was given to supporting operations in the Indies under ABDA.

Brett, who was already on MacArthur's bad side for having allowed him to wait four days to be rescued from Mindanao, incurred further wrath by arguing that missions against the Philippines were impractical. They pushed the limits of a handful of already strained aircraft, he said, while they were unlikely to render any serious damage to the enemy. MacArthur's retort, according to William Manchester, was that a bombing mission would prove to the Filipino people that "they have not been forgotten."

In the meantime, General Wainwright, on Corregidor, had requested air cover for ships carrying supplies into Corregidor from the Philippine island of Cebu, which was not yet fully occupied by the Japanese. Brigadier General Ralph Royce volunteered to lead this mission personally. The former air attaché at the US Embassy in London, he had been reassigned to the FEAF in January and had arrived before the evacuation of Java.

The "Royce Mission," as it came to be known, took off from Darwin on April 11, flying 1,500 miles to Del Monte Field on Mindanao with the idea of running a series of missions out of Mindanao over several days before returning to Australia. Three B-17s were accompanied by ten B-25s of the 3rd Bomb Group – one of them flown by Pappy Gunn – which were fitted with external fuel tanks to extend their range. The B-25s would be disbursed to camouflaged fighter fields, while the B-17s operated from Del Monte.

On April 12 and 13, the Royce Mission bombers attacked the Japanese on Cebu and at their main base at Davao on the southern side of Mindanao. Some of the B-25s even flew north to Luzon for a bittersweet attack on Nichols Field outside Manila, once the home of FEAF operations, but now a hub of Japanese air activity.

More than two years would pass before American aircraft again darkened the skies over Manila.

5

Battle Line at Port Moresby

On May 7, 1942, Lieutenant General Jonathan Wainwright had surrendered and was taken under guard to radio station KZRH in Manila that evening to broadcast his orders for all Filipino and American troops in the Philippines to lay down their arms. By then, the Imperial Japanese Army had accomplished the impossible – or at least what any reasonable Allied strategic planner would have called "impossible" when the war began.

Just as the German blitzkrieg stunned its opponents in 1939–40, so too did the Japanese "blitzkrieg" of 1941–42. Yet, the six countries of Western Europe conquered by Germany in 1939–40 comprised a land area that was only a third the size of the land area conquered by the IJA in just seven months. From the Philippines to Hong Kong, from Thailand to Malaya, the Japanese were in control. They had captured Singapore in a week; they now controlled the Dutch East Indies with all its oil wealth. Now, Wainwright – with a gun literally to his head – had surrendered the Philippines.

With 20–20 hindsight we know, too, that May 7 *also* marked the crescendo of the battle of the Coral Sea, which was to be a crucial milestone in the ultimate reversal of fortune for the ambitions of Imperial Japan, but at the time, Emperor Hirohito's war machine still seemed invincible.

On the chessboard of the intersection between Southeast Asia and the Southwest Pacific, both sides recognized that the only obstacle between the unstoppable Japanese juggernaut and Australia was New

Guinea. This island, the second-largest in the world, was divided in two, with its western half being part of the Dutch East Indies, and its eastern half being administered by Australia since 1919 under a League of Nations mandate.

In fact, the outside "control" of New Guinea amounted to just a scattering of outposts along its shoreline. Its unforgivingly inhospitable interior was largely unexplored. The island is more than twice the size of Japan, but in 1942 it had fewer census-counted inhabitants than Kobe, Cleveland, or Coventry – and scarcely half as many as Sydney. In the mid-20th century, New Guinea's largest city, Port Moresby on the Australian side, was home to barely 2,000 people.

In February 1942, the Japanese captured New Britain in the Bismarck Archipelago – only 100 miles *east* of New Guinea – with its strategic port of Rabaul. Meanwhile, there came the largely unopposed Japanese occupation of western New Guinea. Next, the Japanese began working their way westward across the northern side of the huge island.

Any look at a map from the Allied side could see that the next objective for Japan in the region was Port Moresby, which was only 300 miles from the Cape York Peninsula in the Australian state of Queensland. As early as 1938, the Imperial Japanese Navy had begun drafting plans for its capture as part of anchoring the sea lanes at the southern edge of their empire.

New Guinea was essential to the Japanese strategy of containing Australia, though to Australians in 1942, there was the assumption that the Japanese planned not to *contain* Australia, but to *invade* it. Scarcely anyone in Australia believed that an invasion was *not* about to come, and defensive plans were already being drawn up that involved fighting the enemy on Australian soil.

MacArthur, however, rejected this notion. Instead, he adopted a strategy of, as he wrote in his memoirs, making "the fight for Australia beyond its own borders," adding that "if successful, this would save Australia from invasion and give me an opportunity to pass from defense to offense, to seize the initiative, move forward and attack."

The strategy for the Japanese, who *had* the initiative, was to continue moving forward to capture Port Moresby. The initial Japanese objectives were the twin coastal villages of Lae and Salamaua at the head of Huon Gulf, about 200 miles due north of Port Moresby across the Owen Stanley Mountains, from which air support operations could be launched. After these bases were captured in March, the next Japanese moves were to take place across the Coral Sea on the islands of Tulagi and Guadalcanal in the Solomon Islands chain. These islands would position Japanese forces much closer to Australia's east coast. Air bases here could threaten not only Australia itself, but also its ocean supply lines from the United States.

Troopships were loaded and warships assembled for this great undertaking. It was the largest Japanese naval force assembled in one place since the operations across the Java Sea during the latter half of February had erased Allied naval power in the region and rung the death knell for ABDA.

One Japanese invasion force landed unopposed on Tulagi during the night of May 3/4, while the rest, under the command of General Tomitaro Horii, set sail for an amphibious landing at Port Moresby on May 7 under the cover of massive air attacks from three aircraft carriers as well as from the airfields at Lae and Salamaua.

What should have been another installment in an unbroken chain of Japanese victories going back to December did not go as planned. The US Navy's Task Force 17, commanded by Rear Admiral Frank Fletcher, was in the Coral Sea with two carriers of its own and as many cruisers as the Japanese. Two days of maneuvering led to the joining of a remarkable battle on May 7.

The battle of the Coral Sea was unlike anything that had yet been seen in naval history. No ships of either side came within striking distance of the other. Throughout May 7 and 8, the offensive battle was waged entirely by aircraft – mainly carrier airpower. Each side lost one of its carriers sunk, and suffered damage to its surviving flattops, while both sides lost a destroyer. It was a statistical draw, but, although neither side would have thought so at the time, it was a strategic turning point. Japanese momentum, heretofore unstoppable, had stumbled. The amphibious invasion of Port Moresby was postponed twice, then cancelled. Horii decided to attack overland instead.

In July, Japanese troops landed at the coastal villages of Buna and Gona, just 100 miles across the Papuan, or "Bird's Tail," Peninsula to the northeast of Port Moresby. On paper, it looked like a sound strategy. Unfortunately, to travel those 100 miles, they would have to cross the impossibly rugged Owen Stanley Mountains, a mass of steep razorback ridges that includes numerous peaks that rise above 10,000 feet. Virtually devoid of anything remotely approaching level terrain, the Owen Stanleys are covered with thick, tangled jungles growing up through mud and muck.

Initially, the Japanese ground forces would be opposed only by a small number of Australian troops, but their greatest opponent would be the land itself, and it was no friend to the Allies either. At sea and in the air, it was no less challenging, although by the time of the battle of the Coral Sea, the Allies were *beginning* to amass the strength – in both machines and manpower – to blunt the Japanese onslaught. It was far from being the beginning of the end of Japan's juggernaut, but it was, to paraphrase Winston Churchill, perhaps the end of the beginning.

By the summer of 1942, the proverbial "line in the sand," which many had assumed just a few months earlier would be drawn across the middle of Australia, was now a line drawn across a thousand-mile arc of oceans and islands and anchored in the east by Guadalcanal, and in the west by Port Moresby. The Allies were determined that neither should fall.

While US Navy carrier aircraft were taking center stage in the battle of the Coral Sea, the USAAF was otherwise engaged. It will be recalled that this was the week that Java fell, and the Army airmen were still fighting the rearguard actions there. Meanwhile, the Royce Mission to the Philippines, demanded by MacArthur and resisted by George Brett, was still in the planning stages for the following week.

However, the USAAF airmen did play a role in the battle of the Coral Sea with attacks made against the IJN air bases at Lae and Salamaua from Seven Mile Field at Port Moresby. Staging through Port Moresby was complicated by the necessity of refueling the aircraft by hand pumping the avgas from 55-gallon drums. Gradually, the airfields around Port Moresby were expanded and improved, with prefabricated runways made of Marston Matting, or perforated steel planking (PSP), which was manufactured in the United States. Over the coming months, Marston Matting would be shipped extensively to the islands of the Pacific – as well as to airfields across New Guinea – where it was a fast and easy alternative to paved runways.

The missions against these enemy air bases, as well as against Japanese shipping across the 600-mile breadth of the Bismarck Sea, between New Guinea and New Britain, had begun before the Coral Sea battle, and would continue to be the stock and trade of the USAAF in the area for more than a year.

Based at airfields generally in an arc from Brisbane to Townsville, and inland to Charters Towers, the USAAF in Australia in the spring of 1942 consisted mainly of three bombardment groups and three pursuit groups – which were officially redesignated as fighter groups in May 1942.

The 3rd Bomb Group continued the fight with its A-24s, purloined B-25s, and eventually Douglas A-20 Havoc attack bombers. The 19th Bomb Group, which had been in the thick of things since the opening day of the war, continued to operate as the only heavy bomber group, with its B-17s and LB-30s.

On April 5, the recently arrived 22nd Bomb Group, based at Townsville, Australia and staging though Seven Mile Field, ran the first B-26 mission in the Pacific, an attack on Rabaul. This was the first of many, which continued through May 27. For these three-day missions, the aircraft would fly up from Australia on the first day, run a round-trip to Rabaul on the second, then return to Australia on the third.

On June 9, one of the missions flown against Lae by the 22nd Bomb Group was notable for a man who flew as an observer on that flight. In 1942, Lyndon B. Johnson, later President of the United States, was a third-term Democrat congressman from Texas and a lieutenant commander in the US Naval Reserve when President Roosevelt, also a Democrat, asked him to conduct a fact-finding mission to the Pacific.

Johnson reported to MacArthur, asking to be an observer on an operational mission. His request granted, Johnson flew up to Seven Mile Field from Townsville aboard a B-17 on June 8. The following morning, he was assigned to fly aboard the B-26 piloted by Lieutenant Willis Bench, but the observer's seat was taken, so he joined the crew of the Marauder flown by Lieutenant Walter Greer.

By some accounts, Greer's B-26 was attacked during the mission and an engine was damaged by enemy fire. The log book, however, shows the aircraft suffering generator trouble and turning back before reaching the target. Bench's aircraft was shot down with the loss of all aboard. In any case, on MacArthur's recommendation, Johnson was awarded the Silver Star for "gallantry in action," and the congressman reported to Roosevelt that the SWPA deserved a higher priority in the war materiel that it received – both qualitatively and quantitatively.

Meanwhile, the fighter groups were also forming in Australia and becoming combat ready. The 35th, wiped out in the Philippines, was reconstituted in Australia with a new headquarters (briefly assigned to India before moving back to Australia), and rebuilt with new squadrons and personnel. It was joined by the 8th Fighter Group, which reached Brisbane in March. Both of these groups were equipped with Bell P-400 Airacobras, the export variant of the USAAF P-39. They had been ordered by the RAAF, but when they reached Australia, they were taken over by the Americans and thereafter generally referred to as P-39s. The P-39/P-400 was a fighter that was already being considered as obsolescent, though with the "Germany First" doctrine prevailing in Allied strategic planning, they were what could be expected at the end of the supply chain – and were clearly better than nothing. By the end of April, the Airacobras were based in Port Moresby and flying strafing missions against the Japanese at Lae and Salamaua.

The 49th Fighter Group was the first fighter group to reach Australia as an integral unit, with all of its personnel and aircraft. They had shipped out of San Francisco in January, equipped with Curtiss P-40Es and bound for the Philippines. Like so many units thus dispatched, they learned at sea that they had been diverted down under. Once in Australia, about three dozen of the group's aircraft were diverted again, this time to Java aboard the USS *Langley*. On February 27, they were lost when the *Langley* was scuttled after being damaged in a Japanese air attack.

Meanwhile, the unit – still the 49th *Pursuit* Group – was sent north to Darwin after the February 19 Japanese air raids to fly air defense missions. On March 4, Lieutenant Robert "Bob" Morrissey became the first pilot in the 49th to shoot down a Japanese aircraft. That night, as George Kenney recalled, Colonel Paul Bernard "Squeeze" Wurtsmith, the group commander, "produced a magnum of brandy which he announced they would open when the 49th achieved its 500th official destruction of a Japanese airplane in air combat."

On March 14, alerted by coastwatchers on New Guinea's southern shore, nine P-40s of the 49th's 7th Pursuit Squadron intercepted a large formation of IJN Mitsubishi G4M bombers en route from Lae to attack the RAAF field on Horn Island at the tip of the Cape York Peninsula in northeast Australia. The squadron claimed one of the bombers and four of the A6M Zero fighters escorting them – one of which was rammed by Lieutenant A.T. House, who landed at Horn Island with 3 feet of one wing missing. One P-40 ran out of fuel over the Gulf of Carpenteria, but the pilot bailed out, washed ashore, and survived.

The organizational umbrella under which these groups operated was still the Allied Air Forces, commanded by George Brett, now a brevet lieutenant general, and seconded by Air Vice Marshal William Bostock. According to USAAF records, the Fifth Air Force continued to exist on paper, but had not had an assigned headquarters, or an assigned commander, since Lewis Brereton had departed for India in February.

Brett's air forces, both USAAF and RAAF units, were growing and evolving from where they had been when Brereton retreated from the Philippines and Brett himself retreated from Java, but they were still a shoestring force. They were running some offensive missions, but they were scraping together a half dozen bombers here or perhaps a dozen bombers there, and they were still coming up short in terms of truly measurable successes.

To say that MacArthur had lost confidence in his air commander is an understatement. Ever since MacArthur was left cooling his heels at Del Monte waiting for Brett to send a B-17 to pick him up – and certainly since Brett had argued against the Royce Mission – MacArthur's confidence in him had been irreparably ruined. The relationship had soured to the point that MacArthur communicated with Brett mainly through his intractable chief of staff, Richard Sutherland.

Brett was comfortable in his headquarters at Victoria Barracks in Melbourne, so when MacArthur announced that he was moving the SWPA command headquarters on July 20 to Brisbane, 1,200 miles closer to New Guinea, Brett insisted that the capital of the state of Queensland was unsuitable because it lacked adequate infrastructure.

This made little impact on the situation. MacArthur had already asked Chief of Staff General George Marshall and USAAF Commanding General Hap Arnold to send him a replacement air commander.

6

Hitting the Ground Running

Major General George Churchill Kenney received the news on the afternoon of Sunday, July 11, 1942. He had just arrived in Washington, DC from San Francisco, where he commanded the Fourth Air Force, one of the USAAF's four stateside numbered air forces. Reporting in to USAAF headquarters, he met Major General Joseph McNarney, deputy to George Marshall, who told Kenney that he was "going to Australia," and proceeded to paint a grim picture of the situation from which George Brett was being relieved. MacArthur wanted to be rid of Brett, and when he had discussed replacements with Marshall and Hap Arnold, they had settled on Kenney.

Kenney recalled in his memoirs that during a Monday morning meeting with Marshall and Arnold, he was startled to learn that:

> … their analysis of the problems that I would be up against not only confirmed what I had heard from McNarney but sounded even worse. The thing that worried me most, however, was the casual way that everyone seemed to look at the Pacific part of the war. The possibility that the Japanese would soon land in Australia itself was freely admitted and I sensed that, even if that country were taken over by the Nipponese, the real effort would still be made against Germany.

As talk turned to the friction among Douglas MacArthur, Richard Sutherland, George Brett, and their quarreling staffs, Marshall admitted, "there were a lot of personality clashes that undoubtedly were causing a lot of trouble." When Kenney said that he "didn't believe that much could be done to get moving with the collection of top officers that Brett had been given to work with," he was told that he "would have to work that problem out with General MacArthur." It was now Kenney's problem, not that of the Washington brass.

MacArthur's new air officer arrived in Australia at sunset on July 28, having flown out from San Francisco via Hawaii, Canton Island, Fiji, and New Caledonia. He and his aide, Major General William "Bill" Benn, checked into their new homes at Lennon's Hotel in Brisbane, which had become MacArthur's residence a week earlier. Kenney was greeted by Sutherland, whom Kenney had known since 1933, when they were both at the Army War College.

As MacArthur's right hand man, Sutherland was the man to be reckoned with in MacArthur's inner circle. In this position Sutherland had amassed great power, and by all accounts, an ego to go with it. As Kenney recalled, "an unfortunate bit of arrogance combined with his egotism had made him almost universally disliked. However, he was smart, capable of a lot of work, and from my contacts with him I had found he knew so many of the answers that I could understand why General MacArthur had picked him for his chief of staff."

Sutherland proceeded to brief Kenney on all the negative traits of his outgoing predecessor, George Brett, telling Kenney that "nothing that [Brett] did was right … none of Brett's staff or senior commanders was any good, the pilots didn't know much about flying, the bombers couldn't hit anything and knew nothing about proper maintenance of their equipment or how to handle their supplies."

Sutherland added that the Australians "were about as undisciplined, untrained, overadvertised, and generally useless as the Air Force."

The following day, Kenney went down to the SWPA GHQ at the AMP Life Insurance Building, a nine-story structure which had been taken over by the Allies. He called at the fifth floor office occupied by the Allied Air Forces. He talked to Brett, who did not accompany him when he went upstairs to report to General MacArthur.

As Kenney recalled, MacArthur proceeded to tell him about the shortcomings of the air force that he was about to inherit from Brett, adding that he believed that "his own staff could take over and run the Air Force out here better than it had been run so far."

Kenney sensed MacArthur's intense frustration with the entire strategic situation in the Pacific, writing that "he wanted to get going but he hadn't anything to go with."

After a half-hour tirade, MacArthur finally yielded the floor.

"I told him that as long as he had had enough confidence in me to ask for me to be sent out here to run his air show for him, I intended to do that very thing," Kenney said. "I knew how to run an air force as well or better than anyone else and, while there were undoubtedly a lot of things wrong with his show, I intended to correct them and do a real job. I realized that so far the Air Force had not accomplished much but said that, from now on, they would produce results."

After listening to Kenney without expression, MacArthur put his arm on Kenney's shoulder and told him, "George, I think we are going to get along together all right."

Kenney probably impressed MacArthur when he said that he was planning to fly up to Port Moresby immediately to get a sense of the situation in New Guinea.

When Kenney had told Brett of his plans, the outgoing air boss had offered him the use of the airplane that he had commandeered as his personal transport. This B-17D was nicknamed *The Swoose* for half swan and half goose because it had been patched up so many times with cannibalized parts. The story of the airplane had become a well-known element of wartime folklore back in the United States. Indeed, *The Swoose* would be mentioned prominently in the 1943 best-seller *Queens Die Proudly*.

Kenney learned at Port Moresby that the failures of which MacArthur complained had a basis in fact, and that the root cause was the poor weather and poor weather prediction. A large percentage of bombing missions failed either because they had to turn back en route, or because the crews could not see their targets. He watched a mission head out to Rabaul and, ten minutes later, a Japanese bombing mission strike Seven Mile Field while he was standing on it.

He also got a feel for life at the end of the supply chain – the primitive living conditions, the lack of engines and spare parts to keep the aircraft flying, and the mosquitoes that lacked for nothing to keep *them* flying.

A story circulated that one night, a mosquito landed in the dark and was so huge that crews filled it with 20 gallons of avgas before they realized it was not a P-39.

On his way back to Brisbane, Kenney made stops at Townsville and other bases from which the USAAF operated. He found morale low and a chain of paperwork and red tape that ran through Melbourne and still required weeks for anything to get done – even the delivery of spare parts. He returned to Brisbane on August 3, determined to shake things up.

The following morning, Brett left at dawn. He was supposed to take *The Swoose* as far as Hawaii and send it back, but he took it on to Washington, where it was commandeered for a war bond tour. Its pilot, Colonel Frank Kurtz, a two-time Olympic swimmer (1932 and 1936), became a minor celebrity for having made several record-time Pacific crossings – including his chauffeuring of Lyndon Johnson – in the aircraft. Plane and pilot became so closely identified that Kurtz named his only daughter – future Hollywood star Swoosie Kurtz – after the B-17D.

Kenney assumed command of Allied Air Forces as soon as Brett left on August 4. As his first action, Kenney planned a maximum effort raid on the Japanese bomber base at Vunakanau near Rabaul. He told MacArthur that he planned to put 16–18 B-17s of the 19th Bomb Group over this airfield on August 7 – to coincide with the landing on Guadalcanal by the US Marine Corps. He found MacArthur "very enthusiastic."

That afternoon, however, orders came down from the SWPA headquarters concerning air support of the South Pacific Area Command for the Guadalcanal operation. Kenney was dismayed to learn that "instead of ordering the Allied Air Forces to support the show by a maximum effort against the Japanese airdromes in the Rabaul area," the Allied Air Force was tasked with "maintaining reconnaissance."

This precipitated a showdown between Kenney and MacArthur's gatekeeper.

As Kenney recalled, he told Sutherland that he was running the Air Force because "I was the most competent airman in the Pacific and that, if that statement was not true, I recommended that he find somebody that was more competent and put him in charge… Let's go in the next room, see General MacArthur, and get this thing straight. I want to find out who is supposed to run this Air Force."

It was Sutherland who blinked, rescinding the orders while complaining that he was used to writing orders for the Air Force because nobody on Brett's staff would do it.

As it turned out, 18 heavy bombers, led by Lieutenant Colonel Richard Carmichael, launched on the April 7 mission and 13 reached the target. Only one was shot down by the Zeros that intercepted them, but others turned back due to other causes. Kenney's recollection was that the B-17s destroyed around 75 enemy aircraft on the ground. In any case, the mission disrupted the ability of the IJNAF to interfere with the landings on Guadalcanal.

It was still a two-sided war. Ten days later, Japanese bombers destroyed 11 aircraft and 200 drums of fuel at Seven Mile Field, leaving a number of time-delay bombs that continued to explode for two days.

In the meantime, Kenney had begun the work of reorganizing the Allied Air Force. Retaining it as an umbrella, he moved away from the integrated American–Australian joint command structure, going back to having parallel American *and* Australian components with distinct chains of command.

On the American side, he revived the Fifth Air Force – which had been leaderless since Lewis Brereton's departure – and assumed command of it, as well as retaining command of the Allied Air Forces headquarters. As his deputy at Allied Air Forces, Kenney picked recently arrived Brigadier General Ennis "Whitey" Whitehead, while Brigadier General Donald Wilson became Kenney's chief of staff. RAAF Air Vice Marshal William Bostock, who had been Brett's chief of staff, took over as head of the parallel Australian component. Kenney then closed down the sprawling bureaucracy that Brett had built up in Melbourne, streamlined the logistics process, and moved everything to Brisbane.

Within his Fifth Air Force, Kenney reactivated the V Fighter Command and V Bomber Command and picked Paul Wurtsmith of the 49th Fighter Group, now a brigadier general, and Brigadier General Kenneth Walker, respectively, to command them. Wurtsmith had arrived in the SWPA as combat commander, but Walker, like Whitehead, was a staff officer who had come to Australia shortly before Kenney.

On paper, the Fifth Air Force had more than 500 aircraft, but this included many that were awaiting repair, or even being salvaged for parts. Kenney reckoned that there were only 75 fighters and 43 heavy bombers, along with 37 B-25 and B-26 medium bombers, that were combat capable. With the organizational issues within his chain of command under control, Kenney would now need to get his combat forces into shape.

Among the fighters, standard equipment for the Fifth Air Force remained the Curtiss P-40 Warhawks, though a number of P-39 and P-400 Airacobras were still in service. By late summer, faster and more capable twin-engine Lockheed P-38 Lightnings had started to reach Australia. The 35th Fighter Group forward deployed to New Guinea in July 1942, with the 8th following in September. The 49th remained at Darwin, mainly in an air defense role, before moving north to Port Moresby in October.

Most of Bostock's RAAF fleet consisted of trainers or aircraft earmarked for antisubmarine patrols. However, the RAAF deployed two fighter squadrons, No. 75 and No. 76, and an attack squadron, No. 4, to Port Moresby. Each fighter squadron was equipped with around 25 Curtiss Kittyhawks, the export variant of the USAAF P-40, while No. 4 flew Commonwealth Wirraways.

As Kenney turned to offensive operations against the Japanese, the central focus was against the shipping that was necessary for maintaining and supplying their forces in New Guinea and Rabaul. This led to the development of "skip bombing," which was to become a signature of Fifth Air Force operations. In his memoirs, Kenney described what this tactic involved:

> … dropping a bomb, with a five-second-delay fuse, from level flight at an altitude of about fifty feet and a few hundred feet away from a vessel, with the idea of having the bomb skip along the water until it bumped into the side of the ship. In the few seconds remaining, the bomb should sink just about far enough so that when it went off it would blow the bottom out of the ship.

The technique had originated with the British RAF in operations against the Germans in the North Sea. Beginning in 1941, the USAAF began studying the procedure at Eglin Field in Florida, which had become a center for the evaluation of weapons and tactics. Shortly before going overseas with Kenney, Bill Benn had observed the skip-bombing tests at Eglin, and he thought the method would be ideal for the Fifth Air Force.

Kenney and Benn had discussed skip bombing as they crossed the Pacific, and they had even arranged for tests using a borrowed B-26 during their stopover in Fiji. Once in the SWPA, they continued their testing and training program using the shipwrecked SS *Pruth*, which was hung up on a reef offshore from Port Moresby.

For high-altitude bombing, the Fifth Air Force had only the handful of aircraft of the 19th Bomb Group, for which the adjective "war-weary" was an understatement in the extreme. Back in March, these B-17s had been so shopworn that MacArthur had been apprehensive to fly in one, and they had been heavily worked since.

Adding to this arsenal of heavy bombers was like pulling teeth – one or two at a time. The advance echelon of the 43rd Bomb Group had arrived without aircraft, but slowly more heavy bombers flew in. They came mostly from the west, having been ferried across the Atlantic, across Africa, and then across South Asia, gradually filling out the 63rd Bomb Squadron, the 43rd's first squadron. On August 24, when Bill Benn told Kenney that 11 B-17s were on hand with the 63rd, Kenney relieved him of duty as his aide and reassigned Benn to take command of the squadron. He planned to attach it to the 19th while the 43rd was building up its strength.

The following day, the Japanese made a move. Having chosen to abandon their effort to make an amphibious landing at Port Moresby in May, they did so at Milne Bay, the easternmost point on New Guinea, about 360 miles southeast of their base at Lae, and about 250 miles west of Port Moresby. Since June, the Allies had been fortifying this location, and a series of airfields had been constructed for the use of the RAAF.

This led to the Japanese attempt to seize Milne Bay, but their planning was uncovered through the top-secret work of codebreakers hacking into the Japanese Naval Ciphers. MacArthur reinforced Milne Bay with an infantry brigade and Kenney had his P-40s, B-25s, and B-26s overhead when about 2,000 IJN Special Naval Landing Forces came ashore. In the ensuing battle, which lasted through the first week of September, Australian and American ground troops defeated the

Japanese and forced them to withdraw. In his memoirs, MacArthur wrote that they "had fallen into the trap with disastrous results." It was the biggest Japanese defeat in a land battle to date in the Pacific.

However, the fighting in the hellish terrain of the Owen Stanley Mountains continued. The major established trail then in use between Port Moresby and the Japanese beachhead bases at Buna and Gona on the north side was the arduous Kokoda Track, which climbs, often nearly vertically, to 3,380 feet and winds for around 65 miles through some of the most difficult terrain anywhere. The thick and tangled jungle clinging to the steep hillsides favored neither the Japanese attackers, nor the Australian defenders, presenting one of the most difficult and exhausting battlefields of World War II.

Kenney's air campaign, which had been focused on attacking north shore Japanese airfields from Lae and Salamaua to Buna and Gona, was expanded to include strafing and bombing attacks on Japanese troops making their way along the Kokoda Track.

As skip bombing became effective against shipping, the Fifth Air Force used parachute fragmentation bombs in the airfield attacks. A large quantity of these had been delivered to Australia by the summer of 1942, though there were no bomb racks capable of accommodating such ordnance.

Enter Pappy Gunn, already something of a folk legend around the SWPA. Kenney's description of him as a "gadgeteer par excellance" summarized his role in the Fifth Air Force. He had already designed a quad-.50-caliber machine gun assembly for the noses of medium bombers that would also fit an A-20, and he quickly turned his attention to designing racks for the "parafrag" bombs. He had 16 A-20s thus equipped inside two weeks.

Captain Don Hall of the 3rd Bomb Group's 89th Bomb Squadron led nine A-20s in the first parafrag mission of the war on September 12, destroying 17 of the 22 Japanese aircraft on the ground at Buna. The A-20 attack was followed up with strikes by B-26s and B-17s dropping conventional 1,000-pound bombs. Pleased with the results, Kenney ordered Ken Walker to repeat the strikes, next hitting Lae and Salamaua, and he wired Hap Arnold to send him an additional 125,000 parafrags.

Another method of destroying Japanese aircraft on the ground was invented in the field. It involved wrapping 300-pound and 500-pound general purpose bombs with heavy steel wire. "They looked good," Kenney recalled. He continued:

> The wire, which was nearly one-quarter inch in diameter, broke up into pieces from six inches to a couple of feet long, and in the demonstration it cut limbs off trees a hundred feet away which were two inches thick. The noise was quite terrifying. The pieces of wire whirling through the air whistled and sang all the notes on the scale and wailed and screamed like a whole tribe of disconsolate banshees.

Kenney also was about to become a pioneer in the use of tactical airlift.

MacArthur had "decided that the moment had come for a counterdrive that would clear the enemy from eastern [New Guinea]." His plan for his this counterdrive involved a three-pronged offensive – a frontal assault via the Kokoda Track, a wide flanking maneuver to the east of the Track, and a march westward from Milne Bay along the north shore of the Papuan Peninsula – converging on Buna and Gona.

Australian General Sir Thomas Blamey, the Allied Land Forces commander, would be in direct command of the operation on the ground in New Guinea, which would involve not only the 6th and 7th Australian Divisions, but also the US Army 32nd and 41st Infantry Divisions, which had arrived in Australia and were organized within MacArthur's I Corps, commanded by Lieutenant General Robert Eichelberger. To move these troops to New Guinea, Kenney told MacArthur that he could do by air in hours what would take days by ship.

Kenney recalled:

> General MacArthur asked me how many men I would lose flying them from Australia to New Guinea. I told him that we hadn't lost a pound of freight yet on that route and that the airplanes didn't know the difference between 180 pounds of freight and 180 pounds of infantryman. The General said he hated to hear his doughboys compared to freight but for me to fly a company up there and we would see how long it took and how the scheme worked out.

Having convinced MacArthur that it could be done, Kenney then set about scraping together the transport aircraft to do it. The USAAF 21st

Troop Carrier Squadron had been activated in April 1942 (originally as the 21st Transport Squadron) at Brisbane's Archerfield Airport, and it had a collection of Douglas C-47 Skytrains, as well as Lockheed C-56 and C-60 Lodestars and other types of twin-engine transports. There were even B-18 bombers, and Kenney took some B-17s off their bombing operations to fly troops. He then convinced Australian Civil Aviation Minister Samuel Drakeford to help him secure the use of a dozen airliners from Australian civilian airlines.

On the morning of September 15, the airlift began with a company of the 32nd Division's 126th Infantry Regiment flying out of Amberley Field, near Brisbane. By that evening, Kenney was able to report to MacArthur that everyone who had departed was safely on the ground at Port Moresby. The rest of the 126th went by ship, but MacArthur okayed the idea of flying the entire 128th Infantry to New Guinea. Kenney began commandeering civil transports that arrived from the United States, "civilian ferry crews and all."

He told a story of how two B-17s, "replacements from the United States flown by civilian crews who belonged to the Boeing Aircraft Company, landed at Amberley Field." Kenney continued the account:

> They got out of the planes and asked how they could get into town. I told them the next town they saw would be Port Moresby, New Guinea, as I was loading thirty doughboys in each of those B-17s and they were to fly them to the war at the rate of one load every twenty-four hours. They were tickled to death at the idea of taking part in the show.

Kenney said MacArthur, who flew up to Port Moresby to observe the men of the 128th arriving by air, was "happy as a kid at the way the movement was going." In his own memoirs, MacArthur proudly called this "the first large scale airborne troop movement by United States forces in any theater of operations."

On Kenney's return to Brisbane, he learned from Ken Walker that the last of the 128th Infantry had reached Port Moresby. A total of around 4,500 men had been carried up by air. He smiled when he learned that the balance of the 126th was still at sea, and not due to arrive there for another two days. He continued to smile as he went upstairs to MacArthur's office to share the news about the success of his airlift with his boss. Kenney released the civilian ferry pilots with his thanks and let Drakeford know that he could have his airliners back – for now.

Kenney continued to lobby MacArthur on the idea of using tactical airlift to transport troops across the Owen Stanleys from Port Moresby to Wanigela Mission on the north coast about halfway between Milne Bay and Buna. This would cut down on the time it would take to march to Buna. The swampy coastline on the north side of the Papuan Peninsula was largely uncharted, with numerous shoals that would prevent naval operations close to shore, so an amphibious landing was out of the question, but on land, there were no Japanese in the Wanigela area, and it was wide open. Fifth Air Force airmen had surveyed the area around Wanigela from the air and had determined that the meadows in the area could be turned into landing fields. Kenney even suggested that he could move the whole 32nd Division by air.

MacArthur's inner circle, especially Sutherland, were strongly opposed to a Wanigela airlift. Kenney complained, "It was too bad that his staff hadn't his vision and intelligence. They were the stumbling blocks, not MacArthur."

In the meantime, Kenney learned on September 21 that his *other* boss, General Hap Arnold, the commanding general of the USAAF, was on a secret fact-finding mission to the South and Southwest Pacific. He was currently in New Caledonia conferring with the SOPAC theater commander there, Vice Admiral Richard Ghormley, and he was due in Brisbane to meet Douglas MacArthur on September 25.

When Kenney saw that Arnold was also planning to fly up to have a look at Port Moresby, he promptly rearranged his itinerary. He complained:

> … the worst thing about his schedule was that, in addition to broadcasting it to the whole world, it called for his flying from Townsville to Port Moresby and from there to Guadalcanal in daylight in an unarmed airplane. I rearranged his schedule so that these two flights would be at night. His staff didn't use their heads very well, unless they wanted the Japanese to pull an interception on the Old Man.

Kenney met Arnold and his aide, Major General St. Clair Streett, at Amberley Field, and explained that he had modified his schedule and why, recalling that Arnold "looked a little sheepish and said, 'Okay.'"

Kenney then escorted him into MacArthur's office.

Perhaps influenced by the dangerous scenario painted by his theater air boss, Arnold's impression of MacArthur was of a man on the edge. In his diary that day, Arnold wrote that "thinking it over, MacArthur's two hour talk gives me the impression of a brilliant mind, obsessed by a plan he can't carry out; frustrated, dramatic to the extreme, much more nervous than when I formerly knew him, hands twitch and tremble, shell-shocked."

Arnold proceeded to tick off a series of impressions of MacArthur's commentary. On the tactical situation in New Guinea, he wrote that "MacArthur does not have the troops to hold Japanese, only two Divisions, and those partially trained. Australians are not even good militia. Navy support is nil."

Of the strategic situation in the Pacific, MacArthur conveyed the gloomy pronouncement that the Japanese "can take New Guinea at will, can take Fiji, will then control [the] Pacific for one hundred years."

When it came to the USAAF role in the Pacific, Kenney would have been pleased to know that MacArthur thought that "air has passed from below average under Brett to excellent under Kenney; Walker and Whitehead outstanding; [MacArthur] would not exchange Air Force units for any others."

Arnold's own impressions of Kenney, shared with his diary during his visit, were that "he is a real leader and has the finest bunch of pilots I have seen. All those who were worn out and nervous wrecks are now eager to fight and withdrawing their requests to go home."

After the meeting with MacArthur, Kenney and Arnold spent the remainder of the day going through Kenney's shopping list of needs and wants. MacArthur had told Arnold to give Kenney "anything he wanted," but Arnold chilled the enthusiasm by telling him that no more fighter or bomber groups would be assigned to the Fifth Air Force. Kenney did manage to talk Arnold into a one-for-one swap. Kenney explained that the 19th Bombardment Group, which had been through the worst of the shoestring campaigns in the Philippines and Java, "would have to be pulled out, both combat and ground crews.

They were so beaten down that psychologically they were not worth fooling with."

After he met them, Arnold described the men of the 19th as "war weary; pilots experienced but indifferent; been in war since the Philippines but individualists; too many stars; know all the answers."

Kenney asked to trade the 19th for the 90th Bombardment Group, which was then based in Hawaii, and Arnold agreed. In fact, while the 90th did come to New Guinea, Kenney sent the officers, men, and headquarters of the 19th home, but kept its B-17s. Back in the States, the 19th was rebuilt from the ground up. It would return to the Pacific in late 1944 as a B-29 unit.

Arnold went on to say that he would do his best to provide the Fifth Air Force with replacement aircraft, although he cautioned Kenney that "every time an airplane came out of the factory about ten people yelled for it, with the European Theater getting the first call."

When it came to tactics, Kenney brought up a memo from Arnold's office which had arrived the week before. It complained that Kenney should not be attacking Japanese airfields, but should concentrate on Japanese shipping at the Port of Rabaul, which was within range of B-25s and B-26s flying from Port Moresby.

Kenney proceeded to explain that "bombing airdromes had given me control of the air over New Guinea, allowed me to mess up the Japanese advance over the Kokoda trail, and air-drop supplies to feed the Australian troops there, had deprived the Japanese of air support at Milne Bay, and had made Port Moresby almost a rear area rest camp."

He also reminded Arnold that "on the map it might show that Rabaul was in range from Port Moresby [but] after the B-26 had climbed over the 13,000-foot Owen Stanley range with a load of bombs it just did not have enough gas left to make the trip and get back home."

Finally, Kenney treated Arnold to a description of the unexpectedly successful airlift operations, and an outline of the scheme to fly an entire division across the Owen Stanleys.

"More power to you," Arnold laughed. "If you can put it across, I'll get you some more transports somehow, if I have to steal them."

The Fifth Air Force boss then escorted the commanding general to New Guinea and – along with Richard Sutherland representing MacArthur – flew with him as he returned eastward to Noumea in New Caledonia. Here, there would be more talks with Ghormley, and with Major General Miff Harmon, the USAAF man who commanded US Army forces in SOPAC. Admiral Chester Nimitz, commander of the Pacific Fleet and the entire Pacific Ocean Areas, was also present. Despite the optimism expressed by men such as Kenney, the mood was gloomy. In SOPAC, American troops were on Guadalcanal, but so too was the enemy and the US Navy was taking serious hits in nearby naval actions. Ghormley was especially pessimistic, and like George Brett two months earlier, his days were numbered. Kenney observed that he "looked tired and was tired." Nimitz would soon replace him with Bull Halsey.

As Arnold wrote in his diary on September 27, "It's the seniors who are jittery; the juniors have no doubts and are positive of the action that must be taken."

7

Closing in on Buna and Gona
by Land, Air, and Airlift

Through September and October 1942, the positive action taken by MacArthur's Fifth Air Force saw it gradually moving from being completely outclassed by the enemy air forces to holding its own and being able to make claims of having tipped the balance in the skies over New Guinea.

Nobody talked about fighting the Japanese inside Australia any more. Japanese air raids on the growing complex of bases around Port Moresby, once conducted with virtual impunity, now came less often and at a much higher cost.

As the Fifth Air Force medium bombers and A-20s continued their missions against the Japanese on New Guinea's north shore, and their sorties in support of the Allied advances on the Kokoda Track, the B-17s were tasked with stepping up the raids on Rabaul. In both Washington and Tokyo, the respective war leaders perceived this port as the logistics hub for Japanese forward momentum throughout both the SWPA and the SOPAC – and they were right. Though Rabaul was in the SWPA, the loudest calls for action came from the SOPAC commanders, Ghormley and Harmon, whose Marines and soldiers were on the line in Guadalcanal. Bill Benn's 63rd Bomb Squadron had first hit Rabaul's harbor on September 19 and continued to lead the way into October.

In addition to Rabaul, Fifth Air Force B-17s were also asked by SOPAC to conduct raids on Faisi and other harbors on the southern end of the island of Bougainville, about 325 miles southeast of Rabaul, and about the same distance northwest of Guadalcanal.

It soon became clear that the skip-bombing technique was producing better results against ships than traditional high-altitude strikes, but the latter tactics remained useful for attacks on the airfields, such as Vunakanau, around Rabaul.

On the night of October 23, a half dozen bombers attacked from 10,000 feet, but as the Japanese oriented their antiaircraft guns to address this threat, another half dozen bombers came in at 100 feet to skip-bomb the ships in the harbor. They sank a destroyer with two bombs amidships, and claimed some transports and other warships – including a cruiser – sunk or damaged. MacArthur personally awarded Benn the Distinguished Service Cross, and Ken Walker picked him as his chief of operations at V Bomber Command.

On some Rabaul missions, the strike package included as many as 30 heavy bombers, a far cry from earlier in the year when a half dozen would have been a good showing. During October, Benn's 63rd dropped more bomb tonnage than the rest of the Fifth combined. By the end of the month, Colonel Roger Ramey, whom Kenney described as "a real leader," had arrived to command the 43rd Bomb Group, parent of the 63rd Bomb Squadron, as well as of the 64th Bomb Squadron, which had just become operational.

On October 5, meanwhile, the 21st Troop Carrier Squadron began flying Allied troops into airstrips at Wanigela Mission that had been hacked out of the tall kunai grass the day before. An entire thousand-man Australian battalion, part of the 18th Brigade, was on the ground by sunset along with American engineers who would begin the construction of more permanent air base facilities. Fifth Air Force records show that the whole brigade was airlifted a day later. General Thomas Blamey, the ground forces commander in New Guinea who had supported this operation over the skepticism of many, was pleased. It did not hurt that no Japanese resistance was encountered.

Nearly a thousand troops of the US Army's 128th Infantry Regiment of the 32nd Division arrived on October 14. Others followed during the ensuing days and the regiment began its march westward toward the Japanese stronghold at Buna. Major General Forrest Harding, commanding the 32nd, told Kenney the following day that "the Air

Force had really opened [my] eyes to what could be done with airplanes … I'm drinking the same stuff you guys are these days [referring metaphorically to morale]. I don't know what it is or what it is going to do to me, but it sure tastes good."

After a 50-mile march, most of the way to Buna, the men of the 128th located a place at Pongani where another airfield of sufficient length for a C-47 could be established, and they hacked one out of the tall grass. By November, the 126th Infantry would follow by air, and would establish its headquarters at Pongani.

By the end of October, a larger potential airfield site was located at Dobodura, which was inland and less than 10 miles from Buna. Engineers were flown in and they went to work on what was to become one of the most important Fifth Air Force bases in New Guinea.

Despite the promising operations for Fifth Air Force in the SWPA, attrition was taking its toll on its inventory of aircraft. Some were obviously being lost to enemy action, but others to "friendly fire." What Hap Arnold had not said when he had generously promised replacement aircraft to the SWPA was that he had made the same promise to SOPAC – and because the replacement aircraft passed *through* SOPAC en route to Australia, Ghormley and Harmon could requisition any aircraft that they might need in an "emergency," even if it was earmarked for the SWPA. In October, Kenney noted having lost 15 fighters and some B-17s this way. He also lost ten C-47s that he badly needed to keep up his airlift operations to the north side of the Papuan Peninsula.

Meanwhile, MacArthur complained to George Marshall, telling him that he was "in constant communication with Ghormley coordinating my reconnaissance with his and giving in to his requests for attack." MacArthur continued, "Planes capable of affecting his situation have been used exclusively to that end. Three times within the past week I have ordered missions at Ghormley's request, using every bomber available during the period. My own operations in New Guinea have been supported only by short-range aircraft."

There was also bad news regarding the 90th Bomb Group, which Arnold had promised to relocate from Hawaii. The 90th started arriving during the third week of October with its Consolidated B-24 Liberator heavy bombers, but they were found to have cracks in their nose wheel collars. Welding these only produced more cracking, so replacements had to be ordered from the factory in San Diego, and the time it took for delivery would sideline the 90th.

In turn, when the group finally did get into action it was initially met with disaster. Their first mission, on November 16 to Faisi anchorage on the southern tip of Bougainville, failed to put any bombs on target, but it was on the return that things began to unravel. Most of the B-24s got lost. Two ditched in the Coral Sea – though the crews were rescued – and the others wound up scattered at airfields across eastern Australia. The next day, another squadron from the 90th was tasked with a mission to Rabaul. Ten B-24s took off, but the next one ground looped and exploded, taking two other aircraft with it. Of the survivors, only two reached the target, two disappeared – including the one carrying the group commander – and six returned after having got lost.

"I needed them badly but their training was not what I had been led to believe," Kenney recalled. "If I used them as they were, my losses would be beyond all reason and pretty soon I'd have another broken-down outfit like the 19th."

He ordered Ken Walker to take them out of action and put them "on training status until they had learned more about night flying and navigation and had done some practice bombing and gunnery."

With November upon him, MacArthur began to worry about both weather and momentum. As New Guinea lies but a few degrees south of the equator, there is no such thing as winter, but there are seasons – wet and wetter. The latter typically begins in November or December.

"Rations, ammunition, and equipment were generally transported by the Fifth Air Force from Moresby forward," MacArthur wrote in his memoirs. "Allied lines of communication were stretched 1,700 miles from Australia to the landing strips and supply dumps along the coast of New Guinea … Flying weather was usually bad, and for days at a time supply planes were grounded, unable to penetrate the thick, low-hanging clouds which veiled the mountains."

The monsoon season promised not merely discomfort and logistical problems, but disease. Malaria, dengue fever, and dysentery would come – not if, but when – and they would spread, bringing, at the very least, troops unable to press forward, and at the worst, painful death. For all these reasons, MacArthur feared a loss of momentum. He wrote:

> I had hoped that a coordinated drive of the three Allied forces poised before the last remaining strongholds in eastern Papua would be able to gain an early victory. The Japanese, however, realizing they could no longer retreat without forfeiting the vital air bases along the northern coast, were determined to hold their positions no matter what the cost. They methodically prepared a series of well designed and extremely strong defenses. Every contour of the terrain was exploited, and the driest stretches of land were carefully chosen to be occupied and fortified, making it impossible for the Allies to execute any lateral movement without becoming mired in swamp.

The Australians, fighting their way across the crest of the Owen Stanleys on the Kokoda Track and down the other side, finally reached the hill station of Kokoda itself, and took it back from the Japanese on November 1. They were now around 50 miles from Buna and they had the momentum.

On November 6, as though wishing to personally, through force of will, push his forces onward, MacArthur relocated from his headquarters in Brisbane to the advanced echelon (ADVON) SWPA headquarters at Government House in Port Moresby. He announced that he planned to remain at Port Moresby until the Allies had captured Buna and Gona, and had secured both sides of the Papuan Peninsula. He ordered Kenney to do the same with the Fifth Air Force headquarters.

Two days later, the airfield at Dobodura was open for business and Kenney began an airlift of men and materiel of the 126th Infantry across the Owen Stanleys literally to the doorstep of the Japanese at Buna.

However, the monsoons complicated everything. Rain and cloud cover compromised tactical strike operations, but with airlift operations, it was a matter of survival for the growing number of American troops on the north side of the Papuan Peninsula. Because they were completely isolated by land and sea, the Allied troops needed everything from rations to ammunition to be delivered by air. The naysayers on MacArthur's staff, who decried the day they were first talked into the idea of an airlift, blamed the Fifth Air Force for stranding their men.

On November 20, after a meeting at which his staff discussed an evacuation of the stranded men, MacArthur took Kenney aside and spoke frankly about the desperate situation.

"George," he said, "you know there are a lot of men over there eating their last meal tonight."

"Yes," Kenney replied, "but tomorrow we serve breakfast at six-thirty and by noon I'll have five days' rations over to them."

When MacArthur reminded him nothing had been delivered for three days, Kenney nodded, but replied that "our weather guesser says tomorrow will be fine. However, I don't care what the weather is any more. We have the thing licked now."

He proceeded to explain that his men had worked out a way to defeat the weather. A radio beacon was installed at Dobodura, and transport pilots flying on instruments would home in on the radio station using a radio compass for direction. When the needle of the compass indicated that the aircraft was over the beacon, supplies packed into 300-pound containers would be parachuted out of the aircraft.

The following day, the airmen built up the rations on the north coast to a week's supply, and on November 22, as the weather cleared, they began transporting the 127th Infantry to Dobodura to act as a reserve to the other two regiments. Three days later, the Fifth Air Force put on a maximum effort mission to lug 500,000 pounds of supplies across the mountains. Every transport aircraft made three or four trips.

Having proven itself, tactical airlift could now be routinely relied upon. Activated in Brisbane in November, but moved to Port Moresby a month later, the new 374th Troop Carrier Group absorbed the veteran 21st Troop Carrier Squadron, as well as the 6th, 22nd, and 33rd, which had arrived later. The group, which took over all the C-47s that reached the SWPA, still operated the wide assortment of other aircraft – from C-60 Lodestars to commandeered civilian transports – that Kenney had assembled in April for earlier airlifts.

In the meantime, Fifth Air Force A-20, B-25, and B-26 bombers were relentless in their attacks on Japanese positions across the Papuan Peninsula from Buna and Gona to the networks of trails leading into the Kokoda Track. The RAAF was also active with Kittyhawks employed as fighter-bombers, and with their small handful of Lockheed Hudson light bombers.

A glance at Fifth Air Force records shows that around half of the nearly 50 tactical strike missions flown from the beginning of October through mid-November were against the trails and Japanese forces using them. A major focus was around Wairopi on the broad Kumusi River. This village, which takes its name from a cable, or "wire rope," bridge across the river, was the point at which Australian troops coming down the Kokoda Track linked up with Americans of the 126th Infantry who were crossing the Owen Stanleys farther south. It was also here that the Japanese commander, Lieutenant General Tomitaro Horii, drowned on November 23 while trying to escape across the Kumusi.

In the latter half of November, as the weather worsened, the emphasis shifted away from the trails, which were obscured by fog and low clouds, and 80 percent of the strikes were now against Japanese fixed positions, especially airfields, and were divided equally among Buna, Gona, and Lae, with offshore convoys and supply ships also getting some attention.

On the ground, the Australian 7th Division and the regiments of the American 32nd continued their slow and difficult march through the impossible tangle of jungle toward Buna and Gona. By the middle of November, the last 5,500 Japanese troops had been pushed and isolated into a heavily fortified beachhead roughly 15 miles wide and 5 miles deep, with Gona on the west and Buna in the center.

The fighting was intense, with advances measured in yards, as the defenders dug in to fight to the last man. Though the Allies had control of the skies overhead, the strike missions now required down-and-dirty low-level strafing against ground positions and ships, as the Fifth Air Force turned its attention on Buna and Gona proper.

The Australian 21st Brigade finally took Gona on December 9, and all attention then focused on Buna. The preponderance of tactical air missions, averaging roughly one every other day, were against targets around Buna.

One of the heroes of the low-altitude attack campaign against Buna was a young pilot from San Francisco named Ed Larner. During a strafing run against Japanese artillery and machine gun positions, he came in so low that the bottom of his A-20 – nicknamed *Spook* after his wife – scraped the palm trees.

George Kenney recalled:

… after tearing through the treetops for a hundred yards, he brought
the plane back to Port Moresby with the wings dented in, one engine
full of leaves and branches, and the whole length of the bottom of
the fuselage grooved where the top of a palm tree had been in the
way. The lifting surface of the wings was so badly damaged that he
had a landing speed of nearly 175 miles an hour, but Larner got away
with it, landed, and taxied up to the line. As he got out I gave him a
Silver Star and made him a Captain. That lad was good. He had fire,
leadership, and guts.

In his report, Larner wrote that "following this accident I was able to make
only two more strafing passes before the plane became so unmanageable
that I thought it best to return to base where repairs could be made."

Kenney added, "that plane was one of the worst-looking wrecks to be
still flying that I'd ever seen."

The Fifth Air Force commander noted that shortly afterward, Larner
"came back from a strafing attack around Buna with his tail bumper all
scratched up where he had dragged it through the sand making a 'low'
pass at a Japanese machine gun position which had a heavy coconut log
overhead covering. Larner said he had to 'look in the windows of the
bunker to see what to shoot at.'"

To resupply their beleaguered forces at Buna and other isolated
locations along the coast, the Japanese were employing resupply
operations using fast warships, such as destroyers, to transport
supplies. Dubbed "Tokio Express" by the Allies, convoys of such
vessels were also being used by the Japanese to service their garrison
at Guadalcanal.

To address this situation, Kenney decided that his aircraft needed
to be modified to disrupt the heavily armed ships. He started sending
them down to Pappy Gunn in Brisbane, with instructions to "Pull the
bombardier and everything else out of the nose of a B-25 medium
bomber and fill it full of fifty-caliber guns, with 500 rounds of
ammunition per gun. I told him I wanted him then to strap some more
on the sides of the fuselage to give all the forward firepower possible.
I suggested four guns in the nose, two on each side of the fuselage, and
three underneath."

He theorized that he would then have "a skip-bomber that could overwhelm the deck defenses of a Japanese vessel as the plane came in for the kill with its bombs. With a commerce destroyer as effective as I believed this would be, I'd be able to maintain an air blockade on the Japanese anywhere within the radius of action of the airplane."

By the middle of December, the B-24 heavy bombers of the 90th Bomb Group and their crews were back from their month of training. The group flew its first mission on December 14, sending 23 bombers against Japanese positions around the mouth of the Kumusi River about 15 miles up the coast from Gona, where the Japanese had recently landed supplies and reinforcements. The bombing was apparently ineffective, but the bombers shot down eight of the IJNAF fighters that intercepted them – while suffering no losses themselves – and this was seen as a silver lining. The 90th was next tasked with strikes against the Tokio Express convoys, as well as with flying a series of missions against the Japanese air base complex at Lae, 160 miles west of Buna and Gona, a half dozen of which were launched between December 18 and the end of the year.

By the last days of the year, the noose had been tightened around the Japanese position at Buna. The Australian 18th Brigade arrived by sea, bringing with them a small number of M3 Stuart light tanks, and these were thrown into the fight on December 18. Gradually, as the pocket containing the enemy was reduced, it crumbled into smaller pockets. By January 2, 1943, Buna had been captured. As Douglas MacArthur was well aware, this marked the one-year anniversary of the fall of Manila to the Japanese.

8

On the Rim of the Bismarck Sea

Douglas MacArthur was pleased with his air force. Considering the state in which it had been when 1942 began, and where it was one year later, he had a right to be. Considering what his airmen had done with relatively little, he had much in which to take pride.

"During the entire Papuan campaign, the enormous flexibility of modern airpower was constantly exploited," he wrote in his memoirs. "The calculated advance of bomber lines through seizure of forward bases meant a relatively small force of bombers operating at short and medium ranges could attack under cover of an equally limited fighter force."

MacArthur returned to Brisbane on January 9, 1943 after two months of directing operations from Port Moresby. He had vowed to remain there at his ADVON headquarters until Buna and Gona were under Allied control, and this had been done. Also under Allied control was nearby Dobodura, which was being developed into a major Allied air base complex.

"Each phase of advance had as its objective an airfield which could serve as a stepping stone to the next advance ... Ground, air, and sea operations were thoroughly coordinated," MacArthur recalled. He had now accepted airpower not only as a useful support function, but as an essential building block of his strategy.

MacArthur articulated that his "primary goal" in his war against the Japanese in 1943 would be to neutralize their "menacing airfields" and the "bulging supply bases at Rabaul." In so doing, he reiterated a Joint

Chiefs of Staff directive of the previous July calling for three immediate objectives, one in SOPAC and two in the SWPA.

First was the occupation of the southern Solomon Islands to ensure the safety of lines of communication to Australia, which was satisfied by the seizure of Guadalcanal. The other two were the capture of the northern coast of New Guinea, beginning with the Huon Peninsula and then moving north and west, and neutralizing Japanese bases to the east, especially Rabaul. By February 12, MacArthur had drawn up his Reno Plan to address the former and his Elkton Plan for Rabaul. Elkton, which went through a series of revisions during the early months of 1943, called for the capture of Rabaul itself, as well as other Japanese bases.

When MacArthur looked at a map of the north coast of New Guinea at the start of 1943, the line of "menacing airfields" that he wished to transform into his own "stepping stone airfields" began with the twin cities of Lae and Salamaua on Huon Gulf, about 175 miles northwest of Buna and 200 miles due north of Port Moresby. Next was Wewak, 300 miles west of Lae and about 500 miles northwest of Port Moresby, which the Imperial Japanese Army Air Force (IJAAF) was working to turn into a major complex of air bases.

Also apparent on the map when looking at New Guinea and Rabaul at the start of 1943 was that the battlefields were actually the rims of the Solomon Sea and the Bismarck Sea. In the Solomon Sea, the points on these rims included New Guinea to the west and southwest, New Britain to the north, and then to the east, the Solomon Islands. On the rim of the Bismarck Sea, New Guinea lay to the south, and the islands of the Bismarck Archipelago – especially New Britain – were to the east. In an arc across the north, about 250 miles from New Guinea and New Britain, lay the Admiralty Islands and the islands of New Ireland. The latter included the Japanese logistics base at Kavieng, where existing airfields were being expanded. MacArthur's Elkton Plan envisioned the Allied capture of the Japanese bases on all these islands.

This vast, mainly ocean, battlefield comprised around a half million square miles. Part of it lay in Admiral Halsey's SOPAC, but most of it lay in MacArthur's SWPA. Halsey had a fleet, but MacArthur had the heavy bombers that were the only means of crossing the oceans to strike the Japanese at Rabaul or Kavieng. When Halsey needed to attack the Japanese anchorage at Faisi on the southern tip of Bougainville, where the Japanese marshaled their forces for operations in the Solomons, he called MacArthur, who called on the Fifth Air Force.

As MacArthur studied his maps, so too did his opposite numbers in Rabaul whose battlefields were the rims of those seas. Fleet Admiral Isoroku Yamamoto, the infamous architect of the Pearl Harbor attack and the commander in chief of the IJN Combined Fleet, had moved his headquarters to Rabaul, where his subordinate commands included Vice Admiral Junichi Kusaka's Southeast Area Fleet and Vice Admiral Gunichi Mikawa's Eighth Fleet. Rabaul was also the headquarters of the Eleventh Air Fleet, the top of the chain of command for IJN Air Force land-based bombers and fighters.

On the IJA side, General Hitoshi Imamura set up shop in Rabaul. Previously the commander of the victorious IJA 16th Army in its campaign in the Dutch East Indies, Imamura had been named to head the newly created IJA Eighth Area Army. The Eighth functioned as the umbrella organization for the 18th Army in New Guinea and New Britain, as well as the 17th in Bougainville and the Solomons, which had been active against the Allies on Guadalcanal through much of 1942.

The Bismarck Sea was crucial to the Japanese New Guinea defensive strategy because across it were the Japanese supply lines between Rabaul and New Guinea. Just as important for both sides was the air above, through which ran the Allied means of disrupting those supply lines.

The Allied order of battle was also being updated in early 1943. As MacArthur's air assets had been organized under a numbered air force, the Fifth, a numbered field army, the Sixth, was activated for his SWPA command in January 1943. Lieutenant General Walter Krueger, who had worked under MacArthur before when he was Chief of Staff, was named to command the Sixth, and he arrived in the SWPA in February.

The SOPAC command did not get a numbered army, but in January, Hap Arnold did activate a numbered air force for SOPAC. Commanded by USAAF Major General Nathan Twining, the Thirteenth Air Force, like the Fifth, would be built up gradually. As it was based and operated from remote island locations through its formative years the Thirteenth famously earned the nickname "Jungle Air Force."

Also like the Fifth, the Thirteenth would live in the shadow of the "Germany First" strategic policy when it came to allocation of planes, personnel, and other resources. The air forces of Twining and Kenney would operate independently throughout 1943, separated by the vastness of the Coral Sea.

Meanwhile, March 1943 found the US Navy introducing its numbered fleet system with even numbers in the Atlantic, and odd for the Pacific. In the Pacific Ocean Areas, including SOPAC, was the Third Fleet under Admiral William Halsey – nicknamed "Bull," but also called "Bill." All of the US Navy assets then in MacArthur's SWPA were combined into the new Seventh Fleet under Vice Admiral Arthur "Chips" Carpender, who answered directly to MacArthur. As the Fifth was "MacArthur's Air Force," the Seventh Fleet would be known as "MacArthur's Navy."

Though the existence of the numbered army, fleet, and air force made a prominent showing in the table of organization, they were still operating on a shoestring. The Sixth Army had only one division, the 32nd, fully engaged in combat, though some elements of the 41st Division had reached the front in New Guinea in December 1942.

The Fifth Air Force, meanwhile, was still pulling itself together. Kenney reckoned at the start of 1943 that since September he had lost 143 aircraft while receiving just 89 replacements. His research showed more than a few that had been commandeered as they passed through SOPAC bases.

In January 1943, the Fifth Air Force bomber force lost two of its significant founding fathers. Major Bill Benn, George Kenney's former aide and the man perhaps most responsible for developing skip bombing, took off in a B-25 on a reconnaissance mission on January 18, and disappeared without a trace. The crash site was located in the deep New Guinea jungles in 1956, but it took a year to recover remains.

Brigadier General Ken Walker, the commander of V Bomber Command, personally led a January 5 strike mission against a Japanese convoy that was known from secret radio traffic intercepts to be running from Rabaul with substantial reinforcements for the 18th Army at Lae. Walker – who had been explicitly instructed by George Kenney *not* to fly combat missions – took off from Port Moresby with a half dozen B-17s and a like number of B-24s. They sank one transport, forced another to be beached, and damaged a destroyer. However, the withering antiaircraft fire took its toll on the bombers. Only two were shot down, but one of those was Walker's B-17. No remains were ever found.

Kenney said that if he saw Walker again he would hand him a reprimand, but if he did not, he would recommend him for a posthumous Medal of Honor. He made good on the latter promise. On January 18, Kenney brought in Brigadier General Howard Knox Ramey – no relation to Roger Ramey of the 43rd Bomb Group – to replace Walker as the commander of V Bomber Command.

MacArthur's goal of crippling Rabaul was limited by the weather and by the number of bombers that were able to fly through the holes in that weather when they did appear. On the night of February 14/15, in the largest mission to date, the 43rd Bomb Group was able to put 32 B-17s – accompanied by four B-24s of the 90th – over Rabaul with 50 tons of high-explosive ordnance and 4,000 incendiaries. A planned repeat the following night was stymied by weather.

Despite the victory at Buna, 1943 was off to a menacing start for the Allies on the ground in New Guinea. The big convoy that Walker's force attacked had reached New Guinea on January 8 – less two transport ships – and had offloaded about 4,000 troops, mainly comprising the 102nd Infantry Regiment under Major General Toru Okabe, commander of the IJA 51st Division.

The center of the land action as 1943 began was an unassuming speck in the jungle inland from Salamaua called Wau. The site of a brief prewar gold rush, it had an airfield and it was also on the route that Allied ground troops would take from Buna to Salamaua. It had earlier been garrisoned by a small Australian contingent, and Okabe had been sent from Rabaul explicitly to capture it.

Both sides saw the importance of Wau. Australian General Thomas Blamey, the Allied Land Forces commander in New Guinea, had meanwhile ordered Wau to be reinforced. This was done through January, partly by sea and partly through the services of the 374th Troop Carrier Group. On January 31 and February 4 alone, despite horrible weather, the 374th flew 124 missions into Wau.

The Japanese, meanwhile, came overland. Hacking their way through difficult terrain, they fell behind their schedule and became separated in the dense jungle. Though they were able to surprise the defenders, the exhausted Japanese regiment found themselves outnumbered and incapable of a successful attack. Okabe withdrew by February 4, planning to bring in the rest of his experienced 51st Division and strike again.

The Japanese invasion force departed Rabaul on February 28, making its way westward across the Bismarck Sea with eight destroyers and eight transport ships carrying nearly 7,000 troops, their supplies, and large quantities of fuel. The IJNAF brought in extra fighter aircraft to provide air cover. Allied codebreakers, meanwhile, learned from a Japanese Naval Cipher of this massive operation, and the Fifth Air Force was ready with two medium bomber groups, the 22nd and 38th, and two groups with heavy bombers, the veteran 43rd and the newer 90th.

Severe tropical storms prevented the Allied aircraft from locating the convoy until March 1 and delayed the first major strike until the following day. The B-17s of the 43rd Bomb Group attacked in force, sinking one transport and damaging three. Two destroyers, having rescued survivors from the sinking, left the convoy to use their greater speed to press through to disembark at Lae before returning to escort duty.

As George Kenney later recalled, the "big brawl" began at 10:00hrs on March 3 in the Bismarck Sea about 125 miles southeast of Lae, "right where we planned it."

The slow-moving convoy was attacked in waves by B-17s and skip-bombing B-25s, as well as by Bristol Beaufort torpedo bombers of RAAF No. 100 Squadron. The waves washed over the Japanese in a running battle that lasted from morning to dusk.

Captain Ed Larner, the pilot who had scuffed up the bottom of his A-20 flying low over Buna, now led the 90th Bomb Squadron of the 3rd Bomb Group. They skip-bombed the convoy, scoring 17 direct hits with 500-pound bombs.

One by one, each of the seven transports that had survived the previous day was crippled or sunk. The destroyer *Arashio* was struck, and in turn it rammed the transport *Nojima Maru*, disabling both. Of the eight destroyers, four were sunk and only one escaped serious damage. The destroyers managed to rescue 2,700 troops and return them to Rabaul, but most perished. On the darker side, the Japanese were guilty of shooting at Allied airmen parachuting from crippled aircraft, while the Allies strafed Japanese troops escaping from sinking ships.

The battle of the Bismarck Sea was an outstanding victory for the Fifth Air Force and Allied airpower, and a severe blow to the Japanese. A dozen Japanese ships out of 16 had been erased from the IJN roster without the presence of Allied warships. Only around 17 percent of the Japanese troops managed to reach Lae, greatly limiting the capability of the IJA on the New Guinea battlefront. This was only the beginning. Historian Eric Bergerud wrote that postwar analysis of Japanese records revealed that through the war, they lost 20,000 troops crossing the Bismarck Sea.

Douglas MacArthur, in his SWPA press release of March 4, bragged that his command "achieved a victory of such completeness as to assume the proportions of a major disaster to the enemy. Our decisive success cannot fail to have most important results on the enemy's strategic and tactical plans. His campaign, for the time being at least is completely dislocated."

It was not mere hyperbole, though. As noted in Volume II of the postwar US Strategic Bombing Survey *Interrogations of Japanese Officials*, IJN Commander Yasumi Doi, a member of the staff of the Southeast Area Fleet at Rabaul, revealed that after the battle, "all attempts at running large transports into Lae were abandoned and the hungry enemy garrisons in eastern New Guinea had to be satisfied with the thin trickle of supplies and replacements carried in by destroyers, barges, or submarines."

The day after the "Big Brawl," George Kenney, Richard Sutherland, and a gaggle of staff officers departed the SWPA, embarking on a previously planned two-week mission to Washington, DC, where the progress of the war in the Pacific would be discussed with the President and the Joint Chiefs of Staff (JCS).

Reporting in, they found the media and the public greatly enthralled with the outcome of the battle of the Bismarck Sea. Kenney would recall that Secretary of War Louis Stimson and the senior War Department leadership:

... wanted to know all about the show in New Guinea and were most sympathetic about helping me out, but in the final analysis, [USAAF Commanding General] Hap Arnold would have to give me the airplanes and the crews to fly and maintain them. He in turn had to deal with the Joint Chiefs of Staff of the United States, whose policies were decidedly influenced by the Combined Chiefs of Staff of the United States and Great Britain, and they in turn heard from and listened to President Roosevelt and Winston Churchill.

For Kenney's concerns, the so-named Pacific Military Conference was a disappointment. He noted:

> … everyone was really stubborn about giving me airplanes, or even replacements for my losses. I warned them that if they didn't keep me going, we would be run out of New Guinea, as supply of our troops there was impossible unless we maintained at least local control of the air, I suggested that maybe they might let me have ten per cent of the aircraft factory output and let the rest of the war have the remainder. The answer was still No.

At the time, the Fifth Air Force actually did possess 10 percent of the USAAF-deployed heavy bomber groups, 21 percent of medium and light bomber groups, and 11 percent of fighter groups. USAAF records for March 1943 reveal the details for how assets were being allocated under the "Germany First" paradigm. The Eighth Air Force in England, which was being built up for the strategic air offensive against Germany, had one third of all heavy bomber groups, but only a single medium bomber group and the same number of fighter groups as the Fifth.

The Mediterranean Theater of Operations (MTO), where the major American land and air offensive action was then taking place, had a quarter of USAAF medium and light bomber groups and nearly two thirds of fighter groups. SOPAC, meanwhile, had the same number of heavy bomber and fighter groups as the Fifth, but no light or medium bombers. Smaller numbers of all types were assigned in the Western Hemisphere and even smaller numbers in the China–Burma–India Theater.

Kenney also complained that the JCS had difficulty grasping what the Fifth Air Force had been able to accomplish. For example, when MacArthur's plan to capture Lae and Salamaua was presented, he described their response:

[They] were dubious about our ability to supply our forces in the Lae area, as it was doubtful if sufficient shipping could be made available for that purpose. Sutherland made a point of the possibilities of using the road across the Owen Stanley Mountains that the Aussies were then working on ... My personal opinion was that this road would never be finished in time for this war. I didn't tell the conferees that but assured them that if necessary I could handle the whole supply problem by airlift.

He added:

... in spite of the demonstration of what could be done along this line with a handful of cargo airplanes, which we had just shown them during the Buna campaign, neither [US Army Chief of Staff General George Marshall] nor [Chief of Naval Operations Admiral Ernest King] seemed to appreciate the real capabilities of airlift or how flexible a means of supply it was. They listened, but I don't believe they were entirely sold. This business had to be seen to be believed.

As might have been expected, Kenney found Washington to be consumed by political battles that affected people and operations far from the capital.

"Sometimes our discussions became quite heated," he wrote in his memoirs. "The location of the boundary line between SWPA and SOPAC was a source of almost endless discussion in and outside the conference room. SOPAC wanted to move it west and SWPA representatives looked upon that as not only an infringement but an attempt to keep SOPAC in business."

Along with the question of demarcation was that of the rims. The Navy-run SOPAC focused on the rim of the Solomon Sea because the Navy and Marine Corps were so heavily involved in the Solomon Islands. MacArthur's SWPA was concentrated on the rim of the Bismarck Sea because of their objectives across the north side of New Guinea – from Lae and Salamaua to Wewak – and the Japanese supply lines that fed this area passed through the Bismarck Sea.

What both had in common was an understandable obsession with Rabaul, and when that word was mentioned in any of the meetings, all eyes turned to George Kenney, for his Fifth Air Force then possessed the only means of attacking Rabaul.

MacArthur had chosen not to attend the conference, though in retrospect, he probably should have. He understood strategy on a theater-wide scale, while Kenney was a tactician. Furthermore, his eloquence and stature, not to mention his skill at working a conference room, would have been useful in making and closing the case for the resources that both he and Kenney sought.

"The whole business of rigid and fixed boundary lines, particularly between SOPAC and SWPA, seemed silly to me," MacArthur wrote in his memoirs. "There should have been one Supreme Commander out there." Of course, he meant himself. Had MacArthur been in Washington that week, he might well have sold this argument.

The silliness Kenney encountered in Washington occasionally verged on the absurd. Before he left Australia, Kenney had mailed Arnold a set of drawings showing the changes that Pappy Gunn and the Fifth Air Force field crews had made in B-25s to make them into skip-bombing, strafing, "commerce destroyers." He asked Arnold to request that these modifications be done at the North American Aviation factory in Inglewood, California to lift the burden that was placed on the Townsville depot.

In Washington, Arnold introduced him to "a battery of engineering experts" from the Air Materiel Command at Wright Field, "who explained to me that the idea was impracticable. They tried to prove to me that the balance would be all messed up, the airplane would be too heavy, would not fly properly, and so on."

Kenney recalled that he "listened for a while and then mentioned that twelve B-25s fixed up in this manner had played a rather important part in the battle of the Bismarck Sea and that I was remodeling sixty more B-25s right now at Townsville. Arnold glared at his engineering experts and practically ran them out of the office." Arnold told Kenney to wire Pappy Gunn and order him to come to California to show North American Aviation how it was done.

On March 25, Kenney was present at the White House when President Roosevelt made the posthumous award of Ken Walker's Medal of Honor to a teenaged Kenneth Walker, Jr. Afterward, the President took Kenney aside and asked him about "the airplane situation," and whether he was satisfied with the promises he had been given.

"If I got a million more planes, I'd probably want more," Kenney admitted candidly, adding that he was "extremely grateful and glad to get what I had, and was quite sure we would get real dividends out of them."

"I'll be watching the reports," Roosevelt said, "as soon as you get them out in the Pacific."

9

Fighter Boys

The first mention of Lieutenant Richard Ira "Dick" Bong by General George Kenney is on the first page of the first chapter of his memoirs. In this anecdote, it is July 1942 and Kenney is still in San Francisco as commander of the Fourth Air Force. Bong is introduced with Kenney having called him on the carpet for making a low-level pass down the city's Market Street in his P-38.

Rather than tearing him apart verbally and grounding him indefinitely, the general regards the aggressive but unassuming pilot as a father would scrutinize an errant favorite son. Kenney, in his early 50s, eagerly embraced his adopted role of father figure. In his diary and memoirs, Kenney, like MacArthur, frequently referred to "his" twenty-something officers as "kids," "boys," or "youngsters."

"In walked one of the nicest-looking cherubs you ever saw in your life," Kenney wrote in his memoirs. He continued:

> I suspected that he was not over eighteen and maybe even younger. I doubted if he was old enough to shave. He was just a little blond-haired Norwegian boy about five feet six, with a round, pink baby face ... Someone must have just told him how serious this court martial thing might be. He wanted to fly and he wanted to get into the war and do his stuff ... Why, he might be taken off flying status or even thrown out of the Air Force! He wasn't going to try to alibi out of it, but he sure hoped this General Kenney wasn't going to be too rough ... He didn't know it, but he had already won ... We needed kids like this lad.

In fact, the lad was of Swedish extraction, a 21-year-old farm boy from Wisconsin who had earned his wings in January and who had begun training in Lockheed P-38 Lightnings at Hamilton Field north of San Francisco in May 1942.

It was not so much who he *had been*, but who he *would become*. Dick Bong was destined to go out to the SWPA as a fighter pilot, to score his first two aerial victories over Buna in December 1942, and to become the highest-scoring American ace of World War II and of all time. Of course, the point of Bong's story is not that Bong stands so much taller than those around him, but that he *did not*. He was surrounded by the heroic fighter pilots of the Pacific War. He was a symbol, not an anomaly.

The 35th and 49th Fighter Groups had begun transitioning from P-40s to twin-engine Lockheed P-38 Lightnings around the time that Bong arrived in Australia in early September 1942. The P-38 was a gamechanger in a game that had heretofore been dominated by the Japanese. Fast and powerful, it was the ideal fighter for the theater because of its range and the reliability factor, and the advantage over the P-39 and P-40 of having *two* engines. Though it looked ungainly with its twin fuselage layout, the P-38 was fast and maneuverable. With a 20mm cannon and four .50-caliber nose-mounted machine guns, it was also deadly. It was the fighter to match and surpass the Japanese in the contest for air superiority over the Southwest Pacific.

For the better part of a year, the Japanese, especially the IJNAF, had ruled the skies with their Mitsubishi A6M Zero and a large number of remarkable pilots. Arguably the best fighter pilots in the IJNAF were those who flew with the Tainin Kokutai, or Tainin Air Group. They included Hiroyoshi Nishizawa, considered to have been the top-scoring Japanese ace of the war, as well as Toshio Ota and Saburo Sakai.

The Tainin Kokutai was based in Formosa as the war began and decimated the American FEAF in the skies over the Philippines in the early months of the war. After seeing action in the Dutch East Indies, it became a component of the 25th Air Flotilla, based at Rabaul, in March 1942. In April, the Tainin Kokutai was forward deployed to Lae in New Guinea, where it joined other IJNAF units, such as the 582nd Kokutai, as well as the 11th Sentai of the IJAAF. These organizations had already become the nemesis of Allied fighter groups forward deployed to Port

Moresby – often strafing their fields and dueling with them over the Papuan Peninsula.

When the 35th Fighter Group arrived at Port Moresby in July 1942, it found its P-39s a less than even match for the more maneuverable Zeros, so the conversion by the 35th and 49th to the Lightning was awaited with great interest and anticipation. However, the transition was not smooth. The P-38s reached Australia not fully assembled, and their complexity made getting them ready to fly more time-consuming than had been hoped. Next, they were a more complicated aircraft to fly, and the learning curve for pilots used to single-engine aircraft was also steeper than anticipated. Lightnings were flying patrols over New Guinea in November, but did not see combat until late December. The first unit to become operational with the new aircraft was the 39th Fighter Squadron of the 35th Fighter Group, and Dick Bong, with his previous P-38 experience, was temporarily assigned to the group.

Douglas MacArthur would later observe that Bong "ruled the air" over New Guinea, but he was one of many "boys" who became aces – scoring more than five aerial victories – in the Pacific. Flying a P-40, Buzz Wagner had become the first American ace in the Pacific, with five aerial victories over the Philippines in December 1941. A year later, there was Lieutenant Thomas Joseph "Tommy" Lynch, the commander of the 39th Fighter Squadron.

On December 27, 1942, word came in that a Japanese strike force was headed for the new Allied air base at Dobodura, 100 miles to the east of Port Moresby across the Owen Stanley Mountains. Lynch led a dozen P-38s – including one piloted by Dick Bong – toward the intercept. Lynch himself was the first to score, claiming two dive bombers, which added to three kills he scored while flying a P-39 to make him an ace. Bong, in his baptism of fire, also claimed two enemy aircraft.

On New Year's Eve, Lieutenant Hoyt Eason became the first pilot to down five Japanese aircraft in a P-38, making him the first "Lightning ace," and the 39th Fighter Squadron ended the year with 20 Lightning victories. Within two weeks, there were five Lightning aces in the 39th Fighter Squadron, including Tommy Lynch, who had now added eight to the three he had scored flying the P-39.

Dick Bong got two more on January 7, 1943 and he scored his fifth, to achieve ace status, the following day. On January 11, he returned to the 9th Fighter Squadron of the 49th Fighter Group, which was now operational with the Lightning.

The first squadron in the 8th Fighter Group to transition to the P-38 was the 80th, and it possessed a pilot of note. Lieutenant George Welch had been with the 47th Pursuit Squadron at Wheeler Field on December 7, 1941 when the IJNAF had come calling, and he had knocked four of their aircraft out of the skies over Pearl Harbor. Welch had finally become an ace a year later over New Guinea while flying P-39s with the 8th Fighter Group. Now he joined the ranks of the Lightning boys.

Though the P-38s and their pilots proved themselves superior to their opposition when they met them, the Lightnings were still few in number. In his Washington visit in the aftermath of the battle of the Bismarck Sea, George Kenney registered his displeasure with the Fifth Air Force's getting the short end of the stick as the USAAF rationed its Lightnings, and dug in his heels when asked to accept more P-40s.

Eventually, he secured a pledge of two new fighter groups by summer – the 348th and the 475th. The 348th Fighter Group, originally scheduled to go to the European Theater of Operations (ETO) with Republic P-47 Thunderbolts, would be diverted to the Fifth Air Force. There currently were only enough P-38s in the SWPA to equip one squadron in each of the fighter groups, but the 475th was to be the first all-Lightning group in the theater. But summer was a long way off.

During the battle of the Bismarck Sea on March 3 and 4, the Lightnings of the 35th and 49th Fighter Groups flew top cover for the strike force that destroyed the Japanese convoy. The fighter boys were there to peel the layers of Japanese fighters away so that the bomber boys could do their work. Among the 13 enemy aircraft shot down by the P-38s, Dick Bong and Tommy Lynch each got one and Lieutenant Paul Stanch claimed three. However, three Lightning pilots, including Hoyt Eason, did not come back from this intense aerial battle.

By the middle of February, the fighters based at Port Moresby were starting to use the airfield that had been built at Dobodura as a forward operating base, and ground crews were reassigned there. By March, port facilities at nearby Oro Bay had been constructed to supply the base by sea, and the 49th relocated its headquarters to Dobodura. Kenney also activated his First Air Task Force at Dobodura to provide a higher level

of command authority when communication between there and Port
Moresby was down.

As the monsoons gradually tapered off, both sides were able to up
the tempo of their respective air offensives against both shipping and
opposing airfields.

On April 1, Fleet Admiral Isoroku Yamamoto, commander of
the IJN Combined Fleet, ordered his Eleventh Air Fleet to initiate
a two-week air offensive known as *I-Go Sakusen*. As naval historian
Samuel Eliot Morison notes, this operation involved the largest
number of Japanese strike aircraft assembled for single-day missions
since Pearl Harbor. Their opening day gambit, against Allied shipping
in the Solomon Islands, especially around Guadalcanal, involved
177 aircraft.

In the SWPA, the focus was on Port Moresby, but the Japanese
were especially anxious to disrupt operations at Dobodura, which
was not only a fighter base, but also a hub for Fifth Air Force airlift
operations, which were important for the resupply of ground troops.
On April 11, 94 Japanese aircraft were engaged over Oro Bay off
Dobodura by 50 P-40s and P-38s. The Americans claimed 17 of
the attackers, but not before they managed to score hits on Allied
supply ships.

The next day, the Japanese assembled a 174-plane strike package
for the biggest raid to date against Port Moresby. Each Fifth Air Force
fighter group contributed its P-38 squadron to the defense. Official
USAAF records show the loss of 15 G4M bombers and at least nine
A6M Zeros as cheering American troops watched from the ground. The
Fifth Air Force lost two aircraft in air-to-air combat, and four destroyed
on the ground.

During this time, the veteran 49th continued to have their eyes on
a prize. As noted in Chapter Five, little more than a year earlier, Paul
Wurtsmith, then the group commander, had presented a magnum of
brandy to be opened when they downed their 500th Japanese aircraft.
As George Kenney recalled, "The group was still carrying that huge
bottle around as if it were a household god. It was not even a very
good grade of brandy … but that made no difference to the kids. They
were not thinking about how it would taste. It had become a symbol
of a goal that they were shooting for and which they were certain they
would reach ahead of any other group."

Over Oro Bay, Lieutenant Grover Fanning was credited with shooting down number 200. Kenney noted that "the kids were saying that it wouldn't be long now, if the Japanese would just keep sending over shows like the one they had just tangled with. Only three hundred to go."

On April 14, the largest Japanese strike of *I-Go* targeted Allied facilities at Milne Bay with 188 aircraft. Among the Japanese aircraft lost that day was a G4M that became Dick Bong's tenth victory.

Four days later came what is perhaps the most famous P-38 mission of World War II – though it did *not* involve Lightnings of the Fifth Air Force. As it took place in the SOPAC, it was run by the 347th Fighter Group of Nate Twining's Thirteenth Air Force, but it is worth mentioning because of its overall effect on the war in the Pacific.

Through decryptions of the Japanese Naval Cipher, it was learned that Admiral Yamamoto would be departing Rabaul on an inspection tour of the northern Solomon Islands. The idea of intercepting and killing the mastermind of the Pearl Harbor attack was sent up the chain of command, possibly as far as President Roosevelt. In turn, Secretary of the Navy Frank Knox ordered POA commander Admiral Chester Nimitz to order SOPAC commander Admiral William Halsey to initiate the strike. Since no naval aircraft had the range to conduct the mission, Thirteenth Air Force P-38s got the job.

Early on April 18, the mission launched from Guadalcanal. The 18 Lightnings were specially equipped with larger external fuel tanks for longer range on a flight of about 1,000 miles and the longest fighter intercept mission of the war. Two P-38s dropped out, but 16 reached the vicinity of Balalae Island near Bougainville after a flight of two hours and spotted two G4M bombers exactly as the codebreakers had deduced.

Mission commander Major John Mitchell ordered Lieutenant Rex Barber and Captain Thomas Lanphier to attack the G4Ms, not knowing which contained Yamamoto. Other pilots engaged the A6M Zeros that were escorting them. It is possible that Barber shot down what turned out to be Yamamoto's aircraft, though Lanphier also claimed credit – and this would remain a heated controversy for decades. The other G4M was downed by Lieutenant Besby Holmes, and six A6Ms were also claimed. On the long flight back, one of the P-38s ran out of fuel and was lost and another made an emergency landing in the Russell

Islands. Yamamoto's body was found by a Japanese search party the next day, but the official Japanese announcement was not made until May 21.

Back in the SWPA, the daily routine of air combat during the first half of 1943 had developed an almost predictable tempo. The fighters on each side alternated between escorting bombers on strike missions, and air defense, the interception of the other side's strike missions.

The newly formed 348th Fighter Group and its P-47s, under the command of Lieutenant Colonel Neel Kearby, began arriving in Australia in mid-June. George Kenney was on hand to greet Kearby on June 20 and immediately sized him up as a man who knew what he was doing. He described Kearby as:

> … a short, slight, keen-eyed, black-haired Texan about thirty-two [who] looked like money in the bank to me. About two minutes after he had introduced himself he wanted to know who had the highest scores for shooting down Japanese aircraft. You felt that he just wanted to know who he had to beat. I told him to take his squadron commanders and report to General Wurtsmith [now heading V Fighter Command] at Port Moresby for a few days to get acquainted and then come back to Brisbane, where we would erect the P-47s [shipped with wings not attached] as fast as we got them off the boats.

The latter was easier said than done. Assembling the aircraft took longer than expected, and the process was stymied by the absence of external fuel tanks, which would be necessary to give the fighters adequate range for their intended missions. When two sample tanks, immediately requested from the United States, finally arrived a week later, Kenney found that "neither held enough fuel, they both required too many alterations to install, and they both were difficult to release in an emergency. We designed and built one of our own in two days. It tested satisfactorily from every angle and could be installed in a matter of minutes without making any changes in the airplane."

Fortunately, the Fifth Air Force now had a streamlined maintenance and depot system that was working well. Maintenance for fighters could be handled at Port Moresby, with heavy overhaul for bombers taking place in Australia. The 4th Depot Group at Townsville had built

16 warehouses and seven repair hangars. If supplies and parts existed in Australia, they could be made available promptly. The Fifth Air Force even had a network of Australian suppliers who were manufacturing parts. External fuel tanks for existing fighters were being produced at a rate of 1,200 a month, and Kenney contracted with the Ford Company of Australia to make them for the P-47s. Deployment of the 348th would be delayed until the end of July, but at least the Fifth Air Force logistics chain was taking care of its own.

However, to the men of the Fifth Air Force, the delay of the P-47 was not its biggest shortcoming – and there were a lot of those on the list. Rumors abounded that it took too much runway for takeoff, that it had poor maneuverability, that it would not pull out of a dive, that the landing gear was feeble, and that the reliability of its Pratt & Whitney R-2800 radial engine, when compared with a P-38's twin Allison V-1710 inline engines, was questionable.

With this in mind, Kenney ordered Kearby to "sell the P-47 or go back home."

Kenney proposed a mock dogfight between Kearby and Lieutenant Colonel George Prentice, the veteran P-38 pilot whom Kenney had picked to command the 475th Fighter Group when it arrived in the SWPA. In their simulation, the attributes of the Thunderbolt shone, and Prentice admitted that Kearby "shot me down in flames" a half dozen times.

Prentice asked for a rematch, but Kenney told them to "quit that stuff and tend to their jobs of getting a couple of new groups into the war." He had the result he wanted. The P-47 had been "sold" to the Fifth Air Force. The 348th was in Port Moresby with 115 P-47s by the end of July.

Hap Arnold had originally told Kenney that the all-Lightning 475th would arrive in September, but Kenney had convinced him to move that forward to June. The advance echelon did arrive in June, but the group was not operational with its three squadrons, the 431st, 432nd, and 433rd, until the first week of August.

In addition to Prentice, Kenney integrated a number of veteran P-38 pilots into the 475th along with newly arriving pilots. There were also P-38 pilots who had come over as replacements, or had arrived early earmarked for the 475th, who now filled its ranks. One such man was Lieutenant Thomas Buchanan "Tommy" McGuire, a 22-year-old who had been born in New Jersey and who had grown up in Sebring, Florida. He had earned his wings in February 1942 and had spent several months flying P-38s in Alaska before coming to the SWPA in April 1943.

McGuire had spent six weeks attached to the 9th Fighter Squadron for familiarization and had amassed 50 hours of time in the skies over New Guinea. A "new guy" in the spring, he brought the hand of experience to the 475th in summer.

Speaking to the assembled men of his new group at Amberley Field south of Brisbane just before they headed north to New Guinea on August 8, Prentice summarized what they were about to undertake.

In remarks preserved in the group's daily history, he said:

> I know some of you have been in New Guinea for 16 months or more, trying to keep the Japanese from taking the whole damn place. Hanging on and being pushed around are things of the past. With your help we will run the Japanese out of New Guinea. We will start at Port Moresby on the Southeast end of New Guinea and we will strike the Japanese hard and often. We will destroy their air force and soften their ground positions. When our infantry lands, we will cover their landings. When new areas are secured we will move up and extend our flying range still further. We will drive the Japanese off of New Guinea and into the sea 1,500 miles northwest of where we started. General MacArthur has told the Philippine people that he will return. We are vital to that promise.

As each of the three fighter groups then in New Guinea possessed just a single P-38 squadron, the arrival of the 475th in Port Moresby doubled the number of Lightning squadrons overnight.

The first missions flown by the 431st Fighter Squadron mirrored what McGuire had already experienced with the 9th, mainly escorting C-47 transports across the Owen Stanley Mountains. McGuire was off, however, on August 16, the day that his squadron had its baptism of fire. Coincidentally, Neel Kearby's 348th Fighter Group was also part of the escort, and this action marked the first use of P-47s in combat in the Pacific. Around 25 Japanese fighters jumped the transports and the American fighter pilots reacted, destroying a dozen enemy aircraft.

Disappointed at having missed that action, McGuire was in the air the following day, escorting Fifth Air Force bombers in the first raid in some time against the growing Japanese air base complex around Wewak. They struck in two waves, beginning with 50 Fifth Air Force B-17s and B-24s before dawn. Next came around 30 B-25s, plus 80 P-38s – drawn from all six Lightning squadrons – in a midmorning strafing attack. Though he had already been flying in New Guinea for months, Tommy McGuire listed this day in his logbook as his "first raid."

The bomber boys also had an interesting day on August 17. George Kenney would later tell the story of Lieutenant Colonel Don Hall of the 3rd Bomb Group, who had led the first parafrag bomb mission over Buna in September 1942. On August 17, he led his B-25s in a line-abreast attack on Wewak's Borum airfield.

"Coming in over the tops of the palm trees, Don saw a sight to gladden the heart of a strafer," Kenney recalled with dramatic prose. He continued:

The Japanese bombers, sixty of them, were lined up on either side of the runway with their engines turning over, flying crews on board, and groups of ground crewmen standing by each airplane. The Japanese were actually starting to take off and the leading airplane was already halfway down the runway and ready to leave the ground. Off to one side fifty Japanese fighters were warming up their engines ready to follow and cover their bombers. Hall signaled to open fire. His first burst blew up the Japanese bomber just as it lifted into the air. It crashed immediately, blocking the runway for any further Japanese takeoffs. The B-25 formation swept over the field like a giant scythe. The double line of Japanese bombers was on fire almost immediately from the rain of fifty-caliber [incendiary rounds] pouring from over 200 machine guns, antiaircraft defenses were smothered, drums of gasoline by the side of the runway blazed up, and Japanese flying crews and ground personnel melted away in the path of our gunfire, in the crackle of a thousand parafrag bombs, and the explosions of their own bomb-laden aircraft. We hit them just in time. Another five minutes and the whole Japanese force would have been in the air.

In his memoirs, Kenney called August 17 the day that "the big take-out of the Wewak airdromes began." The Japanese called it the "Black Day."

Coincidentally, across the world in the ETO, August 17, 1943 was one of the darkest days yet experienced by the USAAF Eighth Air Force. General Ira Eaker had planned a "maximum effort" mission against German industry involving 16 bombardment groups. In simultaneous strikes against the Messerschmitt factories at Regensburg and the ball bearing industry at Schweinfurt, the 376 B-17s that went out suffered 60 bombers shot down, or unsustainable 16 percent losses. With 600 empty bunks in the barracks that night, it was a staggering blow that nearly derailed the Eighth's strategic air campaign against the Third Reich.

In the Pacific, Kenney reported losing two B-24s out of a strike force that included 41 B-24s plus a dozen B-17s.

August 17 had come as a surprise to the Japanese around Wewak, with their fighters caught on the ground, but the following day, they were ready when the Fifth Air Force tried it again. The strike package included more than 70 bombers, as well as nearly 100 P-38s, again representing all the squadrons.

As they arrived in the morning light, around two dozen IJAAF fighters tore into the Americans. Three men from the 431st – Lieutenant Ed Czarnecki, Captain Verl Jett, and Lieutenant Lowell Lutton – each claimed a pair of enemy Nakajima Ki-43 Hayabusa fighters.

Tommy McGuire did not wait to be attacked, but picked out a Ki-43 and turned into a head-on attack. He made a two-burst firing pass and sent the burning foe tumbling earthward. A moment later Lieutenant Francis "Fran" Lent warned McGuire to "check his six" as he had a fighter on his tail.

McGuire broke left, used the Lightning's power and maneuverability to reverse his situation, and began his pursuit. Joined by Lent, he chased the Ki-43 until it was on fire. The two Americans then turned into another Japanese fighter, which Lent shot down as McGuire seized upon a Kawasaki Ki-62 that was attacking a B-25. The crew of the American bomber watched their attacker become McGuire's third aerial victory in his first day of air-to-air combat.

Three days later, again over Wewak, Tommy McGuire shot down a pair of Ki-43s, becoming an ace after just two aerial battles. Equally momentous was that the new 475th Fighter Group had claimed more than 50 Japanese aircraft in less than two weeks in combat.

And there was heroism among the bomber boys. Major Ralph Cheli of the 38th Bomb Group was leading a low-level attack on Wewak's Dagua airfield when a gaggle of Japanese fighters ganged up on him. His B-25 was a torch long before he reached the target, but he bore on, not wanting to disrupt the formation by climbing to parachute altitude. After leading a very successful strike, he turned the squadron over to his wingman and attempted to ditch in the ocean offshore. He almost made it.

As Kenney bragged that his boys had destroyed "practically the entire Japanese air force in the Wewak area," Cheli was being written up for a posthumous Medal of Honor.

Cartwheel over the Bismarck Rim

At the Pacific Military Conference in Washington in March 1943, the Pacific strategy had been discussed, dissected, deconstructed, and reconstructed, but when it was over, the Allied battle plan was essentially the same as Douglas MacArthur had envisioned in his series of Elkton plans at the start of the year. In fact, Admiral Ernest King, the Chief of Naval Operations, had even proposed a plan very similar to MacArthur's – but under US Navy command.

Finally, a compromise was reached and MacArthur was given strategic command of ground forces in both SWPA and SOPAC, while command of the naval forces at sea remained with Admiral Chester Nimitz leading the Pacific Fleet and the POA command, and direct command of the Third Fleet in the Solomons remained with Admiral William Halsey, the SOPAC commander.

Although politics may have reigned in Washington, in the distant reaches of the Pacific, MacArthur (West Point Class of 1903) and Halsey (Annapolis Class of 1904) apparently shared a mutual respect and had a good working relationship.

It began on April 15 when Halsey arrived in Brisbane for a summit conference that was arguably more substantive than the one in Washington a month earlier.

"Five minutes after I reported, I felt as if we were lifelong friends," Halsey wrote in his memoirs. "I have seldom seen a man who makes a quicker, stronger, more favorable impression."

In his own memoirs, MacArthur wrote that Halsey was "one of our great sailors ... Blunt, outspoken, dynamic, he had already proven himself to be a battle commander of the highest order. A strong advocate of unity of command in the Pacific, there seemed always to be an undercurrent opposed to him in the Navy Department ... I placed the greatest confidence in his judgment. No name rates higher in the annals of our country's naval history."

The new battle plan for the "MacArthur–Halsey Theater" was formally adopted by the Joint Chiefs of Staff on April 26, to be implemented under the name Operation *Cartwheel*. Complicated by more than a dozen sub-operations, *Cartwheel* called for a continuation of what had been ongoing since 1942 when MacArthur first drew his line in the sand at Port Moresby in the SWPA and the US Marine Corps went ashore in Guadalcanal in the SOPAC. MacArthur would continue his march across the rim of New Guinea, while Halsey's SOPAC forces worked their way in a northwesterly direction through the Solomon Islands to Bougainville.

The capture of Rabaul continued to be the keystone to the entire Allied strategy in the region. The great center of Japanese power, it was garrisoned by as many as 100,000 battle-ready troops and protected by hundreds of aircraft.

In the near term, the only means of striking Rabaul continued to be MacArthur's Fifth Air Force. From five heavy bomber missions against Rabaul in March and just two in April, the Fifth was able to fly eight in May and nine in June.

The turning point coincided with an unexpected change of command. On March 26, Brigadier General Howard Ramey, who had led V Bomber Command since the loss of Ken Walker in January, took off from Port Moresby in a B-17 flying a seven-hour reconnaissance mission. He was never seen again. On April 19, after an exhaustive search, George Kenney replaced Ramey with another, unrelated, Ramey. Brigadier General Roger Ramey had served as commander of the 43rd Bomb Group, and had recently become Howard Ramey's chief of staff.

The Rameys and their bomber boys, like the fighter boys on the cusp of a critical mass of P-38s, were still outmatched by the Japanese air forces. Writing in Volume 4 of *The Army Air Forces in World War II*,

Richard Watson summarized that in May, the War Department had "fixed the level of bombers to be maintained in the Southwest Pacific at 197," and that "sufficient aircraft would be 'in pipeline' to maintain actual strength at 197 bombers," though by August 1, the effective date had been pushed back to September 15. *I-Go Sakusen*, the Japanese air offensive of April 1943, showcased superior Japanese numbers in the skies over New Guinea and the rim of the Bismarck Sea that the Fifth Air Force and the RAAF could not equal. The Japanese could put an average of more than 150 aircraft over targets for three days running, and they still had the capability to go deep, striking Australia a half dozen times in May 1943 alone.

Yet *I-Go Sakusen* was a major effort that yielded little in the way of strategic results. Had it occurred half a year earlier, when the Japanese war machine was still an unstoppable juggernaut, it might have dealt a crippling blow.

Naval historian Samuel Eliot Morison faulted the Japanese for investing heavily in a massed effort, contrasting it to the steady, more methodical campaign being waged by the Fifth Air Force. In his memoirs, Kenney criticized them for piecemeal attacks with no follow-up, writing that they lacked imagination and "did not understand air warfare [nor] how to handle large masses of aircraft."

Kenney noted that the Japanese "had no good heavy bomber that could fight its way to the target and back. We had both the B-17 and the B-24. When surface means of supply were lacking or insufficient, we had the air cargo planes and knew how to use them. The Japanese had no air cargo service and would not have known what to do with it." Kenney had certainly demonstrated that he understood tactical airlift.

The Japanese, though, did understand and depend upon sealift – and since the battle of the Bismarck Sea, they had come to understand that sealift was their Achilles heel when it came to the Allied bomber boys. The enemy had developed such a dread of Fifth Air Force bombers that instead of transport ships, supplies coming into northern New Guinea were being sent on coastal barges and motor launches that could be hidden along the jungled shorelines by day. By hugging the rim, coastal shipping could reduce its open-seas exposure. The 90-mile run across the Vitiaz Strait from Cape Gloucester on New Britain to Finschhafen on New Guinea's Huon Peninsula was a target-rich environment for the bombers. The daily routine for the Fifth involved barge-hunting and skip-bombing missions across the rim of the Bismarck Sea, as well as the strikes on key Japanese bases at Lae, Salamaua, and Finschhafen.

It was at the conclusion of one of these missions that Major Ed Larner, commander of the 90th Bomb Squadron, lost his life. Larner, who earned a Silver Star over Buna flying so low that one engine came back full of palm tree fronds, had become one of the Fifth Air Force folk heroes. On April 29, he was returning from a mission against Japanese positions up the Markham River from Lae, when his B-25, *Spook II*, crashed on landing at Dobodura. Hap Arnold had called him "a man who didn't know the meaning of the word quit," and he hadn't – right up to the end.

The Operation *Cartwheel* ground offensive began with a series of simultaneous Allied actions from New Guinea to the Solomons on June 30, 1943. After the absence of major ground action in New Guinea since the battle of Wau in January, American and Australian troops landed at Nassau Bay near Salamaua, as well as on New Georgia in the Solomons, and on the Solomon Sea islands of Woodlark (now Muyua) and Kiriwina. The latter, being about 350 miles from Rabaul, compared with Port Moresby's 500 miles, would provide bases for fighters escorting bombers against Rabaul.

The next major element of the Operation *Cartwheel* ground offensive was to be Operation *Postern* in early September, a pincer operation aimed at capturing the key Japanese bases around Lae. To prepare the way, V Bomber Command was called upon to begin softening up Japanese defenses in late July. The field of air action centered on Lae, but included Salamaua, while ranging east to Finschhafen and north to Madang and to the big base complex at Wewak far to the northwest. On July 27, one of the largest missions yet against a single SWPA target saw 35 B-25s and 18-B-24s over Salamaua. The missions on August 13 and September 1 each entered the record as the heaviest Fifth Air Force bombing raids to date in the SWPA, the latter exceeding 200 tons of bombs.

The first jaw of the *Postern* pincer went forward on September 4 with amphibious landings near Lae supported by Fifth Air Force B-25s, while two dozen B-24s pummeled the Japanese bases in the area with 96 tons of bombs. Japanese fighters flying out of Madang managed to make just a single fast strafing attack against the beachhead that morning, and a strike force from Rabaul arrived in the late afternoon.

The enemy bombers were greeted by Neel Kearby and his 348th Fighter Group. They were divided into three flights, with Kearby himself leading the third. Spotting the IJNAF coming in for a pass at 2,000 feet, Kearby led his men in a diving attack from 25,000 feet. He and his wingman, Lieutenant George Orr, lined up behind a G4M "Betty" bomber accompanied by a pair of escort fighters. As Kearby made a fast firing pass, Orr watched the G4M explode and a wing rip from one of the fighters. They pursued the remaining Japanese fighter, which disappeared into the clouds.

When the aerial battle was over that day, the P-38 pilots could claim 21 Japanese aircraft shot down, while among the P-47 pilots of the 348th, there were only two victories to count. Both were Kearby's, his first aerial victories. More would follow.

That night at Port Moresby, Kenney and MacArthur discussed the second jaw of the *Postern* pincer that would be engaged the next day. The 503rd Parachute Infantry Regiment was to descend into Nadzab, about 15 miles west of Lae in the valley of the Markham River. The 1,700 Americans, who had never jumped in combat before, would be accompanied by a handful of Australian artillerymen who had never even worn parachutes before, and who would be jumping *with* their artillery pieces.

Kenney casually mentioned to his boss that he planned to fly in one of the bombers supporting the airborne operation "to see how things went off."

When MacArthur told him that he didn't think Kenney should go, the Fifth Air Force commander replied that he had obeyed MacArthur's orders to keep out of combat, but that he didn't expect any trouble. He added that they were "my kids and I was going to see them do their stuff."

"You're right, George," MacArthur replied. "We'll both go. They're my kids, too."

"No, that doesn't make sense," Kenney argued. "Why, after living all these years and getting to be the head general of the show, is it necessary for you to risk having some five-dollar-a-month Japanese aviator shoot a hole through you?"

"I'm not worried about getting shot," MacArthur said. "Honestly, the only thing that disturbs me is the possibility that when we hit the rough air over the mountains my stomach might get upset. I'd hate to get sick and disgrace myself in front of the kids."

"I inspected them and found, as was only natural, a sense of nervousness among the ranks," MacArthur recalled about the following morning. "I decided that it would be advisable for me to fly in with them. I did not want them to go through their first baptism of fire without such comfort as my presence might bring to them. But they did not need me."

September 5 opened in the skies from Nadzab to Lae with six squadrons of B-25s attacking at 1,000 feet, each with eight .50-caliber machine guns blazing and five dozen fragmentation bombs – a total of 32 tons. They were followed at 500 feet by six A-20s flying in pairs to lay smoke as the last bomb exploded.

The C-47 transports of the 54th Troop Carrier Wing followed at 2,000 feet in three columns of three-plane elements, each column carrying a battalion. Fighters flew top cover at 3,000 feet. Kenney recalled of the mission:

> ... the seizure of Nadzab by the paratroopers on September 5th went off so well that it is still hard for me to believe that anything could have been so perfect. At the last minute the Australian gunners who were to man the battery of 25-pounders decided to jump with their guns ... Even this part of the show went off without a hitch and the guns were ready for action within an hour after they landed.

Kenney told Hap Arnold in a memo that he penned that night:

> I truly don't believe that another air force in the world today could have put this over as perfectly as the Fifth Air Force did. Three hundred and two airplanes in all, taking off from eight different fields in the Moresby and Dobodura areas, made a rendezvous right on the nose over Marilinan, flying through clouds, passes in the mountains, and over the top. Not a single squadron did any circling or stalling around but all slid into place like clockwork ... the operation really was a magnificent spectacle.

Kenney couldn't resist telling Arnold that MacArthur was "in a B-17 over the area watching the show and jumping up and down like a kid," even though he was not in the same B-17 to witness this.

Upon his safe return to Port Moresby, MacArthur – who had *not* lost his breakfast – pronounced the drop to be "the most perfect example of discipline and training" that he had ever seen.

By the end of the day, the paratroopers had secured 3 miles of the trail into Lae, using flamethrowers to burn off the tall kunai grass to get the Nadzab airfield ready to start accepting C-47 flights that would be airlifting the Australian 7th Division. The 35th Fighter Group would have two P-39 squadrons operating out of Nadzab by the end of October.

Within a few days of Operation *Postern*, the Japanese position began to crumble. On September 11, the enemy defenders of Salamaua fell back to Lae, but the Japanese evacuation of Lae, through the jungles to the north, had already begun. Australian forces entered Salamaua on September 11, and were occupying Lae five days later. The Australians landed at the key port of Finschhafen, on the tip of the Huon Peninsula, on September 22 against initially heavy Japanese opposition, but the town was secured by October 2. It would soon be transformed into an important Allied staging base.

By October, the Japanese were withdrawing from throughout the Huon Peninsula. As at Lae, they were not going quietly, but they were going, and they were abandoning large amounts of equipment as they went. It was a rout. Overhead, Allied airpower kept up the pressure on the retreating enemy, while Fifth Air Force troop carriers continued to airlift Australian and American troops into the Markham Valley upstream from Lae.

Only small numbers of Japanese aircraft were in the skies to interfere. Even George Kenney was mystified by the feeble response by Japanese bombers to the Allied presence in the Huon Peninsula and Markham Valley. The lack of enemy air action was, he recalled, "puzzling," in light of their still robust force at Rabaul.

Cartwheel over Rabaul

O n the Pacific strategic planning maps, all roads led to Rabaul, and by October 1943, the strategic planners were ready to pull the trigger. Douglas MacArthur and George Kenney hoped that Operation *Cartwheel's* climactic takedown of Rabaul could be accomplished during the last two weeks of the month.

On September 10, as the Lae–Nadzab operations were successfully past their initial phase, MacArthur hosted a meeting in Brisbane for leaders of both the SWPA and SOPAC. By now, Kenney's Fifth Air Force had a critical mass of bombers and P-38 escort fighters to launch a maximum effort air campaign. Advance operational bases from Lae to Dobodura to Woodlark Island were ready.

According to the minutes of the September 10 meeting, the Fifth Air Force "would attack airfields and shipping at Rabaul with the object of destroying shipping and neutralization of enemy air" in advance of Admiral Halsey's SOPAC landings on Bougainville, scheduled for November 1. Though Bougainville lay geographically within MacArthur's SWPA, the troops to be used were those who had been working their way north through the Solomons, so Halsey retained operational control. According to naval historian Samuel Eliot Morison, the purpose of capturing Bougainville was to provide bases for the ultimate capture of Rabaul.

October 15 was planned for the start date of the Rabaul air operation, but reconnaissance flights had just come back with aerial photos that turned heads and changed minds. Rabaul was so target-rich that the initial strike date was moved to October 12. On the runways of the airfields, there were 124 bombers and 145 fighters – all of which either had attacked the Allies in New Guinea or potentially could do so. In Rabaul's Simpson Harbor there were a heavy cruiser, a light cruiser, ten destroyers, five submarines, and 26 merchant vessels. With a thumbs up from the weather forecasters, the October 12 mission was on.

"By the time you get this letter you should have read some headlines about the show on Rabaul," Kenney wrote to Arnold in Washington on October 10. He continued:

> This is the beginning of what I believe is the most decisive action initiated so far in this theater. We are out not only to gain control of the air over New Britain and New Ireland but to make Rabaul untenable for Japanese shipping and to set up an air blockade of all the Japanese forces in that area ... In the past we have averaged around five percent of direct hits on shipping from high altitude. Our daylight bombing during the past three months on Salamaua, Lae, and Wewak has improved our accuracy tremendously. I expect to sink between 20 and 30 ships in this attack.

It was to be the largest air attack yet seen in the Pacific, with nearly 350 aircraft in the strike force. Crews were meticulously briefed on timing and routing so as to coordinate the massive effort.

The B-25s were tasked with opening the show, strafing, and dropping parafrags after a tree-top, low-level penetration. Having mustered at Dobodura, 115 B-25s took off early in the morning, flying east en masse at a thousand feet to Kiriwina Island, then dropping to wave-top altitude for the final run to the mouth of New Britain's Warangoi River, 22 miles southeast of Rabaul. Here they would split up and go after Rabaul's three main airfields.

Major Don Hall's 3rd Bomb Group, with 40 bombers, pointed their heavily armed noses toward Rapopo airfield. Meanwhile, Lieutenant Colonel Lawrence Tanburg's 38th Bomb Group and Colonel Clinton True's 345th Bomb Group headed to Vunakanau. True himself was piloting one of those aircraft.

The bombers entered their target areas in shallow "Vs," 12–15 aircraft abreast, with each V separated from the others by about a mile. Apparently, the first waves caught the enemy completely by

Lieutenant General Douglas MacArthur presides over the induction of the Philippine Army Air Corps (PAAC) into the US Army Forces in the Far East (USAFFE) at Camp Murphy near Manila on August 15, 1941. Behind MacArthur, from left to right, are Lieutenant Colonel Richard Sutherland, Colonel Harold George, Lieutenant Colonel William Marquat, and Major LeGrande Diller. (US Army)

Officers of the USAAF 3rd Pursuit Squadron in front of a Boeing P-26 Peashooter at Clark Field on Luzon in the Philippines, c. 1937. (USAAF)

In 1942, MacArthur left Manila in defeat, vowing to return. This picture shows him back in the city in early 1945 as the five-star commander of the victorious US Army command that liberated the Philippines from the Japanese occupation. (NARA)

General Lewis Hyde Brereton was a military aviation pioneer who began World War II as a major general commanding the Far East Air Force (FEAF) in the Philippines. He saw action as a senior commander in four major operational theaters. (USAAF)

Two North American A-27s of the 17th Pursuit Squadron at Nichols Field in the Philippines in 1941. The United States commandeered ten such attack aircraft ordered by Thailand when it became apparent the aircraft would fall into Japanese hands. All A-27s were destroyed when the Japanese attacked the Philippine Islands in the first days of the Pacific War. (USAAF)

A B-17D of the FEAF 19th Bombardment Group being loaded with 100- and 500-pound bombs, probably at Del Monte Field on Mindanao in the Philippines, early in 1942. (USAAF)

Allied commanders in New Guinea, c. October 1942. From left to right are Frank Forde, Australian Minister for the Army; General Douglas MacArthur; Australian General Sir Thomas Blamey, commander of Allied Land Forces; Lieutenant General George Churchill Kenney of the Fifth Air Force; Australian Lieutenant General Edmund Herring, the Allied logistics organizer; and Brigadier General Kenneth Walker of the Fifth Air Force V Bomber Command.
(Wikimedia Commons)

The Fifth Air Force B-17E bomber *Yankee Diddl'er* taking off from Seven Mile Field at Port Moresby on New Guinea, *c.* 1942. Assigned at the time to the 65th Bomb Squadron of the 43rd Bomb Group, the bomber was later assigned to the 8th Photo Reconnaissance Squadron operating from Port Moresby. (USAAF)

Stretchers are brought out by jeep to meet the B-17F Flying Fortress *The Old Man* of the 65th Bomb Squadron shortly after it landed at Dobodura, New Guinea, on March 8, 1943. The aircraft had been attacked by 13 Japanese fighters during a photoreconnaissance mission over Gasmata on New Britain. (USAAF)

Lieutenant General George Kenney, commander of the Fifth Air Force, with Major General Ennis Whitehead, his deputy commander, *c.* 1944. Whitehead also commanded the advanced echelon (ADVON) headquarters of the Fifth in Port Moresby. (USAAF)

Fifth Air Force leaders at Port Moresby, New Guinea, in 1942: Lieutenant Colonel Richard Carmichael, commander of the 19th Bomb Group; Fifth Air Force commander Major General George Kenney; and Brigadier General Kenneth Walker, commander of V Bomber Command. (USAAF)

A Fifth Air Force Douglas A-20 bomber conducting a low-level strike on a Japanese transport ship during the battle of the Bismarck Sea in March 1943. (USAAF)

Major General George Kenney, commander of the Fifth Air Force, at Port Moresby with Brigadier General Kenneth Walker, commander of V Bomber Command. Walker, who was KIA in 1943, was posthumously awarded the Medal of Honor. (USAAF)

Brigadier General Howard Knox Ramey became commander of V Bomber Command of the Fifth Air Force in January 1943 when Ken Walker was KIA, and led it in the battle of the Bismarck Sea. On March 26, 1943, his aircraft disappeared on a reconnaissance flight over Torres Strait. No trace of it was ever found. (USAAF)

Paul Irvin "Pappy" Gunn helped found Philippine Airlines before the war and joined the USAAF when the Japanese attacked. A fearless pilot, especially in low-level flying, he is best remembered as the Fifth Air Force engineering genius who devised numerous important aircraft and weapons systems modifications. (USAAF)

Paul Bernard "Squeeze" Wurtsmith commanded the 49th Fighter Group early in the war, and in 1943 he assumed command of V Fighter Command of the Fifth Air Force. He later commanded the Thirteenth Air Force during the southern Philippines and Borneo campaigns. (USAAF)

This remarkable photo shows a Fifth Air Force A-20 Havoc making a very low-level strafing pass over the Japanese airfield at Lae, New Guinea, in 1943. Note the Imperial Japanese Navy Air Force Mitsubishi G4M bomber on the ground. (USAAF)

Fifth Air Force B-25 medium bombers during low-level strikes against Japanese installations on the northern New Guinea coastline near Wewak on August 13, 1943. This was a lead-up to the devastating raids that came four and five days later. (USAAF)

A Consolidated B-24 Liberator of the Fifth Air Force 43rd Bomb Group during a high-altitude bombing mission against the Japanese base at Salamaua in eastern New Guinea on August 13, 1943. (USAAF)

24825 A

Aboard these C-47 transports on the steel matting runway at Port Moresby are some of around 1,700 paratroopers of the 503rd Parachute Infantry Regiment who were dropped into Nadzab on September 5, 1943. In the foreground on the left are George Kenney and Douglas MacArthur, who observed the mission from the air. (USAAF)

General Douglas MacArthur, aboard the B-17F *Talisman*, observes the 503rd Parachute Infantry Regiment drop into Nadzab in the valley of New Guinea's Markham River on September 5, 1943. (USAAF)

General Douglas MacArthur shakes the hand of pilot Colonel Harry Hawthorne after disembarking from the B-17F *Talisman*, from which he had observed the 503rd Parachute Infantry Regiment drop into Nadzab in New Guinea. (USAAF)

Left and Below A bomb explodes off the port quarter of a Japanese cargo ship during the November 2, 1943 attack on Simpson Harbor at Rabaul on New Britain. Note the 3rd Bomb Group B-25 on the left and the Japanese heavy cruiser *Haguro* in center distance. (USAAF)

Above These two photos, taken on October 16, 1943, show the B-25D *Red Wrath* of the 498th "Falcons" Bomb Squadron of the 345th "Air Apaches" Bomb Group, piloted by Captain R. W. Judd during a low-level attack on Japanese antiaircraft sites near Wewak and Boram on the north coast of New Guinea. (USAAF)

The B-25D Mitchell bomber *Here's Howe* of the 90th "Pair-O-Dice" Bomb Squadron of the 3rd "Grim Reapers" Bomb Group during a November 2, 1943 strike on Simpson Harbor at Rabaul on New Britain. (USAAF)

A B-25D Mitchell bomber of the 13th Bomb Squadron departing Simpson Harbor at Rabaul on New Britain after the big Fifth Air Force attack of November 2, 1943. (USAAF)

General Douglas MacArthur in Brisbane, Australia, with Lieutenant General Walter Krueger, commander of the Sixth Army (left) and US Army Chief of Staff General George Marshall (right), during Marshall's inspection tour of the South Pacific in December 1943. (NARA)

Captain Richard Ira "Dick" Bong of the 49th Fighter Group in the cockpit of his P-38 Lighting, possibly at Dobodura on New Guinea in 1943. Bong was destined to be the leading American fighter ace in the Pacific. (USAAF)

Colonel Neel Kearby, commander of the Fifth Air Force 348th Fighter Squadron, climbs into his
P-47 Thunderbolt, *Fiery Ginger*, which is marked with flags indicating aerial victories. He added
his 15th flag on December 3, 1943, and eventually raised his score to 22. His last victory came on
March 5, 1944, shortly before he was KIA. (USAAF)

Captain Thomas Joseph "Tommy" Lynch at 14 Mile Field at Port Moresby, New Guinea, in May 1943. Having scored 20 aerial victories, Lynch was a leading Fifth Air Force ace when he was shot down on a strafing mission over New Guinea in March 1944. (USAAF)

A B-25 Mitchell bomber of the 405th "Green Dragons" Bomb Squadron conducting a "skip-bombing" attack on a Japanese ship off the coast of New Guinea in 1944. (USAAF)

Major Thomas Buchanan "Tommy" McGuire wearing his famous signature 500-hour cap and his Colt sidearm. McGuire commanded the 431st Fighter Squadron of the 475th Fighter Group in New Guinea and the Philippines, and was the second-highest-scoring American ace in the Pacific. (USAAF)

Vice Admiral Thomas Kinkaid, General Douglas MacArthur, and Colonel Lloyd Labrbas aboard the cruiser USS *Phoenix* during the bombardment in preparation for the Allied landings on Los Negros Island in the Admiralty Islands on February 28, 1944. (NARA)

General Douglas MacArthur, commander in chief of the South West Pacific Areas (SWPA) command, points out a location on a *National Geographic* map for Admiral Chester Nimitz, commander in chief of the Pacific Ocean Areas (POA) command. The two senior Pacific commanders were meeting at MacArthur's headquarters in Brisbane, Australia, on March 27, 1944. (NARA)

surprise. Antiaircraft fire was light and generally inaccurate. Following the B-25s in strikes against Rapopo and Tobera airfields were a dozen Bristol Beaufighters of the RAAF No. 71 Wing, which was flying out of Kiriwina.

At Vunakanau, a half dozen A6M Zeros managed to get airborne, and one of them succeeded in shooting down the B-25 piloted by Lieutenant Sidney Crews. The remaining bombers departed the target area and headed for home. Except for a few damaged bombers that recovered on Kiriwina, the B-25 force was on the ground at Dobodura by early afternoon.

Damage assessment was difficult because each aircraft was over the target for mere seconds and visibility for later waves was compromised by heavy smoke, but claims ranged as high as more than two dozen aircraft destroyed on the ground at Rapopo alone.

The heavy bombers were timed to go in at high altitude after the medium bombers had made their exit. From Port Moresby, seven squadrons of B-24s from the 43rd and 90th Bomb Groups went east. En route, after a rendezvous over Kiriwina, they would be covered by P-38s from the 39th Fighter Squadron of the 35th Fighter Group, and by the 80th of the 8th. The day got off to a bad start when a force comprised of 25 B-24s and 19 P-38s aborted because of mechanical problems.

The 400th Bomb Squadron of the 90th arrived shortly after noon, coming over Rabaul in six-ship cells. With the element of surprise long dissipated, the IJNAF was now ready, hurling around 40 A6M Zeros at the bombers, downing two. The 321st Bomb Squadron, which came next, was luckier.

The scene below was reported as pandemonium, with Japanese vessels swarming around Simpson Harbor in evasive action and trying to escape to open water. Initial claims had three destroyers and many merchant vessels sunk – figures that Kenney used in his memoirs – though later photoreconnaissance noted just one destroyer and two large transports sunk, along with a number of harbor vessels. Kenney's prediction of sinking "between 20 and 30 ships" was not met, but damage to wharves and port facilities was substantial, and nearly 100 aircraft were probably destroyed on the ground or in the air.

Though the day's operation had not been a knockout punch, it could certainly be called a success – and the headquarters of both MacArthur and Kenney *did* call it that.

Kenney credited Brigadier General Ennis Whitehead, his deputy and commander of the Fifth Air Force ADVON headquarters in Port Moresby, for the success. He later wrote that Whitehead's "planning had been faultless and his detailed instructions had been carried out to the letter. As he said, this was the first team."

"By the time I got through listening to the interrogation of the crews I was proud of the Fifth Air Force," Kenney recalled. He continued:

Their timing, precision, and bombing had been excellent and, in spite of extremely heavy antiaircraft fire, every airplane but one had attacked its assigned target. During the approach to Rabaul Harbor and while still about three miles from the town, one of the B-24s had been knocked almost over on its back by an antiaircraft shell which had burst just under a wing. In order to gain control, the pilot ordered the four-ton load of bombs released. As they hit the ground, a huge explosion occurred and great clouds of smoke billowed up over a huge area. A direct hit had been inadvertently scored on a big Japanese fuel dump that we hadn't known even existed. Even Lady Luck was working for us that day.

Lady Luck had also brought them good weather that day, but she frowned upon them the next. On October 13, 108 B-25s and 70 B-24s were primed and ready, but only the RAAF Beauforts managed to get through to Simpson Harbor. The 70 Fifth Air Force heavies launched early in the morning, but ran into a powerful storm system 150 miles from the target and were forced to abort – though 27 diverted to secondary targets at the western end of New Britain.

It would be more than a week before the weather over Rabaul fully cooperated again. Captain Bernhardt Mortensen, in Volume 4 of *The Army Air Forces in World War II*, wrote that "the Fifth Air Force not only lost flying days, but it lost the cumulative effect of continuous mass raids."

As the Fifth's planners were organizing their own operations, Japanese bombers were not idle. Mortensen reported that the big October 12 attack was interpreted by the enemy as "preliminary to an invasion," which caused them to brave the weather for a series of strikes of their own against Allied shipping in Oro Bay off Dobodura and against Finschhafen between October 15 and 19.

Kenney had used the perceived success of October 12 to nudge Arnold for an increased flow of men and materiel, especially more P-38s. However, the request reached Arnold at a bad time. On October 14 – October 15 in the Pacific – the Eighth Air Force in England had suffered another seriously bad mission to compound the effect of losses suffered two months earlier on August 17 over Schweinfurt and Regensburg. The Eighth had gone back to Schweinfurt, the center of the German ball bearing industry. The idea was that ball bearings are a "bottleneck" component without which many other industries would founder.

The mission had not gone well. Whereas 60 bombers had been lost in August, 77 aircraft – 26 percent of the strike force – went down in October on the day that became known as "Black Thursday." Doubts were expressed whether the Eighth could absorb these losses, and whether the strategic air campaign against Germany could even continue.

At this most inopportune moment, Kenney told Arnold that his own bomber losses were "not being replaced fast enough to keep up with the attrition we were suffering. My bomber availability was also going down fast."

Kenney recalled that Arnold shot back, telling him that "on account of the serious situation in England he could not give me any more [bombers] or any more P-38 pilots for the next two months." Arnold reminded Kenney that it was "Germany First" and that even the campaign against Germany was in jeopardy.

The Fifth attempted a smaller follow-up Rabaul mission on October 18, but the high-altitude heavy bombers and their P-38 escorts were again forced to turn back. Coming in at low level, though, around 50 B-25s managed to squeeze under the weather. Among these, Clinton True's 345th Bomb Group did especially well in two passes over Rapopo that cost the Japanese around two dozen aircraft on the ground. The group's 500th Bomb Squadron hit Simpson Harbor, upending two transport ships and destroying a corvette.

The B-25 piloted by Lieutenant Ralph Wallace, named *Tondelayo*, was damaged, lost an engine, and fell behind. Two other bombers held back to try to protect him from the swarms of Zeros that were trying to finish him off. Both of the "good Samaritan" aircraft, piloted by Captain Lyle Anacker and Lieutenant Harlan Peterson, were shot down, but the men of *Tondelayo* survived 200 miles of constant Japanese fighter harassment to make an emergency landing on Kiriwina. Wallace's crewmembers credit his skillful low-level flying with actually outmaneuvering at least four Japanese fighter pilots to the extent that they crashed into the ocean trying to catch him. Each of *Tondelayo*'s crewmen was awarded a Silver Star.

For the day, the 38th and 345th Bomb Groups claimed three ships sunk, along with 41 aircraft destroyed on the ground and 38 in the air. One of the transports actually survived and a damaged corvette was later repaired. Japanese records admit the loss of 11 aircraft.

True was reprimanded for continuing the mission after the escorting P-38s turned back, though apparently he was violating procedure rather than disobeying a direct order.

Kenney recalled that True "pretended that he didn't hear the fighters say that they were leaving and kept on flying just over the waves until they hit the New Britain coast."

Kenney went on to say that he called True "over to headquarters and bawled him out for disobeying our standing instructions that bombers were also to turn back if the fighters had to. I told him that if he repeated the offense I would chase him home and then gave him a Distinguished Service Cross."

After congratulating him on the success of his mission, Kenney said, "Now that it's all over, tell me. True, didn't you hear the P-38s say that they were going home?"

"General," he replied, looking Kenney in the eye, "I didn't hear a word."

Knowing that True was lying, he said, "Okay, we'll forget it, but don't do it again."

In retrospect, Kenney admitted that "I had a suspicion he didn't have a single regret, in fact, was rather proud of himself. As a matter of fact, I was kind of proud of him, too."

While the scale of the October 12 mission was not repeated, Whitehead's crews were able to at least achieve some form of continuity. For the rest of the month, attacks with medium bombers would alternate with those using heavy bombers on the next day that weather permitted.

In the meantime, when Rabaul missions were not possible because of weather, the Fifth Air Force was keeping busy expending its ordnance in missions all across the northern side of New Guinea from the edge of the Allied perimeter north of Lae to Wewak.

Whatever losses the Japanese had suffered in the big October 12 and 18 attacks, reconnaissance indicated that their fighter strength at Rabaul was back up to at least 211 by the time that the weather finally cleared. Kenney and Whitehead put a mission on the schedule for October 23, combining a high-altitude attack by 57 B-24s on Lakunai and Vunakanau with a fighter sweep by three P-38 squadrons.

Lady Luck had teased them with a good weather forecast, then punished them with bad weather over Lakunai and Vunakanau, but gave them clear skies over Rapopo, allowing them to divert the strike mission to that location. Despite confusion over the changed target, Kenney reckoned 45 bombers dropped their ordnance, and USAAF records estimate 20 Japanese aircraft destroyed on the ground. The P-38s shot down between 13 and 20 enemy aircraft by USAAF records, and lost one. This American pilot was rescued by indigenous islanders and lived with them for an extended period before returning to his squadron.

Having developed a rhythm of alternating heavy bomber missions with those by medium bombers, Kenney and Whitehead dispatched a mixed B-25 and P-38 force to Rabaul on October 24, and 61 B-24s with 81 escorting P-38s the next day. They ran into rapidly worsening weather, and an announcement on the command frequency ordered an abort. Many heard it, but others, including 50 bomber crews, did not or chose to ignore it.

Supported by the P-38s, the heavy bombers worked the target area, especially the Lakunai airfield, for the better part of an hour. The Intelligence Summary reported the loss of a 403rd Bomb Squadron B-24 that emerged from the raid heavily damaged and falling behind, thereby becoming low-hanging fruit for Japanese fighter pilots. Two other bombers boxed it in for protection, but after a time, they had to break away. Amazingly, the stricken B-24 held on for at least 15 minutes of a low-altitude, running gun battle before breaking up and falling into the sea. Everyone but the two pilots survived to be recovered by a PBY search and rescue plane.

The climax of the air campaign against Rabaul would come at last as part of a vast interlocking series of air and naval actions that unfolded across the region during the first five days of November 1943.

The great battle began on November 1 when the 3rd Marine Division, supported by elements of Halsey's Third Fleet, landed at Cape Torokino on Empress Augusta Bay on Bougainville, northernmost of the major islands of the Solomons.

In response, Vice Admiral Tomoshige Samejima, commander of the Japanese Eighth Fleet, and his boss, Admiral Mineichi Koga, who had succeeded Yamamoto as commander in chief of the IJN Combined Fleet, felt the need for decisive action. From Rabaul, Samejima dispatched a sizable naval counterforce to Empress Augusta Bay. Under the direct command of Vice Admiral Sentaro Omori, it included two heavy cruisers, two light cruisers, and 11 destroyers, with five of the latter as troop carriers.

Koga, who had been concentrating the majority of his fleet in the Solomons and farther east, hoping for a decisive naval battle with the US Navy in the Central Pacific, now committed seven heavy cruisers to join Samejima's force. Meanwhile, Koga made a fateful decision. His best pilots were those assigned to his aircraft carriers, but he began pulling both planes and pilots from his carrier force to beef up his air strength at Rabaul.

Thanks to codebreakers and aerial reconnaissance, both MacArthur and Halsey were well aware of what was happening, and a major Fifth Air Force mission against Rabaul was planned for November 2.

That morning, as so often in recent weeks, the mission had to be scratched on account of weather. However, later in the day, reconnaissance aircraft reported that the skies over Rabaul were clear. Photo interpreters also counted 237 Japanese aircraft, as well as seven destroyers and no fewer than 20 freighters in Simpson Harbor.

The Fifth Air Force scrambled to reassemble the mission that had stood down that morning. Clear weather must not be wasted.

The show opened with P-38s of the 39th and 80th Fighter Squadrons making a low-level sweep over Lakunai and the harbor. Next came four squadrons of B-25s from Clinton True's 345th Bomb Group, escorted by P-38s of the 431st and 432nd Fighter Squadrons, with orders to destroy the antiaircraft guns around Rabaul using white phosphorus bombs. The antiaircraft guns thus suppressed, two B-25 squadrons of the 3rd Bomb Group and three from the 38th hit the ships in Simpson Harbor with 1,000-pound bombs.

Lieutenant Colonel John "Jock" Henebry led the 3rd Bomb Group strike force that day. Kenney later wrote that they "swept across the harbor at mast height with a rain of machine gun fire and heavy bombs that sank or damaged every ship in its path, in spite of an intense concentration of fire from the 18 naval vessels and 20 merchant ships under assault. Of the 38 vessels in Rabaul Harbor that day, 30 received direct hits in the toughest, hardest-fought engagement of the war."

The Fifth Air Force press release claimed that their bombers had sunk three destroyers, eight large freighters, and some coasters. The aggregate total of 50,000 tons that was initially estimated was later revised downward to 13,000. There were at least 16 Japanese aircraft destroyed at Lakunai, and estimates of enemy fighter aircraft shot down ranged up to 68 in official estimates.

It was a costly day for both sides. Eight of the 345th's B-25s in the initial strike were hit, of which three never came home. Five other B-25s went down, as did nine P-38s. The Fifth Air Force lost 45 crewmen either killed or missing.

One of the B-25s lost was piloted by Major Raymond Wilkins. His posthumous Medal of Honor citation summarized the experience of many that day:

> [His aircraft] was hit almost immediately, the right wing damaged, and control rendered extremely difficult. Although he could have withdrawn he held fast and led his squadron in to the attack. He strafed a group of small harbor vessels, and then, at low level, attacked an enemy destroyer. His thousand-pound bomb struck squarely amidships, causing the vessel to explode. Although anti-aircraft fire from this vessel had seriously damaged his left vertical stabilizer, he refused to deviate from the course. From below mast-head height he attacked a transport of some nine thousand tons, scoring a hit which engulfed the ship in flames.

As Wilkins began to withdraw his squadron, a heavy cruiser barred their way, so to neutralize the cruiser's guns and attract their fire, Wilkins "went in for a strafing run. His damaged stabilizer was completely shot off. To avoid swerving into his wing planes he had to turn so as to expose the belly and full wing surfaces of his plane to the enemy fire; it caught and crumpled his left wing. Now past control the bomber crashed into the sea."

Kenney reported that Jock Henebry's airplane, "riddled with bullet and shell holes and with one engine gone, landed in the water just short of Kiriwina. Jock and his whole crew were rescued that day." Henebry later commanded the 3rd Bomb Group.

In his memoirs, Kenney bubbled over with hyperbole, calling the November 2 mission a "big event ... destined to be compared with the Bismarck Sea Battle and the take-out of the Japanese air force at Wewak on August 17."

Early on that same morning of November 2, as the Fifth Air Force was preparing for the initially postponed Rabaul mission, the IJN struck the American invasion fleet off Empress Augusta Bay. Halsey was outgunned, but he went on the offensive, achieving a decisive naval victory over Omori, who lost a half dozen major warships damaged or sunk.

Halsey had not planned to attack Rabaul, but he decided to exploit the momentum of his Empress Augusta Bay victory – so he brought up Rear Admiral Frederick Sherman's Task Force 38, which included the carriers USS *Saratoga* and USS *Princeton*, and did just that.

A perfect storm broke over Rabaul on the morning of November 5, just as the retreating Japanese ships reached Simpson Harbor. The two American carriers launched nearly 100 aircraft, half of them dive bombers and torpedo bombers, and they tore into the Japanese ships. About an hour later, a coordinated Fifth Air Force attack came over with 27 B-24s of the 43rd Bomb Group and 67 P-38s drawn from various groups. When it was over, four cruisers were badly damaged – but the storm was not finished.

After the climactic battering of November 5, Halsey contacted MacArthur, and they decided upon a coordinated aerial coup de grâce against Rabaul for November 11. Halsey was bringing in the carrier air groups of the USS *Essex*, USS *Bunker Hill*, and USS *Independence*, as well as his "SOPAC air force," Nathan Twining's Thirteenth Air Force, which would contribute its own B-24 heavy bombers to the overall effort.

As far as the USAAF was concerned, the baton for the Rabaul strikes passed from the Fifth to the Thirteenth that day, as the latter's

B-24s made their first strike against Rabaul, flying from Munda on New Georgia, 450 miles to the southeast. They were supported by fighter escorts operating out of advanced fields on newly captured real estate in Bougainville. The Thirteenth Air Force would continue the air campaign against Rabaul until March of the following year, but the once great bastion of Japanese power in the Southwest Pacific was already withering on the vine.

Mineichi Koga had already made the decision to withdraw his naval presence from Rabaul.

In aerial battles, the Americans were achieving victories at a ratio of three or four to one as the Japanese were running short of well-trained pilots, who were not being replaced by the training programs in Japan. The nature of the IJN Air Force pilots, who were once recognized by the Americans as both skilled and aggressive, had changed. They were running out of steam.

The nature of this tipping point was perhaps best summarized in a line from the Fifth Air Force Intelligence Summary of October 29 that said of the enemy fliers, "the eager pilots were not experienced; and the experienced not eager."

12

The Race of Aces

The climactic showdown in the skies over Rabaul and the Bismarck Rim that unfolded through the fall of 1943 saw the gradual demise of the experienced pilots who had made the IJAAF and the IJNAF so formidable for so long. Neither service was able to meet the demand for replacement pilots, and as flight training programs were trimmed from months to weeks, the skill level of newer pilots declined.

At the same time, the flight training program in the United States was expanding and the pool of qualified airmen grew. New planes and new pilots, promised to MacArthur and Kenney by Hap Arnold in the spring, arrived through the summer, and began to make a big difference in the fall.

One of the first questions asked by Neel Kearby when he had arrived in June to take command of the all-P-47 348th Fighter Group was "who had the highest scores for shooting down Japanese aircraft?"

The competitiveness inherent in that question was present throughout the Fifth Air Force, and as the number of aces grew, there was obviously talk of a race among them for the highest score. If there was a race, the P-38 pilots were definitely in the lead. Dick Bong, in the 9th Fighter Squadron of the 49th Fighter Group, scored his 16th aerial victory on July 28. George Welch, the hero of Pearl Harbor, matched this score by early September, and Tommy Lynch, with the 39th Fighter Squadron of the 35th Fighter Group, reached 16 on September 16.

Kearby and his fellow P-47 Thunderbolt pilots were not to be outdone. Having scored twin victories over the Hopoi Beach landings on September 4, Kearby was leading the 348th flying top cover for C-47 airlifters ten days later over Nadzab when someone reported an unidentified aircraft ducking into a cloud. Kearby and six other pilots began pursuit of what was soon identified as a Mitsubishi Ki-46, a twin-engine IJAAF reconnaissance aircraft. Kearby opened fire at 300 yards and blew it out of the sky.

The P-47s of the 348th could not match the P-38s of the other groups for range, so they did not fly the Rabaul missions. Instead, they spent a lot of time flying top cover for the C-47 transports crossing the Owen Stanley Mountains, coming and going from Port Moresby. By the end of September, though, they were flying fighter sweeps over northeastern New Guinea, hoping to lure Japanese fighter pilots into dueling with the more powerful Thunderbolts.

Such was the case on October 11, the day before that great maximum effort mission to Rabaul that looms so large in the annals of Fifth Air Force history.

Kearby was leading a four-ship patrol up the coast toward Wewak with three of the group's best pilots, including Major Raymond Gallagher, who commanded the 342nd Fighter Squadron, as well as Captains John Moore and Bill Dunham. Reaching Wewak in the late morning, they spotted an IJAAF Ki-43 Hayabusa fighter flying far below and Kearby dived to attack. Opening fire as he approached, he sent the enemy fighter spiraling down in a column of smoke and fire. It was later determined that Kearby's fourth aerial victory had been against Lieutenant Colonel Tamiya Teranishi, the experienced commander of the IJAAF 14th Hikodan (equivalent of a US fighter group).

As the Americans turned eastward, they found the sky filled with enemy aircraft – around a dozen fighters below them and a formation of 36 bombers farther below, returning to Wewak from a mission against American positions around the Huon Peninsula.

With Dunham on his wing and Moore flying top cover, Kearby made a steep firing pass exploiting the speed and firepower of the P-47. As they passed through the Japanese formation like a scythe, Kearby opened fire and watched two Ki-43s explode in rapid succession. The first one made him an ace. Within moments, he had maneuvered behind another Japanese fighter and made it his fourth for the day.

As the scythe emerged from the Japanese formation, Kearby the hunter became Kearby the hunted as a Ki-61 fighter seized upon him. Luckily, Dunham lined up behind the Japanese fighter and took him out.

Moore attacked another of the Ki-61s and shot him down, but had two more gang up on him. Seeing this, Kearby raced to intervene. Opening fire, he literally shot one of the enemy aircraft in two, leaving the other tumbling downward trailing smoke.

With this, and with their fuel situation critical, the four Americans left Wewak skies to refuel at Lae and fly on to Port Moresby.

Douglas MacArthur was at the Fifth Air Force ADVON headquarters when they landed. He was meeting with Kenney about the big bomber mission scheduled for the next day when Neel Kearby came in. Asked to tell how the day had gone for the men of the 348th, Kearby replied that Moore had gotten two, and the others one each. He added that he had downed seven Japanese fighters – although he learned later that his gun camera had run out of film just as his tracers started to impact the seventh.

Both MacArthur and Kenney congratulated Kearby, and Kenney said that he wanted to write Kearby up for the Medal of Honor. MacArthur said that he "would approve it and send it to Washington."

Meanwhile, Bong, the leading ace in the SWPA, had been on a long furlough in Australia as others in the "race" were gaining. He scored his first victory since the summer over Gasmata on October 2, but it was not until the Rabaul offensive that he began once again to run up his score.

On October 29, the 9th Fighter Squadron launched 13 of the 53 P-38s that went out to escort the B-24s. The Lightnings were met by around 40 enemy interceptors, and at least eight of these jumped the 9th at 22,000 feet. Bong went into a dive to escape a pair of the Zeros, eluded them, and wound up at about 1,000 feet. Confronted by another Zero, he quickly shot it down and looked for more. He chased a pair and claimed one before he broke off to go home. Of the enemy planes claimed by the squadron, Bong and Lieutenant John "Jump" O'Neill each scored two.

On November 5, Bong was part of that perfect storm that broke over Rabaul as the Fifth Air Force and the aircraft of two US Navy carriers converged. The 9th Fighter Squadron contributed 11 of the five dozen P-38s escorting the heavy bombers, and these were met by around 15 Zeros. Leading the squadron's Red Flight, Bong lined up one Zero from behind, and went after a second when the first exploded. Two kills that day raised Bong's overall score to 21.

On November 7, Dick Bong flew his last mission before he joined Tommy Lynch in going back to the States on leave. George Welch also departed the SWPA in November, stricken with malaria.

This left Neel Kearby as the top-scoring USAAF ace still in the SWPA. He had raised his tally to 12 in mid-October, and added three more on December 3.

Kearby had also changed jobs. He had been promoted to colonel, relieved as commander of the 348th Fighter Group, and kicked upstairs to serve as commander, albeit temporarily, of V Fighter Command, a post in which he was still able to fly combat missions.

Emerging into the top tier of P-38 aces when Bong, Lynch, and Welch departed were Gerald Richard "Jerry" Johnson, who flew with Bong in the 49th, and Tommy McGuire of the all-P-38 475th Fighter Group. Referred to by George Kenney as the "thin little black-mustached lad," McGuire had brought his total to seven by the end of August and added two more over Wewak on September 28.

On October 15, both McGuire and Johnson were in action over Oro Bay near Buna and Dobodura, defending Allied shipping from determined attacks by Japanese bombers escorted by fighters. Alerted only moments before to the approaching strike force, the P-38s tore into a formation of IJNAF dive bombers and Zero fighters, with Jerry Johnson claiming three victories.

As their ground crews at Dobodura watched and cheered, the 475th Fighter Group alone shot down 21 of the attackers. Of these, ten were downed by the 431st Fighter Squadron, two by Lieutenant Fran Lent, and another by McGuire.

Two days later, the IJAAF, flying Ki-48 twin-engine bombers, repeated the attack on Oro Bay attempted by the IJNAF.

When the alert was sounded and there was an urgent scramble to get airborne, McGuire realized that his own aircraft was undergoing maintenance, so he "borrowed" the aircraft belonging to the commander of the 431st Fighter Squadron, Major Franklin Nichols. When the major's crew chief tried to stop him, McGuire quipped that he feared the Japanese more than the wrath of Nichols. McGuire joined Red Flight, led by Major Marion Kirby, and as they climbed they spotted 15 enemy fighters. McGuire selected a target and attacked, breaking off when he had fatally damaged the aircraft. It was later observed to have exploded.

Trying to rejoin Red Flight, McGuire was twice attacked, once by a pair of Japanese fighters, and once by three. He got away both times by nosing over into a steep dive, but it left him separated from Red Flight. As he was climbing back, he saw seven Japanese fighters ganging up on a single P-38, so he intervened. He managed to down two enemy aircraft and chase away the others, but he had been hit in the wrist by a Japanese machine gun round, and the controls in the P-38 were unresponsive.

McGuire abandoned ship in a steep dive only to discover that his parachute's ripcord had been damaged. He finally got the chute deployed a few hundred feet before he fell, bleeding profusely, into the shark-infested waters of Oro Bay. Luckily, a PT Boat picked up McGuire and returned him to his base, where Franklin Nichols bawled him out for stealing his aircraft and then recommended him for his second Silver Star.

McGuire, who was sent to Australia to recuperate from his injuries, returned to Dobodura in mid-December having been promoted to captain. He flew about 70 hours through the latter half of the month, but did not see combat until the day after Christmas.

Flying top cover for the American landings at Cape Gloucester on December 26, McGuire flew more than seven hours, returning to Dobodura twice to refuel and reload. During the day, he was credited with shooting down four D3A dive bombers, but "gave" one of the credits to a P-47 pilot who had also claimed it. Not so lucky that day was Major Edward "Porky" Cragg, a 15-victory ace and commander of the 80th Fighter Squadron. He claimed a Japanese fighter, but lost his own life.

Talk of a "race of aces" had inevitably been ongoing at the fighter bases across the SWPA throughout the latter half of 1943, but with the beginning of 1944, it began to be noticed by war correspondents and made its way into popular culture at home. After double victories on both January 3 and January 9, Neel Kearby had reached 21, matching the score of the absent Dick Bong and exceeding that of Tommy Lynch.

Kearby's Medal of Honor was authorized by the War Department on January 6, but according to George Kenney, the news did not reach the SWPA until January 20. Kenney recalled:

Neel happened to be in my office when it came in. I immediately rushed him up to General MacArthur's office and had the decoration ceremony done by the Old Man himself. The General did the thing up right and so overwhelmed Neel that he wanted to go right back to New Guinea and knock down some more Japanese to prove that he was as good as MacArthur had said he was.

As Brigadier General Paul Wurtsmith resumed command of V Fighter Command on January 13, Kearby remained on the command staff. Here, he was joined by Tommy Lynch, who returned to the SWPA in January, having been in Pennsylvania to marry his college sweetheart. As Kearby had been relieved as commander of the 348th Fighter Group, Lynch was no longer commander of the 39th Fighter Squadron. Likewise, when Dick Bong arrived back in the SWPA in February, George Kenney attached him directly to the V Fighter Command staff rather than having him return to the 49th Fighter Group.

Now that they were staff officers, the initial and obvious interpretation is that the three top-scoring aces in the theater had been relegated to desk jobs. But this is not what Kenney had in mind. Without group or squadron commitments, they were now permitted to "freelance," in the old knightly sense of the term, meaning that they could fly operational missions of their own choosing.

Though he often said that he discouraged a race of aces, Kenney's actions tell the opposite story.

Bong and Lynch, the two P-38 pilots among this remarkable trio, formed what they called a "Flying Circus," and flew patrols on their own, or while attached to larger missions. Lynch downed a Ki-48 bomber near Wewak on February 10 while it was just the two of them, and Bong claimed a Ki-61 fighter five days later while they were flying with A-20s on a strike mission to Kavieng. On February 28, Bong attacked a G4M bomber while it was landing at one of the Wewak airfields, but he refused to accept credit because the airplane had rolled to a stop before it blew up.

March 3 proved to be the best day for the Flying Circus. The two men were on a hunting trip when they spotted a Ki-21 bomber flying at low level near Tadji, an IJAAF airfield located about 100 miles west of Wewak. Lynch damaged the aircraft while Bong finished it off. They then engaged several Ki-61 fighters, downing one of them before attacking a pair of Ki-21s. The scores for Lynch and Bong now stood at 19 and 24, respectively.

For Bong, the race of aces now took on a new dimension. At the beginning of the year, as the scores of American aces had mounted, there had been a great deal of interest in the American media – not to mention American fighter bases around the world – in who would be the first American ace to match the score of Eddie Rickenbacker. America's "ace of aces" in World War I, Rickenbacker had downed 26 German aircraft. Unfortunately for the USAAF, the first man to reach that count in World War II was Captain Joe Foss of the US Marine Corps. Flying out of Guadalcanal with Marine Fighter Squadron VMF-121, Foss had downed his 26th Japanese aircraft on January 15, 1943. However, he had been ordered to return to the United States to collect celebrity status and a Medal of Honor. This meant that the next goal in the race of aces was to *exceed* the Rickenbacker total.

On March 5, the leading USAAF contenders – Bong with 24, Kearby with 21, and Lynch with 19 – were all in New Guinea air space.

Arriving over Wewak's Dagua airfield, Bong and Lynch reported three Ki-43 fighters far below and plunged to strike. Lynch destroyed one of them immediately, and the four surviving aircraft pursued one another through the clouds. Bong claimed one fighter, but his claim was downgraded to "probable" because his gun camera malfunctioned, and because Lynch had not been able to witness it through the clouds.

Kearby reached Dagua himself late in the afternoon, accompanied by Major Sam Blair and Captain Bill Dunham, who had flown with him on the day he downed seven Japanese aircraft and earned the Medal of Honor. They spotted three G3M medium bombers on approach to Dagua and shot them down – but they had not noticed other Japanese aircraft farther back and also on their final approach. Preoccupied by the bombers, the Americans had inserted themselves directly into the sights of three Ki-43 fighters that were now closing on them. Both Blair and Dunham managed to outmaneuver their attackers in the late afternoon light, but they could find no trace of Kearby. They went home to wait, but he never came back. His remains were finally found in 1947 but not identified until 1949.

Three days later, on March 8, Bong and Lynch were out again. It was the morning after they had celebrated Lynch's promotion to lieutenant colonel. They had passed over Tadji airfield and were approaching the harbor at Aitape when they decided to come in low to strafe some of the Japanese coasters that were anchored there. As they made a pass just 20 feet off the water, Lynch's P-38 caught a hail of gunfire which ignited his right engine. He climbed to 2,500 feet and turned toward home. Bong watched Lynch jump from the burning aircraft just before it exploded, but never saw his parachute open. Tommy Lynch is still classified by the US Air Force as MIA.

Dick Bong continued to freelance, mainly flying alone. On April 3, he attached himself to the 475th Fighter Group, one of three groups contributing P-38s to escort a maximum effort mission over Hollandia, 250 miles west of Wewak. When the Americans were jumped by around 60 Japanese interceptors, Bong found himself in a twisting, spiraling dogfight with a skilled enemy pilot. Both pilots managed a few bursts that found their mark before Bong scored the fatal hit. His was one of more than two dozen aerial victories scored by the P-38 pilots that day.

On April 12, Bong was over Hollandia again, this time attached to a bomber escort mission being flown by the 80th Fighter Squadron of the 8th Fighter Group. As they entered the target area just before noon, they were challenged by a mix of Ki-43 and Ki-61 interceptors. After his flight leader downed one, Bong chased another through the clouds, firing at him until he crashed into Tannemerah Bay. Pulling up, he intervened against a Ki-43 that was attacking another P-38 and took him out. Bong then dove on another Ki-43 and chased him at low level, shooting at him until he crashed.

That day, Dick Bong matched and surpassed Rickenbacker and Foss, as well as the top aces of the Eighth Air Force in Europe. Those three confirmed victories made him the top-scoring American ace in the world.

13

Stepping Stones to Hollandia

D ouglas MacArthur, in his memoirs, had described his plan for 1943 by saying that each phase of advance had an objective which "could serve as a stepping stone to the next advance." He began the year with a step to Buna, and as the year unfolded steps were made across New Guinea to Lae, Salamaua, Nadzab, and beyond. To the east, in the SOPAC, Halsey had stepped up from Guadalcanal to New Britain.

As 1944 began, it became apparent that by isolating objectives, he would not have to step on *all* the stones to get to the end of the path. In 1943, all the arrows of strategic direction in the Pacific had led to Rabaul, but as 1944 began, the paradigm had shifted to embrace the notion that Rabaul, neutralized by aerial bombardment in late 1943, could be a stone upon which the Allies need not step.

The idea of bypassing, rather than capturing, Rabaul originated in August 1943, when President Franklin Roosevelt and Prime Minister Winston Churchill, along with their Combined Chiefs of Staff, met in Quebec for the Quadrant Conference. Instead of attacking Rabaul, with its vast IJA garrison, the Allies could just *isolate* it.

MacArthur was quick to embrace this concept and to apply it elsewhere as he pressed forward through 1944. He articulated a strategy "to avoid the frontal attack with its terrible loss of life; to bypass Japanese strongpoints and neutralize them by cutting their lines of supply; to thus isolate their armies and starve them on the battlefield." This evolved into his famous "island hopping" approach – also to be used by Nimitz in the Central Pacific.

Along with Rabaul, the Allies also chose to bypass the Japanese stronghold at Kavieng on New Ireland. However, it was decided that airfields on Los Negros in the Admiralty Islands north of New Guinea should be captured. Allied strategy determined at the Sextant Conference called for this operation to take place in April, but MacArthur executed it ahead of schedule on the last day of February. Supported by Fifth Air Force bombers, the Sixth Army landings were successful, and ground troops managed to capture Momote airfield inside two hours with minimal interference from Japanese aircraft.

MacArthur wrote that with Rabaul bypassed, his plan for 1944 would be:

> ... a westward drive along New Guinea. Up to this time the axis of my advance had been northward, but it was now to bend sharply to the west. The route of a return to the Philippines lay straight before me – along the coast of New Guinea to the Vogelkop Peninsula ... I was now in a position to carry out with increasing speed the massive strokes against the enemy which I had envisioned since the beginning of my campaigns in the Southwest Pacific Area.

Looking westward across New Guinea's north coast, it was obvious that MacArthur's next stepping stone would be the great Japanese air base complex at Wewak that had been a thorn in the side of his air and ground operations for the better part of a year. The V Bomber Command had devoted a large proportion of its strike missions to Wewak, and the Japanese built up their resources proportionally to defend it. Lieutenant General Hatazo Adachi, commander of the Imperial Japanese Eighteenth Army, expected MacArthur at Hansa Bay and Wewak, and he prepared his defenses accordingly.

Across the world in Washington, the JCS could also clearly see MacArthur's obvious next stepping stone on *their* maps – that is, until MacArthur informed them that he intended to *bypass* both Hansa Bay and Wewak. His new plan was now to leap forward 250 miles beyond Wewak to Hollandia (now Jayapura, Indonesia) in the western half of New Guinea that had been part of the Dutch East Indies. It was a bold move that was designated – appropriately from the perspective of MacArthur's detractors – as Operation *Reckless*.

MacArthur wrote in a March 5 message to the JCS:

I propose to make the Hollandia area instead of Hansa Bay my next objective, capturing the airfields and base in that vicinity for further support of operations toward the Philippines. The enemy has concentrated the mass of his ground forces forward in the Madang-Wewak area, leaving relatively weak forces in the Hollandia Bay area ... Establishment of our forces in this area will have wide implications. It will hopelessly isolate some 40,000 of the enemy ground forces along the New Guinea coast, will place in our hands airdromes from which our land-based air forces can dominate the Vogelkop, and hasten the advance westward by several months.

In fact, the Japanese troops around Wewak and Hansa Bay were only part of it. Hatazo Adachi had closer to 70,000 Eighteenth Army combat troops scattered across the north coast of New Guinea in garrisons which MacArthur planned to step over and ignore.

MacArthur had shared the Operation *Reckless* plan with Admiral Halsey in SOPAC, and had secured his concurrence. Admiral Nimitz, meanwhile, also acceded to provide Pacific Fleet carrier air support because Hollandia pushed the limits of the range of Fifth Air Force land-based fighters.

Nimitz was nervous. Recalling a March 25 meeting at MacArthur's headquarters in Brisbane, Kenney wrote in his memoirs:

[The admiral] was emphatic about the danger to his carrier force if the Japanese air strength at Hollandia was not greatly reduced by the time he was called on to support our landing ... Nimitz kept bringing up the threat of the Japanese air force at Hollandia and said that he didn't want to send his carriers to Hollandia with two or three hundred Japanese airplanes in there at the time he arrived. I promised to have them rubbed out by April 5th. Everyone except MacArthur looked skeptical.

Through March and into April, the Fifth Air Force kept up the pressure on Japanese installations on the coastline leading up through Hansa Bay to Wewak. Between March 17 and 19, there was a series of missions involving around 100 bombers each day. Later in the month, the V Bomber Command managed to launch missions with more than 200 aircraft. USAAF records indicate that between March 11 and March 27, there were 500 sorties flown by B-24s, 488 by B-25s, and over 500 by A-20s.

These missions were designed in part to create the deception that they were in preparation for imminent Allied landings. Apparently it worked. An SWPA G-2 intelligence assessment dated March 31 reported that the Japanese were "hurriedly strengthening their bases at Hansa Bay and Wewak."

With enemy attention fixated upon these stepping stones, Kenney turned to planning the main event, the assault against Hollandia in preparation for Operation *Reckless*. He sat down with Ennis Whitehead and Brigadier General Jarred Crabb, who had just taken over as head of V Bomber Command at the end of February, and who had once commanded the 345th Bomb Group. They decided to start with a three-day maximum effort utilizing "all available B-24s carrying a maximum load of fragmentation bombs and dropping from an altitude of ten to twelve thousand feet."

In the lead would be the veteran 90th Bomb Group, which would be commanded by a man new to the work of the V Bomber Command. Colonel Carl Brandt, in Kenney's recollection, was "one of the best bomber pilots I had ever seen," but Brandt had other qualities that had made him useful to the Fifth Air Force. He had worked for Kenney in the Air Corps Materiel Division at Wright Field, Ohio, in 1941, and he had come to know "all about the B-24 from his experience as Air Corps representative at the Consolidated Aircraft plant at San Diego and later on at Willow Run, Michigan, where the Ford Motor Company was producing the airplane."

For this reason, when Brandt had first arrived in the SWPA in 1943, Kenney had put him in charge of a new supply and maintenance depot at Port Moresby "to run it and straighten things out."

Kenney admitted that "Carl looked a bit disappointed. I said that when he got the depot running properly and had trained a successor capable of taking over, I would consider letting him go to war."

In January 1944, Kenney had pulled Brandt out of the depot and had assigned him as a pilot with the 90th. Though Brandt outranked everyone in the group, Kenney explained that "my groups were commanded by the best leaders. If a youngster had the gift and the ability to lead, I would give him the job and promote him afterward."

Colonel Art Rogers, then commanding the 90th, had flown more than 500 combat hours when "300 was about the number that the average man could take without cracking." Kenney was about to rotate him home and he wanted to replace him with Brandt. Kenney recalled:

[He had] every confidence that Brandt would be the best man to lead that outfit, the kids didn't know it yet, so he would have to prove it to them. Normally when the group commander went home or was killed, the best-qualified squadron commander took over and before I would deviate from this procedure I would have to have a good reason for it … It was up to Brandt to fly with the kids, show them first that he was a better bomber pilot than any of them and then that he was the kind of pilot they would like to have lead them – the kind they had more confidence in than anyone else. Carl took my advice literally. For a whole month he flew formation with youngsters, who were not too good at it. He taught them how to maintain their airplanes, how to get the most out of their engines and, without their really suspecting it, imparted to them a world of knowledge that he had gained in long years of flying experience.

When Brandt was through, all four of the squadron commanders in the 90th Bomb Group came to Kenney and recommended that Brandt was the best man to lead the group.

The first big daylight raids on Hollandia came back-to-back on March 30 and 31, with Carl Brandt leading more than 60 B-24s each day, supported by nearly 100 P-38s.

In his May 30 after action report, Kenney mentioned destroying 25 Japanese aircraft and badly damaging another 65 on the ground. He wrote that "fuel dumps burned all over the lot, with heavy black smoke rising to 10,000 feet and visible 150 miles away. The photos showed that we did quite effective work on the antiaircraft machine-gun positions I was worried about … antiaircraft gunfire was described as slight and inaccurate."

He added that 80 P-38s took on the 40 Japanese interceptors and "our score was ten definite and seven probable. We had no losses. The following day, when 70 P-38s were challenged by 30 interceptors, the

Americans shot down 14 and lost one who became separated from the pack."

US Air Force historian Frank Futrell, writing in Volume 4 of *The Army Air Forces in World War II*, noted that the March 31 attack had destroyed 199 Japanese aircraft in daytime raids, with the results of night attacks bringing the total to 208.

Delayed by bad weather, Kenney launched his third major Hollandia attack on April 3. He described this 300-plane effort as "a final clean-up … opened by the heavies and followed by all available strafers mopping up everything not already destroyed."

In a memo to the JCS, MacArthur described this strike:

… our escorted heavy [bomber] units followed by medium and attack planes at minimum altitude, dropped 400 tons of bombs and expended 275,000 rounds of ammunition on the three airdromes. Our heavies [B-24s] started the attack by destroying or silencing the antiaircraft defenses; our medium [B-25] and light [A-20] bombers followed and in wave after wave swept the dispersal bays, revetments and landing strips. The runways were left unserviceable, and equipment and installations heavily damaged. Smoke from burning planes and fuel dumps totally obscured the target. In the air, we destroyed 26 intercepting enemy fighters for the loss of one plane. The enemy's strong air reserves built up in this area have been destroyed at negligible cost to us. Of the 288 planes present in the area on 30 March all have been demolished or irreparably damaged.

Even at the extent of their range, the American fighter pilots had an exceptional day. Frank Futrell points out that 21 P-38s of the 80th Fighter Squadron shot down ten Japanese aircraft and the 17 P-38s of the 432nd downed 12, while the three dozen Lightnings of the 475th Fighter Group "encountered only three Japanese fighters and shot them all down." One of these three aerial victories was the 26th for Captain – soon to be Major – Dick Bong.

After April 3, according to Futrell, "the Fifth Air Force virtually owned the sky over Hollandia." Despite this, and Kenney's earlier assertion that April 3 was a "final clean-up," Kenney continued the attacks as weather permitted.

On April 5, the Fifth Air Force was able to muster more than 270 B-24s, B-25s, A-20s, and P-38s against Hollandia. The April 12 mission again involved heavy, medium, and light bombers, 180 in all, escorted by 60 P-38s. It was on this mission that Dick Bong shot down three enemy aircraft to match and exceed the score attained in World War I by Eddie Rickenbacker.

Another maximum effort struck Hollandia successfully on April 16, but a heavy and turbulent weather front had moved over their landing fields in eastern New Guinea, and many aircraft got lost and ran out of fuel trying to get home. In what would come to be known within the Fifth Air Force as "Black Sunday," 16 men were killed and another 37 were listed as MIA. Because of the rugged mountains and inhospitable jungles that cover virtually all of New Guinea, almost anyone surviving a crash was doomed.

The maximum efforts against Hollandia notwithstanding, the area between Wewak and Hansa Bay continued to be the subject of substantial raids nearly every day through March and April, while only about a dozen missions – albeit large ones – targeted Hollandia in April. These took a toll greater than merely deceiving the Japanese. By the middle of March, aircraft losses were so great that Lieutenant General Kunachi Teramoto, commander of the IJAAF Fourth Air Army, was compelled to eliminate and consolidate squadrons, and eventually to withdraw all of his fighter strength, as well as his own headquarters, to Hollandia.

Unable to move his ground personnel by air or sea because of the constant Fifth Air Force pressure, Teramoto ordered them to walk the 250 miles to Hollandia through the trackless coastal jungles. The majority never made it, and the survivors arrived after it fell to the Americans, and after Teramoto had moved again, this time to the island of Celebes, 1,400 miles to the west.

The deception effort had been a success. Both Adachi and Teramoto were completely deceived. In the Japanese First Demobilization Bureau report, *Southeast Area Operations Record, Part III: Eighteenth Army Operations*, it had been written that "According to the general situation a landing in the Wewak sector is next in probability … It is also possible that the enemy will land in the Hollandia sector … However, since no signs of the usual pre-landing operations are discernible … Therefore, the probability of a landing in this sector is thought to be minor."

For this reason, Hollandia, the "minor sector," was staffed by around 15,000 mainly service troops, while 70,000 combat troops waited elsewhere for attacks that did not come. In April 1944, they confidently assumed that they still had plenty of time to reinforce Hollandia. This time ran out on April 22.

On that morning, as Douglas MacArthur watched from the cruiser USS *Nashville*, the US Sixth Army's I Corps, under Lieutenant General Robert Eichelberger, landed with the pincers of Operation *Reckless* – the 24th Infantry Division in Tannemerah Bay to the west of Hollandia, and the 41st in Humboldt Bay to the east. Nimitz's promised carrier air support, having been brought south from successful operations at Palau in the Central Pacific, was in the skies, but it was anticlimactic. The Fifth Air Force had already destroyed the IJAAF at Hollandia, and within two days of the landings, the Japanese airfields were under American control. Though sporadic Japanese resistance continued through May, efforts had already begun to make the airfields usable for the Fifth Air Force. The 49th and 475th Fighter Groups, as well as the 3rd Bomb Group, began operating from there in May. During that time, the 54th Troop Carrier Wing airlifted 3,999 tons of supplies into Hollandia.

Douglas MacArthur received congratulatory messages from many people, including both George Marshall and Chester Nimitz. The one from General of the Armies John J. Pershing, who had commanded American armies in World War I, was especially memorable.

"When history looks back to master strategic strokes, your capture of Hollandia will undoubtedly stand out as one of the most masterly," wrote the old soldier. "Seldom, if ever, in history have such important military results been obtained at such small cost to the attacker and with such surprise and disaster to the defender."

14

Leaping North to Leyte

On July 30, 1944, the US Army's 6th Infantry Division landed at Sansapor on New Guinea's far western Vogelkop Peninsula, 1,200 miles northwest of Port Moresby, and 900 miles southeast of Davao on the Philippine island of Mindanao. George Kenney recalled that the operation "was heavily supported by our aircraft, but that wasn't necessary. There were no Japanese in the air or on the ground to interfere."

Having stepped 600 miles westward across New Guinea from Hollandia to Wakde, to Biak Island, to Noemfoor Island in a matter of weeks, American ground troops had effectively conquered New Guinea, while the Fifth Air Force had swept the IJAAF and IJNAF from New Guinea's skies.

Douglas MacArthur now had New Guinea behind him as he prepared to take the next steps toward the fulfillment of his promise to return to the Philippines.

In the Central Pacific, meanwhile, Nimitz's Pacific Fleet warships and Marines had island hopped through the Gilbert Islands in late 1943 and the Marshall Islands in February 1944; and as MacArthur was finishing off New Guinea, they had crossed 1,200 miles of Pacific Ocean to the Marianas to land on Saipan, Tinian, and Guam in June and July 1944. Having achieved naval dominance, they were able to bypass and isolate numerous Japanese island garrisons, including the great and heavily defended naval base at Truk – just as had been done at Rabaul.

In the meantime, the Pacific Fleet had effectively destroyed – in a single battle – the IJN's ability to engage in offensive carrier operations. In the battle of the Philippine Sea of June 19–20, 1944, Pacific Fleet naval aviators shot down 645 Japanese aircraft, while losing 123 of their own. Also lost were three IJN fleet carriers, along with their planes and pilots. The IJN lost so many pilots – these on top of severe losses in the Solomons – that for the remainder of the war, they were barely capable of forming a carrier air group for a single light carrier. For the US Navy, this battle was then and forever known as the "Great Marianas Turkey Shoot."

In an August 1 SWPA command communiqué commenting on Sansapor, Douglas MacArthur announced that "our air bases are now established from Milne Bay along the entire coast of New Guinea. The enemy is no longer able to operate in this area, either by air or sea." He added that Japanese forces remained undefeated in New Guinea, but that most were "now isolated with [their] only possible escape route to the south over hazardous terrain of swamp and jungle."

If the campaign against Rabaul had ended with a whimper, the long and difficult campaign in New Guinea ended with a bang – albeit a small one – on July 11, when Lieutenant General Hatazo Adachi, commander of the remnants of the Imperial Japanese Eighteenth Army, launched a last, failed attack on Allied positions at Aitape. Some Japanese troops held out in the dense jungles, continuing to fight, but effective resistance ended on August 10. Adachi and around 9 percent of his original Eighteenth Army survived in the jungle until the end of the war.

As one Japanese field army essentially evaporated, a new American one had been born. Joining the veteran US Sixth Army within the SWPA command structure, the new US Eighth Army was officially created in June 1944 and formally established in September. Commanding it would be Lieutenant General Robert Eichelberger, who had commanded I Corps of the Sixth, created two years earlier to contain the only two US Army divisions then in the SWPA.

Along with the formation of the US Eighth Army came a complete reorganization of the Allied force structure. On March 25, 1944, with the ground campaign in the Solomons, Bougainville, and New Britain – the SOPAC area of responsibility – largely wrapped up, the Joint Chiefs of Staff had authorized that SOPAC, the South Pacific Area command, be dissolved as an entity. This became effective on June 15, as SOPAC's assets were divided between Nimitz and MacArthur.

Admiral Halsey, who had commanded SOPAC, retained command of the Third Fleet and joined Admiral Nimitz's Pacific Fleet in the POA. The Seventh Fleet under Rear Admiral Thomas Kinkaid remained under MacArthur's command. The six divisions of US Army ground troops in the former SOPAC areas were reassigned to MacArthur's direct command and placed within the Sixth or Eighth Army, or into MacArthur's GHQ Reserve. With the Eighth activated in New Guinea, MacArthur began pulling out the Sixth to act as the spearhead for the upcoming Philippine operations.

Australian General Thomas Blamey's Allied Land Forces command, still part of MacArthur's SWPA command, took on the responsibility for the limited ongoing ground operations in New Guinea, Bougainville, and New Britain.

In the air, the USAAF Thirteenth Air Force, the USAAF component of the SOPAC command since it was formed in January 1943, was transferred to George Kenney's Allied Air Forces, SWPA. Known as the "Jungle Air Force," the Thirteenth had been led since January by Major General Hubert Harmon, the younger brother of Lieutenant General Millard Fillmore "Miff" Harmon, who commanded Army Air Forces, POA under Nimitz. In June, Harmon was succeeded by Major General St. Clair "Bill" Streett, whose previous career had been mainly as a Washington staff officer, and who had not previously held a combat command.

With two USAAF numbered air forces now under the same command structure, a new organization was created to contain them. Known as the Far East Air Forces, it shared an acronym with – but is not to be confused with – the Far East Air Force (singular) that existed before the war and was a predecessor of the Fifth Air Force. In addition to continuing to command the Allied Air Forces, SWPA, Kenney assumed command of the new FEAF and installed Ennis Whitehead, his deputy, as the leader of the Fifth Air Force.

In addition to FEAF, the components of Kenney and MacArthur's Allied Air Forces, SWPA had also contained Air Vice Marshal William Bostock's RAAF command since 1942, and now it also had two other coequal components. These were the land-based US Navy aircraft of

Rear Admiral Frank Wagner's Task Force 73, and Major General Ralph Mitchell's Marine Corps aviation in the Solomons.

On September 1, Kenney formally relocated the headquarters of both FEAF and Allied Air Forces from Brisbane to Hollandia. As he pointed out in his memoirs, the distance was the equivalent to a move from Washington, DC to San Francisco. On August 10, Whitehead had moved the Fifth Air Force headquarters from Nadzab to Owi Island, midway between Hollandia and Sansapor, where runways were being lengthened to support operations by fully loaded heavy bombers. The headquarters of the Thirteenth Air Force, meanwhile, moved from Guadalcanal to Los Negros on June 15, and to Hollandia on September 13. Two days earlier, MacArthur had established his own SWPA ADVON headquarters in Hollandia.

On July 6, as the reorganization was ongoing, Douglas MacArthur received a mysterious message from US Army Chief of Staff General George Marshall ordering him to report to Honolulu on July 26. The memo, a copy of which resides in the National Archives, cautioned him that it was of the "utmost importance that the fewest possible number of individuals know of your expected departure or of your destination."

When MacArthur queried the Chief of Staff on the purpose of traveling nearly 5,000 miles across the Pacific in the midst of his running a theater of war, Marshall replied cryptically, "No further orders are necessary." He did add that MacArthur would be meeting with Admiral Nimitz – whose headquarters was at Pearl Harbor in Honolulu – for a "general strategical discussion," and that "Leahy, etcetera" would also attend.

Leahy was Admiral William Leahy, the man who chaired the Joint Chiefs of Staff, and who served as the military advisor to President Franklin Roosevelt. From this, MacArthur could deduce that he would be meeting with the President, though he followed orders and apparently did not discuss it with anyone.

Roosevelt made the journey aboard the heavy cruiser USS *Baltimore*, MacArthur in a grueling 26-hour flight aboard the B-17 named *Bataan*, which he used as his personal transport. Far from slipping into Honolulu secretly, Roosevelt made a grand entrance, waving to cheering crowds from the deck of the cruiser as he was greeted by the admirals. MacArthur also made a dramatic arrival, in a motorcade from Hickam Field after everyone else was on the deck of the *Baltimore*.

It should be noted that there was a political dimension to Roosevelt's being seen and photographed with MacArthur. The general was immensely popular in the United States. Indeed, 1944 was a presidential election year, and MacArthur's name had been widely mentioned in the stateside media as a possible candidate for the Republican Party presidential nomination – which would have put him on the ballot against Democrat Roosevelt in November. This was, of course, a moot point by July, as the Republicans had already nominated Thomas E. Dewey, and MacArthur had never claimed to be a candidate. Nevertheless, the general, who had not been in the United States since 1937, obviously enjoyed the popularity and media attention that he was receiving in absentia back home.

When the dust of the campaign-style arrivals had settled, the leaders sat down with a large map on the wall of a mansion overlooking Waikiki Beach. Taking a large bamboo pointer, Roosevelt tapped New Guinea on the map and asked, "Well, Douglas, where do we go from here?"

"Mindanao, Mr. President," MacArthur replied as he pointed to the major islands of the Philippines. "Then Leyte, and then Luzon."

Nimitz made the case for bypassing the Philippines and taking Formosa, but MacArthur retorted that a promise had been made to the Philippine people and that, given the status of the Philippines as an American commonwealth, this promise must be kept. Vice Admiral Daniel Barbey, who commanded the VII Amphibious Force in the SWPA and who had managed all of the amphibious landings made in New Guinea, observed that MacArthur felt a return to the Philippines to be "as much a moral issue as a military one."

MacArthur also made the military case that Luzon was too large to be ignored. Japanese bases there could threaten further Allied advances toward Japan itself if bypassed, and if captured, such bases would support the advance.

By the end of the final round of talks on the morning of July 28, Leahy had sided with MacArthur, and finally Roosevelt gave his own endorsement to the general's Philippine strategy.

Philippine President Manuel Quezon, who had formed a government in exile in the United States in 1942, lived to hear the news, but only just. He died of tuberculosis on August 1 at Saranac Lake, New York, and was succeeded by Vice President Sergio Osmeña, who was also in exile.

As preparations for the execution of the Philippine strategy progressed, the plans called for amphibious landings on Mindanao, 600 miles from Manila, on November 15, 1944 and on Leyte, 350 miles from Manila, on December 20.

On September 1, FEAF opened the Philippine air campaign with the first daylight raid on Philippine targets since early in 1942. Kenney's airmen, in 57 Owi-based B-24s, unleashed 105 tons of bombs on airfields around Davao. The following day, 65 B-24s, along with 50 P-38s, had gone back to work over the port facilities at Davao.

By now, the weakness of Japanese air activity on Mindanao, as discovered by the FEAF and carrier aircraft sweeps, indicated that the island could potentially be bypassed. In a memo to Hap Arnold, Kenney theorized that the Japanese had lost their competent pilots and maintenance personnel at Wewak, Kavieng, and Rabaul. Indeed, many of the maintenance people were then starving in the New Guinea jungles.

Meanwhile, Nimitz and Halsey had decided that a number of islands in the Central Pacific, including Yap, would be bypassed and this would free up Third Fleet naval assets to support the Philippines operations. The net result was the decision for the next stepping stone in MacArthur's offensive to be Leyte, with that step being advanced two months to October 20.

On September 14, Roosevelt, while meeting with Prime Minister Winston Churchill at the Octagon Conference in Quebec, signed off on the idea. In political terms, Roosevelt certainly would benefit from a Philippines landing before, rather than after, the November 7 election.

For the Philippines operations, the Sixth Army and the Fifth Air Force would take the lead, with the Eighth Army and Thirteenth Air Force in a supporting role. At sea, the Seventh Fleet, specifically the Central Philippines Attack Force (Task Force 77), with 18 escort carriers, would take the lead with help from Halsey's Third Fleet, which possessed four fast carrier battle groups.

On September 15, the Allies landed against minimal opposition on the island of Morotai, about halfway between Sansapor and Leyte, and began developing airfields which would support Thirteenth Air Force heavy bombers. Indeed, Bill Streett, the Thirteenth commander, would relocate his headquarters to Morotai in October. These fields would be useful in upcoming operations against the Philippines, as well as for striking locations in the Dutch East Indies. The latter missions included strikes on the petrochemical facilities at Balikpapan that are detailed in Chapter 16. In the Indies, they also targeted Japanese airfields on islands such as Ambon, Boeroe (now Buru), Celebes (now Sulawesi), and Ceram (now Seram) from which the Japanese could interfere with the FEAF.

Beginning in mid-October, FEAF operations ranged through the central Philippines, striking targets on the islands of Bohol, Cebu, Negros, and Panay, as well as continuing to hit Mindanao. Frank Futrell, in Volume 5 of *The Army Air Forces in World War II*, shared a vignette of a mission on October 16 in which P-38s of the 35th and 80th Fighter Squadrons "flew to Cagayan on the north-central Mindanao coast, where they fired three vessels in the harbor, strafed and put to flight a troop of mounted cavalry, strafed a [Mitsubishi Ki-21] bomber and a staff car at Cagayan airdrome, and then swept down the highway to Valencia, destroying fifty to sixty military vehicles along the road."

On September 29, FEAF and Third Fleet air officers met in Hollandia to establish a mechanism to coordinate carrier-based and land-based air activities for the upcoming Philippine operation. In turn, aircraft from Nimitz's Pacific Fleet carriers roamed far and wide now, with the IJN reluctant to intervene. On October 10, Task Force 38 ranged as far as Okinawa and the Ryukyu Islands, destroying 93 enemy aircraft on the ground. Two days later they launched a fighter sweep over the northern Philippines, with attacks on Formosa the following day. Between October 10 and 18, the carrier pilots claimed 655 airborne Japanese aircraft destroyed in the air, and 465 on the ground. It was reminiscent of the "Great Marianas Turkey Shoot."

Meanwhile, as the Navy attacked the Philippines, Kenney's FEAF returned the favor by supporting Nimitz and Halsey's operations with B-24 attacks against sites such as Peleliu and in the Marianas where the POA forces were engaged.

Comprising around 600 ships with Task Force 77 as its centerpiece and with Admiral Barbey's VII Amphibious Force running the landings, the Leyte invasion force was the largest naval flotilla yet assembled in the Pacific. It entered Leyte Gulf before dawn on October 20 and began a four-hour naval bombardment of the beaches.

General Walter Krueger's 174,000-man Sixth Army began going ashore at 10:00hrs along an 18-mile front between the two towns of Dulag and San Jose, with XXIV Corps (7th and 96th Infantry Divisions) on the left and X Corps (1st Cavalry and 24th Infantry Divisions) to the north. The terrain proved to be as serious an obstacle as the Japanese defenders, who had apparently failed to occupy many of the concrete defensive positions that they had built.

Douglas MacArthur, who had watched the landings from the USS *Nashville*, decided to go ashore in the afternoon. When the whaleboat in which he and his entourage were traveling grounded in knee-deep water, they were compelled to wade to shore through the surf. MacArthur was initially angered by this, but when he saw photos that had been taken, and realized the dramatic effect, he embraced it as though it had been his idea all along. The photos of MacArthur, flanked by his aide Richard Sutherland, George Kenney of FEAF, Philippine President Sergio Osmeña, and Carlos Romulo – a former MacArthur aide and later a UN General Assembly president – were soon published around the world. The image became so iconic that it is now memorialized by a group of bronze statues on the site.

When he reached the beach, MacArthur broadcast a message in which he announced to the Philippine people:

I have returned. By the grace of Almighty God our forces stand again on Philippine soil – soil consecrated in the blood of our two peoples. We have come dedicated and committed to the task of destroying every vestige of enemy control over your daily lives, and of restoring upon a foundation of indestructible strength, the liberties of your people.

With Kenney, MacArthur then proceeded inland a few miles to Tacloban, which he recalled as having been his first posting in the Philippines after he had left West Point. There were still Japanese snipers being shot out of the palm trees.

Setting aside the hyperbole of the moment and our 20–20 hindsight understanding that things turned out the way that MacArthur intended, it was a fragile and precarious moment. The Americans had come ashore against minimal opposition and stood upon a narrow sliver of beach, but the Japanese had every intention of resisting to the utmost of their ability and of doing so to the last man if necessary.

General Tomoyuki Yamashita, who had earned the sobriquet "Tiger of Malaya" for his swift and triumphant conquest of Malaya and Singapore in 1942, had taken command of Japanese forces in the Philippines less than two weeks before, bringing skillful leadership to the determination with which the defenders would confront MacArthur.

As planned, the advancing American troops moved inland to secure airfields that could be put into service by FEAF. The strip at Tacloban was secured by X Corps on the first day, and the one at Dulag was captured by XXIV Corps the next day. Chaos on the beaches, where supplies and construction equipment were rapidly being unloaded, delayed work on the fields for four days, but the ground echelons of the 49th and 475th Fighter Groups arrived with their tents and gear on October 24.

MacArthur established his new ADVON headquarters at Tacloban the following day, taking over a rambling colonial mansion built around the turn of the century by American expatriate businessman Walter Scott Price. Kenney did not move his own FEAF headquarters to Leyte until November.

At this moment, the Imperial Japanese Navy was about to launch a maximum effort involving more than 60 ships against the American invasion fleet. The ensuing contest – actually a series of battles known collectively as the battle of Leyte Gulf – was to be the largest naval battle in world history. The US Navy Third and Seventh Fleets – with some help from FEAF heavy bombers – delivered a resounding and decisive defeat to the IJN. Though some Japanese ships limped away, three battleships, four carriers, and ten cruisers were among the ships that were lost. Military historian and strategist J. F. C. Fuller, writing in *The Decisive Battles of the Western World*, wrote that after the battle, the Japanese fleet effectively "ceased to exist." Admiral Mitsumasa Yonai, the Imperial Naval Minister, commented that "I felt that it was the end."

For the Imperial Japanese *Army*, however, it was far from being the end. Before and after the Americans landed, Yamashita had pushed 65,000 troops into Leyte, mainly through the port of Ormoc on Leyte's west coast. This port was only about 40 miles as the crow flies from where the Americans had landed, but the intervening terrain was as rugged as the jungles of New Guinea.

Nor was it the end for Japanese airpower, which had now added a fearsome new weapon to its bag of tricks – the *kamikaze*. It was at Leyte that the Japanese first widely used manned aircraft to fly suicide missions against American ships at sea. Apparently, trading a single-engine aircraft and the life of a barely trained pilot for an American escort carrier – the USS *St. Lo* was sunk on October 25 – seemed like a reasonable bargain.

Recognizing that his gunners and carrier pilots were taxed to the max by the *kamikazes*, Admiral Thomas Kinkaid of the Seventh Fleet asked George Kenney for help from his P-38s. The FEAF men pulled out all the stops, with ground personnel aiding engineer and construction crews in laying metal matting at Tacloban, and by October 27, P-38s landed on a new 2,800-foot steel runway. Nearly three dozen Lightnings that arrived the first day were merely the beginning.

Continuing their day and night air attacks – *kamikaze* and conventional – against US Navy ships, the Japanese added Tacloban to their target list, and managed to effect some damage. By the end of the month, Tacloban had a 4,000-foot runway and Northrop P-61 Black Widow night fighters of the 421st Night Fighter Squadron had moved in to aid in the nocturnal air defense mission. The P-47s of the 348th Fighter Group's 460th Fighter Squadron also arrived, as did US Marine Corps F4U Corsairs from the Central Pacific. There were still P-40Es in the FEAF inventory, but these were now being used mainly as fighter bombers.

After the first week of November, Japanese air attacks on the American Leyte airfields came mainly at dawn, dusk, or during the night. While the FEAF P-38s and P-47s were more than a match for the Japanese aircraft that raided by day, at night the P-61s of the 421st Night Fighter Squadron proved too slow to catch the attackers. With this in mind, George Kenney traded them to the Navy for the Marine Corps squadron VMF(N)-541. Based on Peleliu, this squadron was, as Frank Futrell put it, "not fully occupied" because Japanese nighttime air activity out there was minimal. Formed in February 1944 at a time when night fighter technology was still in its early days, VMF(N)-541, appropriately nicknamed "Bat Eyes," operated Grumman F6F-6N Hellcat night fighters.

Tacloban proved to be an ideal location for an air base, and was developed as such, but Dulag was situated on the low-lying flood plain of the Marabang River, too low for adequate drainage and prone to flooding in heavy rains. Nevertheless, engineers made it work. The 475th Fighter Group, which operated from Tacloban initially, was flying from Dulag with all three of its squadrons by late November. General Ennis Whitehead, meanwhile, had established his Fifth Air Force headquarters at Burauen, 8 miles inland from Dulag on higher ground.

15

Air War over Leyte

The air war over the Philippines, which had begun on December 8, 1941, was a lopsided affair. The Japanese had swept the American Far East Air Force and the Philippine Army Air Corps from the skies. Largely erased in the first weeks of war – with 72 percent of its aircraft lost in December 1941 – American airpower had abandoned those Philippine skies to the enemy and had been essentially absent for more than two years.

By the fall of 1944, the equation had shifted. Both the IJAAF and IJNAF had been badly battered and beaten in New Guinea and the Solomons, so by the time the nexus of the air war shifted to the Philippines, their best pilots had been killed and great armies of skilled mechanics had been abandoned in the jungles.

The Americans, on the other hand, were in their ascendancy. With unfettered and uninterrupted air and sea lanes across the Pacific to Australia, and up to the ports of New Guinea and the Marianas, the numbers had steadily grown. USAAF personnel strength in the Pacific had grown from 77,000 at the time of the battle of the Bismarck Sea in March 1943 to 232,000 when MacArthur stepped ashore at Leyte in October 1944.

In February 1942, when the original Far East Air Force (singular) became the Fifth Air Force, it possessed just 23 heavy bombers and three medium bombers, along with 490 fighters, mostly P-39s and P-40s. By the time of the Leyte operations, the Far East Air Forces (plural), incorporating the Fifth and Thirteenth, was a much more formidable force. The new FEAF boasted 617 heavy bombers, 930 light and medium bombers, and 1,252 fighters, of which 436 were P-38s and 336 were P-47s. North American P-51 Mustangs, which had proven to be a significant game-changer in Europe against the Luftwaffe, made their first appearance with FEAF in October, but there remained fewer than 100 of them on hand until after the start of 1945.

When the air war over the Philippines resumed with a vengeance – literally – in October 1944, the FEAF ruled the skies. Estimates by SWPA and Sixth Army intelligence put the total number of Japanese warplanes in the Philippines at 442 fighters and 337 bombers. Because Yamashita's strategy was to conserve his resources for the upcoming battle for Luzon, most of these remained in the north. Intelligence estimates calculated that the Japanese would meet the Americans over Leyte with 152 fighters and 179 bombers.

As the Fifth Air Force fighter groups moved into Leyte, the FEAF medium and heavy bomber groups based on Morotai were ranging far and wide throughout the central Philippines. After October 29, the bombers of the Thirteenth Air Force's XIII Bomber Command were joined by B-24s of the Fifth's V Bomber Command. In large numbers, they were attacking Japanese shipping, especially at the port of Ormoc, where Japanese convoys bringing supplies down from the northern Philippines docked.

As Kenney recalled, on November 3, Japanese fighters intercepted a strike force over Ormoc, but the P-38s from Tacloban "shot down 24 of them without loss to themselves. In the meantime seven more Japanese planes were shot down in combat and ten destroyed on the ground by the B-25s from Morotai in another raid on Cebu. We lost a B-25."

The following day, Kenney noted that 27 P-38s shot down 32 Japanese aircraft "and chased the rest away. Once again we had no losses. The 49th Group had been so busy for the past four days they had forgotten to count. At lunch someone said, 'What is the score? We must be up to 500 by this time.'"

At the 49th, they all knew about that magnum of brandy that the group had been carrying around since March 1942, a magnum that was to be opened at the once-impossible milestone of 500 Japanese aircraft shot down.

"The count was made," Kenney recalled. "It was 535. No one knew who had gotten number 500 or just when." In fact, the 500th victory had been scored by Lieutenant Milden Mathre on October 29.

"Aw, let's open that bottle at 600," said Colonel George Walker, now the group commander. Everyone agreed.

A new chapter in the race of Fifth Air Force aces began in October 1944, as the action in this informal contest was now centered at Tacloban and Dulag.

Richard Ira "Dick" Bong, late of the 49th Fighter Group and a Fifth Air Force "freelancer" after the start of 1944, had officially scored his 28th aerial victory in April and had been back in the States on a publicity tour ever since, but now he was back in the SWPA. Because Bong's status as "ace of aces" made him a minor celebrity, USAAF headquarters in Washington was reticent about having him endanger himself with further combat. With this in mind, George Kenney had assigned him to training duties as a combat instructor to newer pilots, and had ordered him to avoid combat. He told Bong that he was not to shoot *except* in "self defense."

During the earlier iteration of the "race of aces," Bong had been part of a field that included Neel Kearby, Tommy Lynch, and George Welch. Now, Kearby and Lynch were dead and Welch had gone home for good. The new cast of aces was headed by Tommy McGuire, who led the 431st Fighter Squadron of the 475th Fighter Group, and who was now the second-highest-scoring SWPA, with 21 victories. With him in the top tier within the Fifth Air Force and nearing 20 were Gerald Richard "Jerry" Johnson of the 49th Fighter Group, and Charles Henry "Mac" MacDonald, a Pearl Harbor veteran who commanded the 475th Fighter Group. Also approaching 20 was Robert Burdette Westbrook, deputy commander of the 347th Fighter Group, who was the highest-scoring ace in the Thirteenth Air Force.

Kenney had assigned Bong and McGuire to attach themselves to the 49th Fighter Group for escort bombers on missions to the big Japanese-occupied petrochemical complex at Balikpapan in Borneo, which are discussed in detail in the following chapter. It was to be fertile ground for these aces. In the space of just a few days in mid-October, McGuire had shot down three enemy aircraft, while Bong had downed two – in self defense, of course.

Both Kenney and MacArthur were on hand at Tacloban when Dick Bong first flew in around noon on October 27. His arrival among the first wave of P-38s was unexpected and unauthorized because he was under Kenney's orders and pressure from Washington to remain out of the line of fire.

"Bong, come here," Kenney shouted when Bong slid out of the cockpit. "Who told you to come up here?"

"Oh, I had permission from General Wurtsmith and General Whitehead," he answered.

"Did they tell you that you could fly combat after you got here?" Kenney asked.

"No," Bong replied, "but can I?"

As Kenney recalled, "Everybody laughed now, including me. I told him that we were in such a fix that anyone could fly combat that knew anything about a P-38 and had one to fly. Bong saluted happily and went back to his airplane to get it gassed up and ready to go."

At 16:15hrs, Bong, along with Jerry Johnson and Bob Morrissey, were among 11 pilots who took off on a routine patrol, but as soon as they were airborne, they encountered incoming IJAAF Ki-43 Hayabusa fighters.

Bong fired a burst at the lead aircraft but failed to do serious damage. However, Jerry Johnson got on the Hayabusa's tail and shot him down. Bong picked another and sent him tumbling into the waters of Leyte Gulf. By the time that the lone survivor of the IJAAF force escaped into the clouds, Morrissey had scored and Johnson had downed a second enemy aircraft to bring his overall score to 17. Bong had raised his score to 31 within five hours of arriving in the Philippines, and he added yet another the next day while flying with Johnson, Morrissey, and group commander George Walker.

Feeling compelled to explain the situation with the ace of aces to headquarters, Kenney wired Hap Arnold in Washington, telling him that "In accordance with my instructions Major Richard Bong is trying to be careful, but the Japanese won't do their part." He then went on to detail Bong's recent string of aerial victories.

With tongue in cheek, Arnold wired back that "Major Bong's excuses in matter of shooting down three more Japanese noted with happy skepticism by this headquarters. Subject officer judged incorrigible. In

Judge Advocate's opinion, he is liable under Articles of War 122 [willful or negligent damage to enemy equipment or personnel]."

By Kenney's reckoning, the FEAF shot down 350 Japanese aircraft in combat and destroyed 120 on the ground between October 28 and November 4, 1944. During the following two days, Halsey's Third Fleet carrier pilots, flying over Luzon in the north, shot down 113 and eliminated 327 on the ground.

At the same time, despite their losses, the Japanese continued to hammer the Fifth Air Force airfields with undiminished intensity. Air Force historian Frank Futrell observed in Volume 5 of *The Army Air Forces in World War II*:

Damage by the enemy planes which penetrated fighter and antiaircraft defenses was usually severe. On the morning of November 4, for example, 35 Japanese planes made a low-level attack on Tacloban strip which killed four men, wounded more than 30 others, cratered the runway in four places, destroyed two P-38's, and damaged 39 other planes. Two suicide planes crashed into two transports bringing in the ground echelon of the 345th Bombardment Group, killing 92 men outright and wounding 156, 15 of whom died en route to hospitals.

One of the victims of the Japanese at Tacloban was Paul Irwin "Pappy" Gunn, Kenney's extraordinary aircraft modification engineer. He survived an incendiary attack, but would spend the rest of the war recovering in a convalescent hospital.

Tacloban was the most ideally situated American base, the most heavily utilized, and the most often attacked – but it was constantly expanding. The runway was extended to 6,000 feet by November 9, ten days before Dulag was fully functional. As Futrell points out, there was an ongoing battle between operations people at Fifth Air Force who needed as many airfields as possible and the engineers who made them usable.

At Bayug, for example, the engineers "urged that unstable subsurface, poor drainage, and the great engineering effort required to build access roads made its development impracticable." It was used, however, as a fair weather fighter field beginning on November 3. By the end of the year, it had a 4,500-foot Marston Matting runway.

The FEAF bombers, from B-24 heavies to smaller B-25s, were meanwhile taking their toll on the Japanese, with continuing pressure on Ormoc.

From Morotai on November 1, the V and XIII Bomber Commands sent an aggregate total of 54 B-24s and 26 B-25s to, in Kenney's words, "clean up" the Japanese airfields in the central Philippines from Bacolod to Cebu City. They and their 58 escorting P-38s claimed 100 enemy aircraft on the ground and three dozen in the air. The following day, a strike force of similar size hit Japanese ships unloading at Ormoc.

November 10 was an especially busy day over Leyte. During the night, the Japanese had sent several large freighters, shepherded by more than a dozen destroyers and destroyer escorts. To put the Americans on edge, the Japanese also launched a dawn air raid on Tacloban. Kenney recalled that as soon as the runway was repaired, "every P-38 that could fly carried bombs to Ormoc." In addition, 30 B-25s from the 38th Bomb Group flew up from Morotai. Numerous barges and several of the larger ships were sunk. Kenney reported that "We had seven B-25s shot down [but] 18 of their 25 crewmen were later rescued."

In the massive air battles tumbling across the skies over northern Leyte on November 10, Dick Bong, Tommy McGuire, and Jerry Johnson each scored an aerial victory. Bong, who occasionally attached himself to McGuire's 475th Fighter Group, usually flew with the 49th, and so he was doing this day. The group was escorting P-40s that were bombing the ships in the harbor. A number of Ki-43 fighters were observed, both singly and in small groups, but they were ducking in and out of the large, low-lying clouds, so they were hard to catch. Bong himself lost one in the clouds, but at that moment another appeared in Bong's sights and did not escape.

The Ki-43 claimed by Bong on November 10 brought his tally to 34, while McGuire's total now stood at 26 and Johnson's was at 14. The next day, as the great air battle resumed, Bong scored twice more and Johnson got one. McGuire, in turn, added two more on November 12.

It was shortly after this that Kenney considered Bong's achievements, as he later wrote in a biography of Bong:

[I] decided it was time to see General MacArthur about a Medal of Honor. Dick already had every other American decoration for valor and I had given him nothing since he had returned to the theater in

September. I had been saving those victories for this very purpose. Now I figured that eight Japanese aircraft destroyed in a little more than a month, especially when Bong was supposed to shoot only in "self-defense," warranted some real recognition.

Kenney recalled that MacArthur smiled as he was handed the "for conspicuous gallantry" citation Kenney had written up.

"I've been wondering when you were going to bring this matter up," MacArthur said, barely glancing at the paperwork. "It's long overdue. I'll approve this citation and forward it to Washington right away."

On the ground, meanwhile, the Sixth Army was making steady, but slow, progress. Their push across Leyte was reminiscent of the approaches to Buna and Gona in New Guinea two years earlier, in terms of both the difficult jungle terrain and the ferocity of the Japanese resistance.

With the approach of December 7, 1944, the battle of Leyte abruptly intensified. The symbolism of this being the third anniversary of Pearl Harbor was lost on neither side as they each chose the date for a bold move.

Having largely avoided using airborne operations since the first six months of the war, the Japanese suddenly launched assaults on the American airfields using nearly 40 transport aircraft crammed with heavily armed infantrymen. The plan was to destroy American aircraft on the ground to keep them from being able to attack a convoy due into Ormoc on December 7, as well as to blow up fuel and bomb dumps.

Appearing at dusk on December 6, the transports dropped paratroopers in the hills west of Dulag and even made attempts to land on the runways at Dulag and Tacloban. Had it worked, this risky move would have been devastating, but all of the aircraft attempting to land were destroyed in the process and few of the paratroopers got close to a runway. It did take several days, however, for all the enemy to be killed or chased into the mountains. Ennis Whitehead and his Fifth Air Force headquarters at Burauen were briefly cut off from the American lines, but the Japanese never exploited this predicament.

If the Japanese strike was intended as a hit and run – or hit and suicide – mission, the American action on December 7 was aimed at capturing and holding ground. As the Japanese paratroopers were being hunted on the east side of Leyte, the US Sixth Army sent the 77th

Infantry Division on an end run around to the west side of the island to stage an amphibious landing near Ormoc – coincidentally, just as the Japanese convoy was arriving.

As the scene on the ground and at sea was chaotic, so too was the situation in the sky. With the P-38s of the 49th and 475th Fighter Groups flying top cover, the convoy was blasted by nearly four dozen bomb-laden fighter bombers, including P-40s, P-47s, and Marine Corps F4U Corsairs, most flying multiple sorties through the day.

December 7 was an important day in the chronicle of fighter folklore in the skies over Leyte. Dick Bong was flying with the 431st Fighter Group of the 475th Fighter Group, commanded by Tommy McGuire. In fact, on this day, they both flew as part of Daddy Green Flight, with McGuire as the flight leader, along with Lieutenant Floyd Fulkerson and Major Jack Rittmayer.

At 14:50hrs that afternoon, only 20 minutes after taking off from Dulag, Daddy Green Flight took up its patrol station over Ormoc. Bong was the first to spot a Mitsubishi Ki-21 IJAAF heavy bomber flying low above the water, presumably heading toward the American invasion convoy. He broke formation to dive on it, and at 15:10hrs it was seen to crash. Shortly thereafter, Rittmayer engaged and destroyed a lone Nakajima B5N IJNAF attack bomber.

Next, McGuire sighted five Nakajima Ki-44 fighters, which he presumed to be preparing for a *kamikaze* strike against the American ships. They were taking antiaircraft fire, but the fighter pilots dove to attack with McGuire in the lead. He managed to shoot down two of the attackers, with Fulkerson and Rittmayer each claiming one, and Bong picking off the Ki-44 that brought up the rear.

Of the more than 70 Japanese aircraft shot down that day by Fifth Air Force and Marine Corps pilots, seven were shot down by Daddy Green Flight, with Bong and McGuire each scoring a pair. Their respective totals now stood at 38 and 30, making them by far the two highest-scoring American aces in the Pacific.

However, even these remarkable accomplishments were overshadowed by the exploits of Jerry Johnson and Mac MacDonald, who each scored three aerial victories on December 7.

George Kenney described Johnson as "the best shot in the 49th Fighter Group," and he dramatically proved it. The moment that Johnson's formation encountered a swarm of Japanese fighters, he attacked and downed a pair in less than one minute. He then spotted a Nakajima Ki-49 heavy bomber and sent it tumbling into Ormoc Bay.

"One, two, three. Count 'em," he yelled over the radio.

MacDonald flew four missions on December 7 and matched Johnson's score of three for the day. He was also the top scorer in the 475th Fighter Group, which he commanded. After running low on fuel with an improperly fueled tank on his second sortie, he returned to base, but took off again just before noon with Lieutenant Colonel Meryl Smith, the 475th's executive officer, as his wingman. They engaged a trio of Mitsubishi J2Ms and each shot one of them down. When the third Japanese fighter appeared on MacDonald's tail, Smith scored his second for the day.

McDonald's third victory on December 7 came on his next outing. He and Smith, along with two others, were jumped by a group of J2Ms and A6M Zeros, but the Japanese aircraft flashed past without hitting the Americans, who now were able to attack them from behind. MacDonald dispatched one of them, but became separated from Smith. When he found his wingman at last, Smith had a Zero on his tail. MacDonald hammered the Zero until he finally fell, but he could not now find Smith. After refueling at Dulag and not seeing Smith return, MacDonald went back into Ormoc skies, trying in vain to find him.

As for the Fifth Air Force attacks on the convoy in Ormoc Bay on December 7, George Kenney recalled that "at 4:30p.m. a Navy reconnaissance plane from Kincaid's outfit [the Seventh Fleet] reported that all the merchant vessels were sunk or destroyed, one destroyer was on fire all over, one destroyer was on fire and settling fast at the stem, and the three destroyer escorts were all on fire and sinking."

The final attack at 17:30hrs sank five barges loaded with troops and expended their remaining bombs and ammunition in a tree-top attack on Japanese positions north of Ormoc. Meanwhile, Japanese *kamikazes* took their toll, fatally damaging the destroyer USS *Mahan*, as well as two transports.

A few days later, the Medal of Honor that MacArthur had requested for Dick Bong was finally approved by Washington. Kenney proposed that MacArthur should award it in a public ceremony on the Tacloban airstrip. MacArthur refused, saying that he was "not running for any office and was not looking for publicity."

It had been his practice to present medals in his office at the Price House and not in public, and he did not want to break precedent. Kenney argued that the 49th Fighter Group was "one of his favorite outfits. They all knew him and he had met and personally congratulated all the top aces of the group. Also, Bong was their favorite, and I believed that they would be disappointed if they didn't see a show."

"All right, George, I'll do it for you."

On December 12, Kenney put on an elaborate show for his favorite ace, arranging for eight P-38s lined up in a half circle and an honor guard of a dozen aces, each with at least a dozen aerial victories. Bong, who could be "cool as a cucumber" in a sky full of enemy aircraft, was speechless with stage fright.

MacArthur pocketed his prepared speech and ad-libbed what Kenney thought to be "the greatest speech I have ever heard."

In it, he described Bong as having "ruled the air from New Guinea to the Philippines," which was not entirely true. He'd had plenty of help.

Bong's citation was for eight enemy aircraft destroyed between October 10 and November 15, 1944, but by the time the medal was awarded, he had claimed two more, and three days after the award ceremony he added yet another.

By the time that Bong accepted his medal, Ormoc had been wrested from the Japanese. No more reinforcements would be coming, and the Japanese garrison was fighting what they knew was a losing battle. By Christmas, the Sixth Army would turn the battle of Leyte over to the Eighth Army and prepare for the invasion of Luzon. In the meantime, on December 15, American and Filipino troops landed on the island of Mindoro, 280 miles northwest of Dulag and 150 miles south of Manila. Here, the SWPA command engineers would build the airfields that would support the final battles of the retaking of the Philippines. After Leyte, it was anticlimactic. The Japanese had only around a thousand troops on the whole island.

Dick Bong took off for his penultimate combat mission, a fighter sweep over Mindoro, on December 17. At about 16:15hrs, he and Jack Rittmayer spotted a pair of Ki-43 fighters, skinned their external fuel tanks, and climbed to attack. Both Japanese aircraft fell to their guns.

When George Kenney heard the news, he ordered his favorite ace to be grounded. Bong now had 40 aerial victories, making him the highest-scoring American ace in the world, and Kenney wanted him to see the postwar world. He flew one more mission – escorting Kenney's transport on an inspection tour to Mindoro. He was back in the States by New Year's Eve.

The last three months of 1944 were the months that made the careers of the top-scoring USAAF aces of the Pacific War. Bong scored a dozen of his and Tommy McGuire scored 17. Mac MacDonald would score 13 of his eventual 27 aerial victories between November 10 and the end of the year. The three of them would be the highest-scoring aces still in the Pacific.

There was a three-way tie for fourth place, each man with 22. Jerry Johnson got ten during the final months of 1944, and Major Jay "Cock" Robbins scored his last one on November 14. The other man was Neel Kearby, who had died in March of 1944.

In recapping that season of air combat in Volume 5 of *The Army Air Forces in World War II*, Frank Futrell observed that from October 27 through December 31, as the Japanese sent more than 1,033 sorties over Leyte, Fifth Air Force fighter pilots shot down a confirmed 314 Japanese aircraft and 45 probables, while losing only 16 of their own in aerial combat. The US Marine Corps pilots scored 42 confirmed, plus two probables, while losing seven F4Us.

As it had been when Japanese airpower first tangled with American pilots over the Philippines in 1941, a lopsided victory had been achieved, but this time, the data on the balance sheet was reversed.

16

Balikpapan, the Ploesti of the Pacific

O ften overlooked in histories of the air war in the Pacific is the campaign against what was probably the single most economically significant strategic target outside mainland Asia or Japan itself – the oil fields and sprawling petrochemical refinery complex around Balikpapan on the island of Borneo in the Dutch East Indies.

Strategic air warfare, as first theorized by Billy Mitchell during World War I, as refined and institutionalized by the Air War Plans Division (AWPD) of the Air Corps in the late 1930s, and as practiced by the USAAF in World War II, is economic warfare. It strives to degrade and destroy an enemy's ability to wage war through the systematic dismantling of a war economy.

In looking at targets for such a bombing campaign, planners examined elements of that war economy, identifying those that were essential to the war effort. Among the economic sectors highlighted were the manufacturing of war machines, machine tools, and transportation equipment. High on any such list was oil, especially refineries and other petrochemical manufacturing facilities. Though they possessed refineries, Germany and Japan had no oil supply to feed those refineries. Their refineries were dependent upon imported crude oil.

In the 1940s, the world's three largest oil producers were the United States, with 63 percent of global oil production, the Soviet Union with 10 percent, and Venezuela with 9 percent. In the second tier of oil producers were Iran, Romania, and the Dutch East Indies. At the time, each of these three produced more oil than Iraq, Saudi Arabia, and the Persian Gulf emirates *combined*.

The Japanese economy had long depended on massive quantities of California crude flowing in armadas of tankers across the Pacific, but when the war began, the open world market went through dramatic changes. In 1941, even before Pearl Harbor, the United States had embargoed shipments to Japan because of the brutal Japanese misbehavior in China. Also in 1941, Britain and the Soviet Union invaded and occupied Iran, so its oil spigot was no longer available to the Axis powers.

However, wartime Germany and Japan each had a tap upon which to depend. As the Third Reich was allied with Romania after 1940, its oil fields, and its great refinery complex at Ploesti, were available to service the German war machine. For Japan, it was the oil fields of the Dutch East Indies, especially Borneo and Sumatra, and the refineries of Balikpapan.

In a 1944 memo to Minneapolis-Honeywell, R.J. Condon summarized the importance of the Balikpapan complex, writing that it was the "most complete oil refinery outside the continental limits of the United States." Indeed a major element of Japanese strategy in Southeast Asia had revolved around Balikpapan and the Indies oil patch.

By the end of January 1942, with the war less than two months old, the Japanese had occupied all of the oil fields and facilities in Borneo, including those of Sarawak, Brunei, and British North Borneo as well as those of the Netherlands in Borneo.

For the planners of the strategic air campaigns against Germany and Japan, petrochemical capability was a key objective, and Japan appeared to be the most vulnerable. A July 1942 briefing study prepared by the AWPD for Robert Lovett, then the Assistant Secretary of War for Air and a postwar Secretary of Defense, concluded that Japan was "probably more dependent on gasoline and oil in storage than any other country in the world." This meant that the offshore refining capacity upon which it depended was "possibly the Achilles heel" for Japan.

Ploesti and Balikpapan were both obvious targets – albeit hard to reach from bases possessed by the Allies in 1942–43. From North Africa, the USAAF launched two very long and very costly strikes on Ploesti in June 1942 and August 1943, but it was unable to undertake a sustained campaign until bases in Italy became available in 1944. Although the missions against Ploesti are well known, parallel actions against Balikpapan are largely forgotten in the narrative of the war in the Pacific.

While nearly 60 percent of the crude oil destined for the Japanese economy was produced on the Dutch East Indies island of Sumatra, and Penang on Sumatra refined about a third of Indies oil, intelligence reports suggested that because of Balikpapan's immense refining capacity, crude was being sent there from Sumatra for refining.

Balikpapan was reportedly *capable* of producing more than 80 percent of the high octane aviation fuel needed by the IJNAF. Other intelligence reports surmised that Balikpapan refineries were producing as much as 40 percent of all of Japan's aviation fuel, though this was probably an exaggeration.

Because Balikpapan was controlled by the IJN, much of its output supported the needs of ships at sea, though a considerable amount of it was being shipped to Japan rather than being retained solely to serve the needs of the IJN in the southwest Pacific. The petrochemical complex at Milli, on Borneo's western side, was controlled by the IJA.

MacArthur's original Far East Air Force had appeared in the skies over Balikpapan once in February 1942, flying from bases in Java before the Dutch East Indies fell to the Japanese. The B-17s came to attack Japanese shipping, not the oil fields. It would be a year and a half before American heavy bombers were back.

Kenney launched night missions over Balikpapan on August 16 and 17 in 1943, but the situation was like that of the Ploesti mission flown two weeks earlier. The distances were long, the missions grueling, and the damage less than had been hoped. The Ninth Air Force was able to put 162 B-24s over Ploesti in August 1943, but Kenney's Fifth Air Force was hard pressed to put more than a half dozen B-24s over any target at that time. Kenney launched two B-24 missions to Balikpapan during the winter, one in December 1943, and another a month later. Ploesti is 950 miles from Libya, but Balikpapan is 1,200 miles from Darwin and 2,200 miles from Port Moresby.

Balikpapan was like a glittering prize that was just out of reach, close enough to touch, albeit with great exertion, but not close enough to grasp.

Throughout 1943 and into 1944, Kenney held out hope that Hap Arnold would make the very long range B-29 Superfortress strategic bombers available to FEAF to help conquer the distances involved. However, when the B-29 finally became operational in mid-1944, Arnold assigned it only to the newly created Twentieth Air Force, and not to Kenney's FEAF, nor to any other USAAF command, many of which wanted it.

Finally, when the islands of Noemfoor and Morotai were captured in the fall of 1944, it was a game-changer for Kenney. It meant that bases less than a thousand miles from Balikpapan were available.

Kenney was able at last to plan a sustained air campaign against the Balikpapan refineries by shipping large quantities of fuel and ordnance into Noemfoor and Sansapor. He observed:

> … with the heavy concentration of Japanese aircraft in the Philippines, if I could destroy the Edelanu and Pandasari refineries at Balikpapan, the Japanese might not be able to get their planes off the ground to oppose us when we went in. With the sudden increase in aircraft strength in the Philippines during the past two months I doubted that the Japanese had been able to build up sufficient reserve of gasoline to keep going very long.

Outlining his plan to MacArthur, Kenney proposed:

> [to] set up a series of big attacks as soon as the Sansapor airdromes were finished … The distance was too great to have the fighters escort the bombers unless a field could be constructed at Morotai in time. We could not delay too long, as even after I destroyed the Balikpapan refineries and the storage tanks there, it might be a month or two before the pinch would be felt in the Philippines.

MacArthur agreed and told Kenney to go ahead with his plan to attack Balikpapan at roughly four-day intervals beginning on September 30. For the missions, the 90th Bomb Group of the Fifth Air Force and the 5th and 307th Bomb Groups of the Thirteenth Air Force would contribute a total of more than 100 B-24s. Though this was a great increase in numbers compared with the earlier Balikpapan missions, the Fifteenth Air Force had often been putting between 300 and 400 B-24s over Ploesti during the summer of 1944.

FEAF planners were so confident that Japanese interceptor capability at Balikpapan would be minimal that they sent the bombers out on September 30 without fighter escorts. After a flight of more than nine hours from Noemfoor, 68 bombers reached Balikpapan. They had been detected over Celebes, so Balikpapan air defenses were alerted and around two dozen interceptors met them for a running gun battle that lasted for an hour as the bombers were passing through the target area.

Between disruption from the interceptors and intermittent cloud cover, only 34 bombers were able to drop their bombs visually, and then after making repeated bomb runs because of the weather. Many dropped on secondary targets and targets of opportunity. Six aircraft were lost, two each to fighters and antiaircraft fire and two in landing mishaps when they diverted to Morotai on their return.

On October 3, only the two Thirteenth Air Force groups returned, dividing the two main refineries between them – to the Edelanu for the 5th Bomb Group, and Pandasari for the 307th. As three dozen B-24s reached Balikpapan and entered their bomb runs, they were greeted by Japanese fighters. The 307th took the brunt of the punishment, being mauled by around 50 interceptors for more than an hour as they passed through the target area. Entering the target area after the 307th had passed through, the 5th Bomb Group met fewer interceptors. The bombing results of the October 3 mission, as seen in later reconnaissance photos, were better than those from the mission on the last day of September, but the cost was higher. Seven of the 36 bombers that reached Balikpapan did not return, for a loss rate of nearly 20 percent, the highest percentage of any mission ever conducted by FEAF or its constituent air forces.

After these two disasters, with the second worse than the first, Kenney flew to Noemfoor to talk to the crews and to Bill Streett, the Thirteenth Air Force commander. As Kenney recalled, "They were getting close to the breaking point. I got the kids together, discussed the importance of the mission and how it would deprive the Japanese of gasoline and make our job easier in the future."

They all realized that the show must go on, but that the script had to change.

At the top of the list for Kenney and Streett was the decision that the bombers would not go back to Balikpapan for a daylight strike without a fighter escort. Balikpapan was technically beyond the range of P-38s and P-47s, even if flying from Morotai. However, the Far East Air Service Command (FEASC) came up with a scheme to extend the range of P-38s through the addition of a huge 610-gallon fuel tank in addition to their normal pair of 165-gallon tanks. The large, cumbersome tank could be drained first, then jettisoned. A similar arrangement was worked out for the P-47s.

To help train them in fuel management techniques, the fighter pilots had a unique tutor. Charles Lindbergh, the aviation hero of the 1920s, happened to be in the SWPA flying with the fighter groups as an observer. Having flown the Atlantic alone and nonstop 17 years earlier using much more primitive technology, Lindbergh was a practiced expert in long flights with limited fuel and had personally devised fuel management techniques that delivered good results.

The next mission, now scheduled for October 10, would be a maximum effort involving all three bomb groups from September 30, plus the Fifth Air Force's veteran 22nd and 43rd Bomb Groups. They would also increase their ordnance load and switch from 250-pound to 500-pound bombs.

Streett began training his Thirteenth Air Force groups in the box formation that was used by Eighth Air Force bombers over Europe. It was more complicated, but it was better defensively against fighters because interlocking fields of fire from the bombers provided mutual protection.

In the same theme of closing up the formations, Kenney and Streett decided to tighten up the bomber stream and condense the amount of time that the total force would be over the targets – from nearly an hour to as little as ten minutes, which was a challenge for a much larger force. They would also stagger the altitudes of the various groups to complicate things for the defenders.

Added to all this was the decision to add missions between the main missions, involving smaller numbers of bombers going over Balikpapan at low level in the middle of the night, using their bombing radar to hit targets such as Japanese airfields. Everything the Japanese had come to expect about the behavior of their nemesis had now changed.

To the chagrin of the Americans, it would change again when the two sides met on October 10. The P-47s of the 35th Fighter Group arrived as planned, shot down a half dozen interceptors, and departed as the Fifth Air Force bomber groups arrived. The Thirteenth Air Force, however, was late. The Fifth, having expended fuel waiting for it, finally attacked.

The Thirteenth Air Force bombers finally arrived, not knowing they were late, accompanied by the 49th Fighter Group. Ace of aces Dick Bong, flying with the 49th that day, shot down two of the enemy interceptors who rose to meet the second wave. The 49th managed to peel the enemy fighters away from the bombers, which swept over the targets undisturbed.

The two air forces managed to put 104 bombers over Balikpapan that day, and they lost seven too many, but the loss rate was much lower than in the previous missions. Post-strike reconnaissance showed great bombing accuracy, with severe damage noted at Edelanu, Pandasari, and other locations.

On October 14, FEAF returned to Balikpapan using the same basic plan as four days earlier, but more than doubling the fighter protection. An even 100 bombers reached their targets, escorted by nearly that many P-38s and 15 P-47s. Among the fighter pilots involved were leading aces Tommy McGuire and Jerry Johnson, who were the first pilots to shoot down Japanese interceptors on that mission. McGuire would claim three enemy fighters during the Balikpapan campaign.

As on the previous mission, the Fifth Air Force bombers arrived ahead of those of the Thirteenth, but as before, the presence of the large numbers of American fighters meant that the bomb runs were largely free of enemy action. The accuracy was deemed excellent and the results were better even than those of October 10.

A coup de grâce using only Thirteenth Air Force bombers was planned for October 18, though there seemed to be little to finish off. This was a good thing, because heavy weather moved in and only 17 of 52 bombers dropped their bombs on Balikpapan because of poor visibility.

This anticlimax brought down the curtain on the Balikpapan campaign of 1944. FEAF lost 22 heavy bombers on the missions, as well as nine fighters, while claiming 129 Japanese fighters shot down. The American loss rates plummeted after the first two missions. There were 151 Americans killed, but 60 who escaped stricken aircraft were rescued by submarines or PBY Catalina flying boats. The nearly 450 tons of bombs that were dropped did considerable damage to the refineries, as well as to docks, storage facilities, and other petrochemical facilities. George Kenney wrote that after this series of attacks, "we just about finished Balikpapan off for the rest of the war."

The damage had been great, but Kenney's interpretation was tinged with wishful thinking. As had been the case at Ploesti, there was a full-scale scramble to repair the damage. It took many months to repair Pandasari, but Edelanu had to be rebuilt from the charred ground up. The major focus of Japanese petrochemical production shifted to Lutong in Malaya, but a series of Thirteenth Air Force attacks two months later put Lutong off line.

The results of the Balikpapan campaign are hard to quantify. As Major John Bunnell wrote in a 2005 Air University thesis, the Balikpapan production records were lost or destroyed. While Kenney would later claim that difficulties that dogged Japanese airpower in the later Philippines campaigns had direct correlation to the loss of Balikpapan refining capacity, Bunnell points out that Balikpapan had shipped little if any aviation fuel to the Philippines beforehand. Most of it had come from Sumatran refineries. He credits interdiction of tankers transporting fuel to the Philippines as the major cause of later Japanese shortages.

In the meantime, as Germany was turning to the development of synthetic fuel to compensate for petroleum shortages, so too did Japan. Formosa, a Japanese possession since 1895, was a major producer of sugar cane, from which the Japanese were refining butanol, a hydrocarbon fuel that is closer chemically to gasoline than is ethanol, the alcohol derived from corn which is widely used as a fuel today.

During the war, many sugar refineries on Formosa had been converted to the production of butanol for aviation fuel. Logistically this was quite attractive given that Balikpapan is 3,000 miles from Tokyo, while Formosa ports are half as far. Major sugar refining centers at Byoritsu, Eiko, Kori, Kyoshito, Shinei, Taichu, Tenshi, and Toyohara had been converted to butanol production, but it was not until the first quarter of 1945 that these came under attack by the FEAF.

As FEAF bombers had other fish to fry, Balikpapan would be off the target list until May 1945. By this time, bases available to the

FEAF – including those on the Philippine islands of Palawan and Samar – made routine missions possible throughout the Dutch East Indies. Between May 10 and July 11, FEAF bombers struck Balikpapan nearly three dozen times. Soon, most of the rebuilt refineries had ground to a sputtering halt. By now, this was irrelevant because the Japanese no longer had the ability to transport refined petroleum. Most of the later Balikpapan missions in this period were in support of the Australian 7th Division, which landed at Balikpapan on July 1, 1945 and had secured the city and the refinery complex by July 21.

17

The Bloody Road to Manila

O n December 18, 1944, just six days after he pinned the Medal of Honor on Dick Bong at Tacloban, General Douglas MacArthur got a promotion. Through an act of Congress, a process had begun on December 15 by which seven American military officers were promoted – one day apart to establish seniority – to five-star rank, a level in the hierarchy never previously authorized. Four were the members of the Joint Chiefs of Staff – Admiral William Leahy (the chairman), General George Marshall of the US Army, Admiral Ernest King of the US Navy, and General Hap Arnold of the USAAF.

Of the three who were field commanders, Douglas MacArthur was first and most senior, followed by Admiral Chester Nimitz and General Dwight Eisenhower. In American history, only Admiral George Dewey, General John J. Pershing, and General George Washington hold higher ranks, but these were bestowed after the wars in which they distinguished themselves. (Admiral Bill Halsey and General Omar Bradley are the only officers promoted to five-star rank since World War II.)

Also on December 15, American troops began securing beachheads on the island of Mindoro, halfway to Manila. This move was a complete tactical surprise to the Japanese.

Strategically, General Tomoyuki Yamashita knew that Luzon was MacArthur's ultimate prize in the Philippines, and that there would be an intermediate tactical step to secure sites for airfields to support Luzon operations. Yamashita and his planners were sure that MacArthur would land on either Negros or Panay, and they had planned accordingly.

They had planned wrong. The Americans landed on lightly defended southern Mindoro, and by December 20, engineers had a fighter strip with a 5,750-foot Marston Matting runway in operation near the town of San Jose. Known as Hill Field, it was just the first of four.

Determined Japanese air and sea attacks against Mindoro and the American ships offshore began immediately and persisted at a high level into the new year. Nevertheless, Mindoro gave FEAF air bases that were only about an hour's flying time from Manila and the heart of Luzon.

"With our occupation of Mindoro, General Yamashita became greatly concerned over the prospect of an imminent invasion of the southern area of Luzon," Douglas MacArthur wrote in his memoirs. He continued:

> Stationing the Eighth Army off the southern coast of Luzon, I planned to threaten landings at Legaspi, Batangas, and other southern ports, hoping to draw the bulk of the Japanese into the south. Our plans then called for landing the Sixth Army in an amphibious enveloping movement on the exposed northern shore, thus cutting off the enemy's supplies from Japan. This would draw the enemy back to the north, leaving the Eighth Army to land against only weak opposition on the south coast, in another amphibious movement. Both forces ashore, we would then close like a vise on the enemy deprived of supplies and destroy him. No plan ever worked better.

MacArthur's planned invasion site in the north would be Lingayan Gulf, 135 highway miles north of Manila. It was here that Lieutenant General Masaharu Homma's 14th Army had landed on December 22, 1941.

In preparation for the assault, Fifth and Thirteenth Air Force heavy bombers were brought north to Leyte to begin an air offensive against the airfields of Luzon – prewar American and Filipino air bases including Clark and Nichols, which had been used by the Japanese for the past three years.

In the meantime, fighter units had their hands full flying air defense missions over Mindoro while beginning sweeps over Luzon and other islands with Japanese airfields. The object was to capitalize on the growing American qualitative and quantitative superiority in the air to destroy as many Japanese aircraft as possible.

With Bong grounded and packing his bags to go Stateside, Major Tommy McGuire, commander of the 431st Fighter Squadron, found himself the highest-scoring American ace in the Pacific. He was determined to close the gap and perhaps surpass Bong's record of 40 aerial victories. By Christmas, having just shot down a Japanese fighter over Cebu, McGuire's aerial victory score stood at 31.

Christmas was just another day in the air war over Luzon. B-24s were headed north to strike Clark Field, and escort duty interrupted the parties at the Dulag barracks of the 431st. After a 07:55hrs takeoff, P-38s of both the 49th and 475th Fighter Groups rendezvoused with the bombers at 09:15hrs. An hour and 20 minutes later, they were 10 miles from Clark, when 20 IJNAF A6M Zeros attacked the fighters, diving out of the sun. McGuire and his wingman each shot down Zeros almost immediately, and McGuire added two more in rapid succession.

The aerial battle quickly grew as 30 IJAAF Ki-43s piled on. McGuire tried to respond but his guns jammed and he spent a half hour maneuvering through the sky trying to stay out of the line of fire. The pilots from the two groups claimed 42 Japanese aircraft, with both McGuire and Mac MacDonald shooting down three.

It had been fighter on fighter as the B-24s slipped in and slipped out without losing anyone, but three Americans – including Floyd Fulkerson, who shot down two Japanese aircraft – reported that they were stricken and headed down. Fulkerson survived, was picked up by Filipino guerrillas, and spent the coming months blowing up bridges with the covert operatives of the Office of Strategic Services (OSS).

On December 26, all three squadrons of the 475th Fighter Group joined the 49th in another escort mission to Clark Field, the fourth in five days. As on the day before, IJNAF A6Ms dropped out of the sun and into the bomber formation. McGuire downed two out of the initial group of attacking Zeros, but three more appeared. A third fell to his guns and a fourth slid into his sights. This one he chased as its pilot attempted a diving escape. He pursued it downward until it crashed into the ground. In two days, Tommy McGuire had downed seven enemy aircraft to bring his score to 38.

On December 28, McGuire was on hand at Tacloban to bid farewell to Dick Bong as he finally exited the Pacific. Kenney ordered McGuire not to fly again until after Bong had returned home to his hero's welcome. McGuire agreed, but the press had descended. At least in the pages of Stateside newspapers, the race of aces was as conspicuous as ever.

On January 7, 1945, McGuire, along with Jack Rittmayer, Captain Ed Weaver, and Lieutenant Douglas Thropp, was flying a routine low-level fighter sweep over the island of Negros when they were attacked by a single Zero. The Japanese fighter seized upon Thropp's tail, and McGuire maneuvered to attack. The P-38s were each equipped with large external fuel tanks, which extended their range, but also compromised maneuverability. For some reason, McGuire chose not to jettison his tanks, which was standard procedure when beginning an aerial battle. As he maneuvered to follow the Zero, McGuire lost control. He was too low to recover and he impacted the ground at full power. The second-highest-scoring American fighter ace of all time was dead at the age of 24. He would be posthumously awarded the Medal of Honor. His body was recovered from the remote jungle in 1949.

Another ace who made history the week that McGuire died was Captain William Shomo, commander of the 82nd Reconnaissance Squadron. He and his wingman, Lieutenant Paul Lipscomb, were flying a mission near Aparri in northern Luzon when they encountered a dozen Japanese fighters and a G4M bomber. The Americans were flying F-6 Mustangs, the reconnaissance variant of the P-51 fighter, which was still a rarity in the Pacific. Because it had an inline, rather than radial, engine, it looked like no other familiar American single-engine fighter, so the Japanese pilots mistook the planes for IJAAF Ki-61s. The Americans attacked the surprised Japanese, and while Lipscomb got three, Shomo became the only USAAF pilot to shoot down *seven* enemy aircraft in a single engagement. (US Navy pilot Commander David McCampbell had downed nine in one day three months earlier.)

At dawn on January 9, two days after McGuire's death, the American invasion armada entered Lingayan Gulf. As Douglas MacArthur watched from aboard the cruiser USS *Boise*, the first of the 175,000 men of Walter Krueger's US Sixth Army went ashore to begin their march south toward Manila.

"The Japanese, as I had hoped, were deceived, and moved troops in anticipation of an attack [in southern Luzon]," MacArthur recalled proudly in his memoirs. "Not until we had actually landed at Lingayen did General Yamashita move his center of gravity to the north."

Within a week, FEAF fighter, medium bomber, and troop carrier groups were operating out of airfields near Lingayan. Organized into the newly formed 308th Wing, the strike aircraft were able to provide timely and coordinated air support for the ground troops, effectively denying the Japanese the use of roads during daylight hours, and isolating the battlefield from resupply. Through the end of January, escort carriers belonging to Admiral Chester Nimitz's Pacific Fleet continued to provide additional air support to Luzon operations. By early February, nearly 400 FEAF aircraft were operating from Luzon fields, and the Navy was able to withdraw for other operations elsewhere. The Iwo Jima battle, for example, was due to begin on February 19.

XIV Corps, led by General Oscar Griswold, spearheaded the Sixth Army advance, reaching Clark Field by January 23, where it faced stiff resistance for several days from the Japanese defenders of the former American base.

By this time, Japanese air activity in opposition to the American drive had dwindled to practically nothing. With the last of their Philippine bases being overrun by American troops, the only air attacks the Japanese were able to make originated in Formosa. Meanwhile, heavy bombers of FEAF, as well as carrier aircraft from Admiral Bill Halsey's Third Fleet, were already pummeling Formosan fields. The FEAF bombers based in the Lingayan area interdicted Japanese supply ships making the run from Formosa to the beleaguered garrison in Luzon during its final stand, and continued the campaign against Formosa from bases in the Philippines until the end of the war.

At the end of January, George Kenney arrived to survey the damaged Clark Field. He described what he saw:

> [US Army crews] started cleaning up the wreckage of what had once been a powerful Japanese air force and repairing the runways which had been badly cratered by our bombing of the past month. The six airdromes in the Clark Field area had all been treated alike. Wrecked and burned-out airplanes were all over the place. Rusty piles of burned gasoline drums dotted the edges of the field, and hangars, shops, and operations buildings were tangled piles of steel and concrete.

On January 29, XI Corps landed on Luzon's west coast to seal off the approaches to the Bataan Peninsula to prevent the Japanese from withdrawing into it as the ill-fated Americans had done three years before. On that same day, the American flag was raised over Clark Field.

On January 30, Krueger initiated plans for the final assault on Manila, and on the following day two divisions from Lieutenant General Robert Eichelberger's Eighth Army landed south of Manila to create the opposing jaws of a pincer. Like MacArthur three years earlier, Yamashita had already given up on a determined defense of Manila. He had begun moving men and materiel out of the city in December and had relocated his own headquarters to Baguio, the traditional Philippines summer capital, located high in the mountains of northern Luzon.

American troops were on the edges of Manila by February 3, and MacArthur entered the city four days later. It seemed as though the end was in sight, but appearances were deceiving.

As MacArthur had declared Manila an open city before Homma moved in on January 2, 1942, Yamashita had ordered General Shizuo Yokoyama, commander of the IJA Shimbu Group garrisoning the city, to withdraw and not contest the city. However, IJN Rear Admiral Sanji Iwabuchi, heading the Manila Naval Defense Force, had other ideas. Nominally part of Yamashita's chain of command, Iwabuchi decided that his allegiance was to the IJN, not the IJA, and that he would disobey Yamashita's orders. He had about 12,500 barely disciplined naval personnel under his command, along with about 4,500 IJA troops. He convinced them to fight to the death before allowing the Americans and Filipinos to have Manila back.

Kenney remembered:

> ... it had been hoped that the Japanese would evacuate the city without destroying it, but they decided that, if they couldn't have the place, they would cause as much destruction as possible before they left. Practically every building in the city was dynamited or burned during their retreat ... Water lines, sewer lines, and power lines were blown up with land mines, and a city of nearly a million people left without water, electricity or food.

MacArthur made it to within sight of his old penthouse apartment – which still housed much of his personal property – when it exploded in a fireball of destruction.

What Iwabuchi's men lacked in practical military training, they made up for in zealous fanaticism. With machine guns and grenades they fought until they had been killed to the last man. By the time it was over on March 3, the Japanese dead counted within Intramuros, the old walled central city, numbered 16,665. The death toll for the Americans was 1,010, but for the Filipinos Iwabuchi's capricious stunt cost more than 100,000 lives.

"The wanton destruction of Manila was bad enough, but the Japanese earned the undying hatred of the Filipinos for all time by their senseless orgy of pillage, murder, and rape of the civilian population," Kenney added. "People in the houses were called out and shot in the streets, the houses searched for liquor and loot and then set on fire. Crazed with alcohol, Japanese officers and men raged through the city in an orgy of lust and destruction that brought back memories of their conduct at the capture of Nanking several years before, when their actions had horrified the civilized world."

In the meantime, MacArthur's troops recaptured Corregidor, the island fortress in Manila Bay where the Americans and Filipinos had held out last in the spring of 1942. To avoid the bloody urban fighting ongoing in Manila, MacArthur turned the "Rock" over to Kenney's airmen on January 22, 1945.

"I proposed to slug the place to death with heavy bombs and then let the paratroopers take it," he explained. "The General said go ahead … Every airplane that we could spare bombed the Rock. Fifth Air Force and Thirteenth Air Force bombers, strafers, and fighters, and fighters and dive bombers from the Marine Wing … Over 4,000 [actually around 3,200] tons of bombs, hundreds of thousands of rounds of ammunition, and huge quantities of our new weapon, napalm, or liquid fire, slowly crumbled the defenses of Corregidor."

On February 16, Kenney's troop carrier C-47s dropped the 503rd Parachute Regiment on Corregidor, soon to be followed by troops making an amphibious landing. Ferocious fighting ensued, tapering off only after February 21. The Rock was finally declared secured and Manila Harbor officially opened to Allied shipping on March 1.

In March and April, the official center of gravity for SWPA airpower, which had leap-frogged up from Australia to Port Moresby and across the north side of New Guinea and beyond, formally relocated to the Philippines. Having had an ADVON headquarters in Luzon soon after Allied forces landed, Kenney reestablished the formal FEAF headquarters at Fort William McKinley outside Manila. At the same time, the headquarters of the Fifth Air Force was established at Clark Field. Both V Bomber Command and V Fighter Command took up residence at Clark.

The Thirteenth Air Force moved from Morotai to Leyte in March, while its XIII Bomber Command remained in Morotai for the time being, and its XIII Fighter Command moved to Palawan Island in the southwestern Philippines. These organizations were destined to play a role in upcoming operations against the Japanese occupation of the Dutch East Indies. In the meantime, FEAF's Far East Air Service Command (FEASC) continued to operate supply depots that paralleled the forward progression of Allied forces stretching back to Australia.

Under an umbrella of complete FEAF air dominance, Krueger's Sixth Army and Eichelberger's Eighth continued to press Yamashita's forces, which had withdrawn into the difficult mountainous terrain of eastern and northern Luzon. The fighting continued through the summer of 1945, as the Japanese were unwilling to surrender. Yamashita himself did not come out of hiding and surrender until September 2, the same day that the formal surrender of Imperial Japan took place in Tokyo Bay.

An A-20 Havoc of the Fifth Air Force V Bomber Command makes a pass over a Japanese airfield near Hollandia, New Guinea, that is filled with Kawasaki Ki-48 bombers. (USAAF)

This bomb damage assessment photo shows a field of Kawasaki Ki-48 bombers damaged and destroyed at a Japanese airfield near Hollandia in northern New Guinea. (USAAF)

The dramatic sequence of photos on this spread shows a pair of Douglas A-20G Havoc attack bombers of the 387th Bomb Squadron of the 312th Bomb Group striking Japanese positions at Kokas on the Vogelkop Peninsula in western New Guinea on July 22, 1944. In the course of the sequence, the aircraft named *Bevo*, having been hit by antiaircraft fire, loses altitude and crashes. There were no survivors. (USAAF)

An A-20G Havoc of the 312th "Roarin' 20s" Bomb Group exits the target area after its mission supporting the Allied landings at Cape Sansapor on the Vogelkop Peninsula in western New Guinea. The smoke is rising from the water where an American aircraft went down. A US Navy PBY search and rescue aircraft can be seen circling below. (USAAF)

On July 28, 1944, senior leaders met to discuss strategy for the Pacific War at the Honolulu home of the late Chris Holmes overlooking Waikiki Beach that was used as a rest and relaxation facility for US naval aviators. From left to right are General Douglas MacArthur, commander in chief of the South West Pacific Areas command; President Franklin D. Roosevelt; Admiral William Leahy, chairman of the Joint Chiefs of Staff and Roosevelt's military advisor; and Admiral Chester Nimitz, commander in chief of the Pacific Ocean Areas command. (NARA)

Rear Admiral Daniel Barbey and General Douglas MacArthur conducting an inspection of the invasion beaches on the island of Morotai on September 15, 1944. The island would become an important bomber base for operations against the Dutch East Indies, especially Balikpapan, as well as for missions into the Philippines. (NARA)

Senior leaders coming ashore of the Philippine Island of Leyte on October 20, 1944. From left to right in the center row, they are Lieutenant General George Kenney, commander of the Far East Air Forces; Lieutenant General Richard Sutherland, MacArthur's chief of staff; President Sergio Osmeña of the Philippines; and Douglas MacArthur. Carlos Romulo, the Resident Commissioner to the US Congress from the Philippines, is on the left in the foreground wearing a helmet. (US Navy)

General Douglas MacArthur returns to the Philippines, wading through the surf at Dulag Beach on the island of Leyte on October 20, 1944. Philippine President Sergio Osmeña is on the far left, and MacArthur's chief of staff, Richard Sutherland, is to MacArthur's immediate left. Carlos Romulo, the Resident Commissioner to the US Congress from the Philippines, is behind MacArthur and Sutherland. (NARA)

General Douglas MacArthur (center) is accompanied by Lieutenant Generals George Kenney, Richard Sutherland, and Verne Mudge of the 1st Cavalry Division at Dulag Beach on the island of Leyte on October 20, 1944. Philippine President Sergio Osmeña is to MacArthur's right wearing a pith helmet. (NARA)

General Douglas MacArthur glances at his chief of staff, Lieutenant General Richard Sutherland (left), as he prepares to make remarks on the liberation of the Philippines at Tacloban, Leyte, in October 1944. Clutching his own notes, Philippine President Sergio Osmeña is in the center wearing his pith helmet. (NARA)

On December 12, 1944, the men of the 49th Fighter Group gathered at Tacloban Field to watch General Douglas MacArthur award the Medal of Honor to fighter ace Major Dick Bong. FEAF commander General George Kenney is seen here behind MacArthur wearing sunglasses. (USAAF)

General Douglas MacArthur awarded Major Dick Bong the Medal of Honor for "conspicuous gallantry and intrepidity in action above and beyond the call of duty" in actions over Borneo and Leyte between October 10 and November 15, 1944. Bong was the highest-scoring American ace of the war. (USAAF)

A FEAF B-25 Mitchell medium bomber making a very low level pass, nearly at mast level, against an Imperial Japanese Navy destroyer off the China coast in March 1945. (USAAF)

The Japanese destroyer *Amatsukaze* is attacked by a B-25 off the coast of Amoy (now Xiamen), China, on April 6, 1945. The crew managed to beach the ship, but it was unsalvageable and had to be scuttled four days later. (USAAF)

General Douglas MacArthur (second from right) at Atsugi airfield near Tokyo on August 30, 1945, shortly after he flew in aboard his personal C-54 Skymaster named *Bataan*, which is visible in the background. Flanking MacArthur are his chief of staff, Lieutenant General Richard Sutherland, on his right and General Robert Eichelberger, commander of the Eighth Army, on his left. On the left in sunglasses is Major General Joseph Swing, commander of the 11th Airborne Division. (NARA)

General Douglas MacArthur, as Supreme Commander for the Allied Forces (SCAP), signs a document aboard the USS *Missouri* in Tokyo Bay on September 2, 1945, formally accepting the surrender of Japan. Behind MacArthur are Lieutenant General Jonathan Wainwright and Lieutenant General Arthur Percival. (NARA)

General Douglas MacArthur, Supreme Commander for the Allied Forces (SCAP), observes the American Independence Day parade at the Imperial Palace plaza in Tokyo, Japan, on July 4, 1948. (NARA)

Fifth Air Force Douglas B-26 Invader light bombers on a routine training flight over Japan during the occupation of that country following World War II. (USAF)

A Douglas B-26 of the Fifth Air Force 3rd Bomb Group attacks the railroad marshaling yard at Iri (now Iksan), near the strategic port of Kunsan, on Korea's west coast, using "parafrag" bombs. (USAF)

A Fifth Air Force F-80 of the 80th Fighter Bomber Squadron, piloted by Lieutenant John Shannon (call sign "Ice Age Charlie Four"), unleashes a napalm bomb on a North Korean target as a projectile launched from the ground rises to intercept it. (USAF)

B-29 Superfortresses of the Far East Air Forces Bomber Command's 92nd Bomb Group drop their 500-pound bombs on a strategic target in North Korea in September 1950. (USAF)

General Douglas MacArthur in his role as commander in chief, United Nations Command, observes the shelling of Inchon, South Korea, in preparation for the September 15, 1950 invasion. With him, from left to right on the deck of USS *Mount McKinley*, are Rear Admiral James Doyle; Brigadier Edwin Wright, MacArthur's operations officer; and Major General Edward Almond, commander of X Corps. (NARA)

In October 1950, Fairchild C-119 Flying Boxcars of the Far East Air Forces Combat Cargo Command dropped more than 2,800 paratroopers of the 187th Airborne Regimental Combat Team 30 miles north of Pyongyang, to complete the envelopment of the North Korean capital. (USAF)

Paratroopers of the 187th Airborne Regimental Combat Team descend from FEAF C-119s on March 23, 1951 during Operation *Tomahawk*, an attempt to cut off retreating Chinese and North Korean troops north of Pyongyang. (NARA)

On his arrival at an advanced air base in Korea, General of the Army Douglas MacArthur is greeted by Major General Earle "Pat" Partridge, the commanding general of Fifth Air Force. (NARA)

North American Aviation F-86A Sabres of the 4th Fighter-Interceptor Group. The group arrived at Suwon AB in South Korea in March 1951 and later relocated to Kimpo AB near Seoul. The Sabre proved itself to be the best air superiority fighter of the Korean War. (USAF)

Flying high above the Yalu River in his Lockheed VC-121A Constellation aircraft on November 24, 1950, General Douglas MacArthur surveys the frontier between North Korea and the People's Republic of China. General George Stratemeyer, commander of the Far East Air Forces, is on MacArthur's left. (NARA)

General Douglas MacArthur with his personal transport aircraft, the Douglas C-54 Skymaster that he named *Bataan*. He used it when he was Supreme Commander for the Allied Powers (SCAP) during the occupation of Japan. (NARA)

18

The Superfortress

T he Boeing B-29 Superfortress was the supreme manifestation
of strategic airpower in World War II. It was used to execute
the strategic air campaign that would play a pivotal role in the
ultimate defeat of Imperial Japan.

The Superfortress had a much longer range than previous heavy
bombers, such as the B-17 and B-24, and it had a pressurized cabin
that permitted crews to operate comfortably at much higher altitudes –
above weather and enemy interceptors – than other types of bombers.
It also had a much greater payload capacity. Indeed, while the B-17
and B-24 were classed as "heavy" bombers, the B-29 was officially
designated as a "very heavy" bomber.

The US Army Air Corps (USAAF after 1941), as well as various
American planemakers, had studied long-range, high-altitude bombers
in the 1930s, but it was not until 1940, when the German blitzkrieg had
swallowed much of Europe, that things got serious and a secret design
competition was initiated. Consolidated, Douglas, Lockheed, and
Boeing submitted proposals, and Boeing won this with its Model 345,
which was ordered under the designation XB-29. The Consolidated
B-32 Dominator was ordered as a backup very heavy bomber, but fewer
than 100 were built, compared with more than 3,600 B-29s.

After the debut flight of the first XB-29 in February 1942, the
Superfortress flight-test program was beset with numerous teething
troubles because the new aircraft and its Wright R-3350 Duplex
Cyclone turbosupercharged engines embodied advanced and untried

technology. However, General Hap Arnold, the commanding general of the USAAF, was committed to the promise of an aircraft with capabilities far beyond those of existing aircraft, so he pushed the program forward with great determination.

Arnold decided that he would not deploy the Superfortress to the European or the Mediterranean Theaters, where the B-17s and B-24s of the Eighth and Fifteenth Air Forces could reach the heart of Germany from secure bases. He would use it only in the Pacific, where distances demanded the range of a Superfortress.

On his trip to the western Pacific in the fall of 1942, Arnold had briefed Chester Nimitz and Douglas MacArthur on the B-29 and had found them both wanting tactical control of the B-29 within their respective theaters.

However, Arnold felt that operational control of the super weapon should be in the hands of someone who had an eye on the ultimate strategic goal, rather than someone preoccupied with narrowly defined tactical goals within a theater of operations. Moreover, Arnold was determined to use his ultimate manifestation of strategic airpower strictly for a *strategic* mission, that of defeating Japan through attacks *on* Japan itself.

Therefore, he resolved to personally maintain control of the B-29 force from his seat on the Joint Chiefs of Staff. The entire operational Superfortress fleet would be assigned to the USAAF Twentieth Air Force, which was activated in April 1944 and commanded directly by Arnold.

"I could do nothing but retain command of the B-29s myself," Arnold wrote in his memoirs. He continued:

> I could not give them to MacArthur because then they would operate ahead of Nimitz' command; I could not give them to Nimitz since in that case they would operate in front of MacArthur's advance. So, in the end, while everybody wondered why, I kept personal command of the Twentieth Air Force. There was nothing else I could do, with no unity of command in the Pacific. I could find no one out there who wanted unity of command, seemingly, unless he himself was made Supreme Commander.

This decision did not prevent Kenney, on behalf of MacArthur, continuing to lobby for B-29s. When Kenney was in Washington, DC in January 1944, he told Arnold, "I could destroy the oil refineries of the Dutch East Indies and the Japanese would be unable to keep the war going."

He had written to Arnold asking to "let me change over my B-24 groups to B-29 outfits, so that I could drop ten tons of bombs per airplane instead of four."

Kenney recalled that Arnold replied that he "would not make any promises but said that if I had a runway big enough to take them by July he might let me have 50 B-29s at that time." Kenney recalled that he issued orders for "construction of a 10,000-foot runway at Darwin, with parking for a hundred B-29s."

During the last week of March 1944, Major General Lawrence Kuter of the Air Staff in Washington, DC arrived in Brisbane. He had been dispatched on a 32,000-mile globe-circling junket to serve as Hap Arnold's eyes and ears in all the far-flung places that the USAAF was operating.

According to Kuter's biographer, Brian Laslie, "Kuter was supposed to meet with General MacArthur, but MacArthur's chief of staff, Brigadier General Richard Sutherland, stonewalled him and sent him directly to Kenney without allowing him to pay MacArthur a courtesy visit."

Kenney wrote of his own recollection:

[Kuter and] a lot of the Air Corps officers in Washington believed that B-29s, operating from Guam, Saipan, and Tinian against Japan proper, could knock the Japanese out of the war before we could capture Luzon … In spite of the fact that Washington knew that I was ready to operate B-29s out of my new airdrome at Darwin against the oil refineries at Balikpapan, which my information showed was producing most of the aviation fuel for the Japanese.

The 10,000-foot runway at Darwin was completed, but it would never host the B-29s of which MacArthur and Kenney dreamed. Instead of Australia, Arnold would send his Superfortresses to China. Arnold's apparent ambiguity in his conversations with Kenney about an Australian deployment of Superfortresses – like a parallel discussion of sending Superfortresses to the Eighth Air Force in Europe – may have meant that the USAAF chief was actually considering such a scenario. Alternatively, the idea, which was bound to leak from behind closed doors, may well have been encouraged by Arnold as a deliberate obfuscation intended for any ears of Axis espionage that might have been listening.

As he was pushing Boeing to resolve the complex developmental and production issues that dogged the program, Arnold was seeking a place within striking distance of Japan at which to base his big bombers. In the spring of 1944, the only places were in China, and Arnold settled upon Chengdu, which was about 180 miles from Chungking (now Chongqing), Nationalist China's wartime capital, and 2,200 miles from Tokyo.

The initial operational deployment of the B-29s was with the XX Bomber Command of the Twentieth Air Force, commanded by Major General Kenneth B. "KB" Wolfe. As a production engineering specialist with the Air Materiel Command, Wolfe had overseen the technical development of the Superfortress. Under Operation *Matterhorn*, the bombers reached bases in India in early 1944 and gradually forward deployed across the Himalayas – known as the "Hump" to airmen of the time. The first mission was flown on June 5 against Japanese facilities in Bangkok, as Thailand was allied with Japan and it was a conduit for supplies flowing into Burma. In the first mission against a target inside Japan, bombs fell on Yawata ten days later. The next major raid on Japan came on July 7.

In August, dissatisfied by the slow pace of the XX Bomber Command operation, Arnold replaced Wolfe, the technician, with Major General Curtis E. LeMay, a tough, results-oriented leader who had been commanding the 3rd Air Division of the Eighth Air Force.

He took over an impossible situation. Chengdu operations were a logistical nightmare because China was at the end of an infeasible supply chain. Because Japan controlled China's ports and there were no good roads into China, resupply had to be done by air, with transport aircraft flying the difficult route over the Hump. The B-29s transported their own fuel and ordnance over the Hump, and it took six such supply missions for each operational strike mission.

Meanwhile, over the summer of 1944, Guam and the Mariana Islands in the Pacific had been captured though the efforts of the US Marine Corps, and a massive airfield construction program undertaken on Guam, Saipan, and Tinian – which are between 1,480 and 1,580 miles from Tokyo. Arnold activated the XXI Bomber Command, the second B-29 organization within the Twentieth Air Force, and began to deploy B-29s under the command of his former chief of staff, Major General Haywood "Possum" Hansell.

Beginning in October with attacks on Japanese-held islands such as Truk, Hansell undertook a training operation to hone the skills of his aircrews before initiating missions against Japan on November 24. As had been the case with the XX Bomber Command in China, Hansell's XXI Bomber Command got off to a slow and hesitant start, nagged by weather and high-altitude winds. Operational bombers had not previously operated so high as to experience the jet stream.

As impatient with Hansell as he was with Wolfe, Arnold decided to sack Hansell and bring LeMay over from China to head the XXI Bomber Command. Henceforth, the majority of Superfortress missions were flown from Guam and the Marianas. LeMay was succeeded in China by Major General Roger Ramey, who had previously commanded the V Bomber Command under George Kenney's Fifth Air Force. The XX Bomber Command moved back to India and conducted operations against Southeast Asia through March, when its assets were reassigned to the XXI Bomber Command.

Because of disappointing results garnered from high-altitude bombing using high-explosive ordnance, LeMay decided to switch to low-altitude incendiary missions. The object of strategic bombing is to destroy an enemy war economy by destroying industry, and because much of Japanese industry depended upon subassemblies manufactured in urban areas, burning out urban areas was a better way of destroying the economy than bombing larger factories, as had been done in Germany.

As LeMay told this author four decades later:

I made up my mind to make some major changes in the way we were using the B-29s because it was now clear that we couldn't possibly succeed by basing our strategy on our experience from Europe. That system wasn't working. It was a different war with different weather and a different airplane. It called for a different solution. As I looked over the reconnaissance photos, I noticed that there wasn't any low-altitude flak such as we'd encountered in Europe. It looked reasonable to me that we could fly a successful mission with less fuel and a larger bomb load by going in low, particularly if we went in at night. After sizing up the situation and knowing that I had to do something radical, I finally arrived at the decision to use low-level attacks against Japanese urban industrial areas using incendiaries. Even poorly trained radar operators could find cities that were on or near the coast, and going in at between 5,000 and 8,000 feet instead of 25,000 feet would ensure that all the bombs would fall in the target area. This method solved the weather problem because, instead of getting the force ready and then waiting for the right weather, we would go in *under* the weather when *we* were ready.

Earlier XXI Bomber Command missions had averaged around 60 B-29s, bur LeMay decided on overwhelming Japanese defenses with a series of maximum effort missions, each involving around 300 Superfortresses. Between March 9 and March 20, such missions were flown at night against Tokyo, Osaka, Kobe, and Nagoya until stocks of incendiaries were depleted.

LeMay recalled:

... it was April 13 before we had built up large enough stocks of incendiaries to support a full-scale mission, but we flew a lot of smaller-scale missions while we were waiting for more bombs. The Navy scurried around and got some ships, and in six weeks we had the bombs. We never caught up from then on, though. We simply bypassed the bomb dumps, and with the help of the Seabees, some Marines that were supposedly in a rest camp, and anybody else that was around, we brought the bombs from the supply ships directly to the hardstands of the airplanes. Soon we were dropping over 3,000 tons per mission.

"I was not happy, but neither was I particularly concerned, about civilian casualties on incendiary raids," LeMay explained to me candidly. He continued:

I didn't let it influence any of my decisions because we knew how the Japanese had treated the Americans – both civilian and military – that they'd captured in places like the Philippines. We had dropped some warning leaflets over Japan, which essentially told the civilian population that we weren't trying to kill them, but rather that we were trying to destroy their capability to make war. We were going to bomb their cities and burn them down. We suggested they leave for their own safety.

MacArthur and Kenney watched as American airpower finally struck major blows against the heart of Imperial Japan. Although Arnold never gave them the B-29, he *did* give them a very heavy bomber. The Consolidated B-32 was finally operational by the spring of 1945. The Fifth Air Force 312th Bomb Group became a "very heavy bombardment group," and B-32s were sent to Clark Field on Luzon in June 1945.

19

Climax in the Southwest Pacific

I n the spring of 1945, as Hap Arnold's Twentieth Air Force, under the management of Curtis LeMay, took the war directly and incessantly to urban Japan, Douglas MacArthur's Far East Air Forces, under the management of George Kenney, were taking their wrath to strategic and maritime targets in other parts of Japan's East Asia Empire within and adjacent to the SWPA.

The arc of FEAF bomber bases that stretched 1,400 miles from Sansapor on New Guinea's far western Vogelkop Peninsula to Clark Field on Luzon brought Japanese bases from Borneo to South China to Formosa within the range of Kenney's B-24 bombers, as well as the P-38s that escorted them. In Volume 5 of *The Army Air Forces in World War II*, Bernhardt Mortensen put this into perspective, writing that "in their northward progress from New Guinea to Leyte, Mindoro, and Luzon, SWPA forces had bypassed substantial enemy garrisons in the Dutch East Indies, Borneo, and the southern Philippine Islands."

Mortensen added that "continually subjected to air attack, those garrisons had suffered an attrition which greatly reduced their capacity to interfere in any serious way with Allied operations. The invasion of Luzon, moreover, placed US forces, both air and sea, in a position to maintain increasingly effective interdiction of the lines of communication joining enemy garrisons in the south with the Japanese homeland and thus to cut off all hope of their reinforcement."

Cutting off supplies was an important part of the FEAF work load. Kenney wrote in his memoirs that "we had been sweeping the China Sea and the China coast, from Saigon to Shanghai, looking for Japanese shipping. By March first the air blockade had cut the volume of that shipping to one third of what it had been a month before. The kids were complaining that the hunting was getting so poor that they hardly felt like calling it combat time any more."

Mortensen went on to say:

… there was a strong temptation to leave enemy garrisons south of Luzon to wither on the vine, much as previously bypassed forces had been left in the Solomons. The temptation, however, was met by several objections. In planning the Philippines operations it had been evident that air bases in Borneo would add to the effectiveness of the attempt to interdict enemy communications in the South China Sea. Political considerations carried even greater weight.

As MacArthur had repeatedly stated, the strong sense of the obligation the United States bore for the liberation of the Philippines – those "political considerations" mentioned by Mortensen – entailed an obligation to the people of Australian territories and the Dutch East Indies who were suffering under Japanese occupation – not to mention other Philippine islands that had been bypassed in the drive toward Luzon.

Operationally, the US Sixth Army was occupied with Luzon and earmarked for operations farther north. Since the Leyte battles, the US Eighth Army was tasked with operations in the Philippines south of Luzon. Plans for the US Army to reconquer Java, the heart of the Dutch East Indies, were shelved. The Australian I Corps, under Operation *Oboe*, was tasked with recapturing Borneo.

Air operations were a different matter. The Fifth Air Force operated in parallel with the Sixth Army in Luzon, but ranged far to the north and west. The Thirteenth Air Force, meanwhile, supported the Eighth Army but spread its wings across the Indies and into China and Indochina. From bases in Morotai, the Thirteenth attacked Japanese air bases on Borneo, as well as Kendari on Celebes.

Formosa, in Japanese hands since 1895, had always been a supplier of raw materials important to the Japanese economy, and with its

well-developed airfield, rail, and port infrastructure, it had served as
a vital logistical and staging center for the Japanese armed forces. As
noted in Chapter 16, Formosa had also become an important synthetic
fuel resource for Japan given that sugar refineries had been converted to
the production of butanol.

As Mortensen pointed out, "with the single exception of Manchuria,
Formosa was the most highly developed of the Japanese possessions ...
Electrical power plants in the mountainous backbone of the island were
tied to the production of perhaps 10 per cent of Japan's aluminum. Iron,
copper, and salt, together with oil refining, rounded out the island's
industrial contribution to the Empire."

The Fifth Air Force initiated a daylight strategic bombing campaign
against Formosa in January. In his memoirs, George Kenney wrote:

> ... every mission reported airplanes destroyed on the ground, rail
> and motor transportation destroyed, warehouses burned down,
> and railroad yards plowed up, with no interception by the enemy
> fighters. On March 2nd we put over a simultaneous attack with 125
> bombers, fighters, and strafers on six Formosan airdromes, destroying
> another forty Japanese planes on the ground. The operation was
> worth mentioning because a lone Japanese airplane had attempted
> interception of the raid. He was shot down so quickly, with so many
> people shooting at him, that the kids involved finally had to draw
> straws to see who should be given credit for the victory. All our planes
> returned.

Major General Ennis Whitehead, commander of the Fifth Air Force,
was putting as many as 70 or more B-24s drawn from all four of his
bombardment groups on each raid. The primary attacks were against
airfields including those at Koshun, Matsuyama, Okayama, Shinchiku,
Taichu, Tainan, Toko, and Toyohara. These attacks were directly related
to the *kamikaze* threat to American shipping, which was correctly
predicted to be a problem for upcoming operations against Okinawa.
Meanwhile, the Fifth Air Force was making itself a threat to Japanese
shipping. Mortensen wrote that "frequent antishipping sweeps were
run along the east and west coasts of Formosa by flights of from six
to twelve medium bombers, and fighters on escort duty often made
strafing runs along the coast before heading for home."

Many of Whitehead's B-24s were now equipped with H2X radar, an improved version of the British H2S system introduced in 1943. Officially designated as AN/APS-15, this was the precursor to future ground mapping radar, and the first to be used in combat. The H2X permitted Low Altitude Bombing (LAB) missions against enemy port facilities at night because the contrast between land and sea was so pronounced on the radar scope that coastlines were very easy to distinguish. The H2X-equipped "pathfinder" B-24s that led the bomber streams over the targets had their lower ball turrets removed and replaced with large radomes.

In addition to the airfields, the butanol refineries were also high on the target lists, with A-20s and B-25s using napalm and high-explosive ordnance to incinerate them. It was against the butanol plants that Kenney would first use his B-32 Dominator very heavy bombers, which finally reached him in June 1945.

The perils of the Formosa missions of that era, and indeed of bomber missions throughout World War II, are summarized in the story of a young sergeant, Bruce Willingham of McAlester, Oklahoma, who was assigned to the 63rd Bomb Squadron of the 43rd Bomb Group based on Luzon.

Just two months shy of turning 24, Willingham was a waist gunner in a H2X radar-equipped LAB B-24 piloted by Lieutenant Albert Goossens, with Lieutenant Charles Phippen as copilot. On the night of January 30, the mission was against Takao (now Kaohsiung) on the southwest coast, which was then the largest city on Formosa, a major port and home to such Japanese industrial firms as Asahi Electro-Chemical, the Taiwan Electrochemical Manufacturing Company, and the Nippon Aluminum Company.

Just after the ordnance dropped from the B-24's bomb bay, everything went completely and impossibly wrong. Defying all odds, a Japanese antiaircraft gunner put a round directly into the bomb bay, a round that had been fused precisely for the altitude of the bomber, so that it exploded *inside* the open bay. Luckily, it caused so little damage that the bay doors were able to close. Then, a *second* Japanese antiaircraft gunner further defied the odds by putting a *second* round directly into the bomb bay, this one crashing through the doors. A third shell, fired by another lucky or uncannily skilled gunner, knocked the cowling off the Number 3 engine.

The odds of an aircraft being hit three times in rapid succession without disintegrating are astronomical, but fate was not yet through twisting.

While Japanese interceptor activity over Formosa was lessening, and night fighter actions rare, Willingham's bomber was suddenly beset by an estimated *seven* Japanese night fighters, which attacked the Americans from the rear. The tail gunner, Sergeant Charles Trusty, managed to destroy one of the enemy aircraft, but was injured by a 20mm shell that it had fired.

Willingham, who was in the waist gun position, intervened, dragging Trusty out of the tail turret and applying first aid. He then took up Trusty's position in the tail turret and engaged a second Japanese fighter, blowing it out of the sky.

At the same time, Sergeant Willard Ogle, the other waist gunner, was operating both his waist gun and Willingham's until he too was wounded. Again, Sergeant Willingham came forward to bind up the wound before returning to the tail turret to engage and shoot up a third Japanese fighter.

As this was ongoing, Goossens had shoved the yoke forward to dive the big bomber into the protection of a layer of clouds. He had almost made it when a fourth Japanese interceptor struck, shooting out the Number 4 engine.

As he leveled out at 1,000 feet above the choppy waters of the Philippine Sea, Goossens shut off the fuel line to the Number 4 engine, but it continued to spew oil and the propeller refused to be feathered, creating serious drag.

Safe from Japanese fighters inside the cloud, Goossens and Phippen took stock of the situation. The automatic pilot and the hydraulic system had failed and there were holes in both wing flaps. From the rear of the aircraft, Willingham reported gaping cannon shell holes in the left vertical stabilizer.

In addition to damage to both engines on the right wing, there was a massive fuel leak in that wing. As they watched, the oil-starved Number 4 engine overheated and exploded into flame. In another moment of beating the odds, the propeller assembly became so hot that the shaft melted and the propeller that would not feather simply spun off into the darkness, and eventually the fire burned out.

Goossens contacted the recently opened bomber base at Lingayan, north of Manila near the gulf of the same name where the Sixth Army had landed, and requested permission to land, but was told that the base was in the midst of a Japanese air raid.

Finally, after about a half hour of cruising offshore and manually cranking down the landing gear, the bomber received a green light to land and a searchlight was illuminated to guide the way. Goossens and Phippen manually deployed the flaps and touched down only to discover that the left main gear tire was flat and the brakes were gone. The big aircraft slewed hard to the left, its wing knocking the tails from a pair of B-25s parked near the runway, and continued to skid as the two pilots struggled to control it. When it came to a stop, Trusty and Ogle were taken out and transported to the base hospital. As the 63rd Bomb Squadron historian reported, "the rest of the crew sat down with hot coffee to congratulate their pilot and their ship, and to contemplate the solid earth beneath them."

Bruce Willingham finished his tour of duty, took home a Distinguished Flying Cross and an Air Medal, married his high school sweetheart, Helen Ruth Gilpin, in June 1945, and eventually took over the family dry cleaning business. He and Ruth had been together for 54 years when he passed away in 1999.

In the air campaigns against targets in both South China and the South China Sea, the Fifth and Thirteenth Air Forces of the FEAF added their firepower to that of the Fourteenth Air Force. Headquartered at Kunming inside China, the Fourteenth had evolved from the earlier China Air Task Force (CATF) and was commanded by the outspoken Major General Claire Lee Chennault.

A prewar Air Corps fighter pilot, Chennault had been called out of retirement in 1937 to serve as a civilian advisor to the air force of Generalissimo Chiang Kai-shek's Nationalist Chinese government. In 1941, Chennault had convinced President Franklin Roosevelt to allow him to create an American mercenary air force in China composed of American military pilots who were allowed to resign their commissions and hire on as civilian contractors to the Chinese government. Flying as fighter pilots for an entity known as the American Volunteer Group (AVG), these Americans were paid a bonus for every Japanese aircraft they downed – making them *literally* bounty hunters!

The AVG, which became known as the "Flying Tigers," was active from December 1941 to July 1942, fought around 50 major aerial battles against hugely lopsided odds, and never lost one of those contests. By the records of the bonuses paid by the Chinese government, 296 Japanese aircraft were shot down. The AVG lost only ten pilots in combat.

After the AVG was deactivated, Chennault was reinducted into the USAAF and given command of the CATF, a small force comprised of the few USAAF assets in China. As Chennault had learned with the AVG and as LeMay would later learn with his XX Bomber Command, all operations inside China had to be supported by flying personnel, supplies, and replacement aircraft across the Hump from India. For all of their complaints about being at a forgotten extremity of the logistics chain, MacArthur and Kenney always had the advantage of being supplied by ocean shipping, a luxury that Chennault never enjoyed. Because of the tenuous nature of the CATF in China, it remained a component of the Tenth Air Force in India until March 1943, when Chennault finally succeeded in lobbying Roosevelt and Arnold for an upgrade to numbered air force status.

Even after becoming the Fourteenth Air Force, Chennault's force still operated on a relative shoestring, with just a single heavy bombardment group. The size of the Fourteenth Air Force and the scale of its operations roughly mirrored those of the Fifth Air Force of 1943. While the Fourteenth Air Force was suited to operations such as maritime interdiction in the South China Sea and ground support on China's battlefields, it lacked the critical mass of bombers necessary for attacks on highly defended strategic targets. As late as the spring of 1945, being able to put two dozen heavy bombers on a target was a good day. In most strike packages, the numbers were in single digits, while the FEAF could deploy 50–100 heavy bombers on a typical mission. Major General Ennis Whitehead's Fifth Air Force in the Philippines alone had four heavy bombardment groups.

Hong Kong was an especially important target. Captured by the Imperial Japanese Army in December 1941, the erstwhile British Crown Colony had provided the Japanese with the best port, ship repair, and drydock facilities in the Far East between Singapore and mainland Japan. Chennault's bombers had been picking at these sites and at the ships using them for nearly three years, but the effectiveness of these strikes had been limited by the small numbers of aircraft. However, by the spring of 1945 they were joined by aircraft from the fast carriers of the US Navy's Task Force 38 under Vice Admiral John S. "Slew" McCain. The Navy's torpedo bombers had been especially effective against shipping in Hong Kong Harbor.

On April 2, 1945, the Fifth Air Force struck Hong Kong for the first time, and followed up with daily operations for the ensuing three days. The Fifth's 90th and 380th Bomb Groups were able to put nearly 50 B-24s over Hong Kong on the first day, supported by Fourteenth Air Force P-51s and by P-38s of the Fifth Air Force 49th Fighter Group. IJAAF interceptor activity was minimal, but Lieutenant Colonel Jerry Johnson, commander of the 49th's 9th Fighter Squadron, scored his 22nd and final aerial victory over Hong Kong on April 2. It was one of six Japanese aircraft downed. No American aircraft were shot down.

For the next three days, Whitehead sent the B-24s of the Fifth Air Force 22nd and 43rd Bomb Groups to follow up, and a final mission of the series came on April 13. During this five-mission effort, the Fifth Air Force lost no bombers, though many took serious hits from antiaircraft fire. Only one P-38 was lost, but its pilot bailed out over American-held Luzon. Damage done to shipping and to the port facilities exceeded that of previous raids.

For the people of Hong Kong, and for the Allied prisoners being held there, the reaction was bittersweet. The sight of so many Allied aircraft lifted morale, but at the same time, as had been the case with most missions against crowded Hong Kong, there were numerous civilian casualties. As Steven Bailey wrote in his excellent book *Bold Venture*, about the air war over Hong Kong, the Allied prisoners in the Sham Shui Po prisoner of war camp greeted the Fifth Air Force "with a mix of giddy jubilation and unvarnished terror."

As for Indochina, Mortensen concluded that by March, FEAF actions had "virtually stopped seaborne movements north of Saigon [and] the 'take-out' of Saigon started on April 19 when eight Liberators of the Thirteenth Air Force's 307th Bomb Group staged through Palawan and bombed the harbor through clouds [using H2X]." He continued:

On April 22, twenty 380th Group B-24's hit the naval yards and shipping with 1,000-pounders, followed the next day by twenty-four 90th Group planes which scored on the dry docks, warehouses, and oil storage tanks. The two groups joined forces on April 25 and 26 to put forty-six and forty-seven planes, respectively, over Saigon. Hits were scored on dry docks, warehouses, ships at dock, barracks, an alcohol plant, and other installations.

By April, Yamashita's cornered troops on Luzon and a few other holdouts notwithstanding, the Philippines had been secured as a base of operations. US Marine blood and sweat had delivered Iwo Jima as a base from which USAAF fighters could escort B-29s on their missions to the Japanese heartland.

As the focus of American offensive action in the Pacific now turned to Okinawa as a stepping stone to Japan itself, the ocean across the vastness of the SWPA was an American lake beneath an American sky. It was punctuated by island after island with Japanese garrisons – from the once powerful naval base at Truk, to Rabaul on New Britain, with its invincible army, to Java, the erstwhile crown jewel of the Dutch East Indies – but these troops could do little other than stare at empty horizons and dwindling supplies.

The few Japanese ships that still plied these waters did so at considerable peril – from submarines as well as aircraft. Once they had sailed these seas under the protection of the IJN when it was the most powerful navy the Pacific had ever known, but now the IJN was but a shadow of itself, a ghost haunting someone else's waters. Once the convoys had traveled beneath skies controlled by Japanese airpower, but that too was just a memory.

One former Japanese Navy convoy commander debriefed after the war told the US Joint Army-Navy Assessment Committee that by April 1945, "when we requested air cover, only American planes showed up."

20

The Last Stepping Stones to Japan

"By the "way,"" George Kenney said to Douglas MacArthur. "I heard a rumor that you are going to command the show when we go into Japan."

It was the evening of March 26, 1945 and the two men were at MacArthur's headquarters in Manila. After a week in Washington, DC conferencing on behalf of MacArthur and three grueling days of flying across the Pacific, he was briefing his boss on what had been discussed in the halls of power.

"I don't believe it," MacArthur replied quickly. "My information is that Nimitz will be in charge and that I am to clean up the Philippines and then move south into the Dutch East Indies. Who gave you that rumor, anyhow?"

"A man named Franklin Delano Roosevelt," Kenney said. The FEAF commander had spent 90 minutes with the commander in chief on March 20, and had been asked to convey Roosevelt's endorsement of MacArthur for this role.

As Kenney recalled, "MacArthur tried to keep the same expression but it was no use. He was as pleased as I was. He would have taken the decision the other way, like the soldier he is, but, of course, he wanted to lead the final drive on Japan – the biggest drive of the war. I wanted him to lead it, too."

MacArthur asked when this decision would be announced.

"Soon," Kenney replied.

On April 3, the South West Pacific Area (SWPA), MacArthur's vast region of responsibility, ceased to exist as an area of operations. Three days later, the Joint Chiefs of Staff gave him responsibility for a much larger geographic area as commander in chief of the newly created United States Army Forces in the Pacific (AFPAC) command.

In their April 3 directive, the Joint Chiefs reorganized and streamlined the command structure in the Pacific, dividing it between MacArthur and Chester Nimitz, the only two American field officers on that side of the globe to hold five-star rank. The "Area" structure, with MacArthur's SWPA and Nimitz's three Pacific Ocean Areas, was superseded by the long overdue decision to designate virtually the entire 64 million-square-mile region as simply the Pacific Theater.

As the Commander in Chief, Pacific (CINCPAC), Nimitz would command all the Allied naval assets, and MacArthur would command all of the army and air assets – except the Twentieth Air Force, which remained under Hap Arnold's direct control. Aside from his not having control of the B-29 force, the Joint Chiefs had signed off on an arrangement that MacArthur had long been advocating.

MacArthur believed that the only efficient force structure was for all land forces to be commanded by an army officer, and all naval forces by a naval officer, with unity of command derived from joint task forces led by an officer of the service most heavily engaged in a specific operation. As MacArthur had written in a wire to the War Department on January 3, 1945, such an organization "will give true unity of command in the Pacific, as it permits the employment of all available resources against the selected objective."

The invasion of Japan was to be largely a ground operation, so MacArthur would, as Roosevelt had told Kenney, be in charge. However, the April 3 directive stopped short of naming a "*supreme* commander" for the entire Pacific Theater. Across the world, meanwhile, General Eisenhower had been the supreme commander of the Supreme Headquarters Allied Expeditionary Force (SHAEF) in Europe since 1943. In August 1945 MacArthur would at last be given the title of Supreme Commander of the Allied Powers (SCAP), but as it turned out, this came just as the war was coming to an end.

Roosevelt's choosing MacArthur for this task was one of the last things he ever did. On April 12, only six days after the JCS confirmed MacArthur to head AFPAC and the invasion of Japan, the President passed away at Warm Springs, Georgia, of a massive cerebral hemorrhage. Harry Truman, less than three months into his first term as Vice President, was sworn in as the President of the United States who would preside over the end of World War II.

Under the new Pacific Theater arrangement, various units and commands were realigned and reassigned – and, unusually for such a massive bureaucracy, it was done quickly. For example, Admiral Halsey's Seventh Fleet was transferred from MacArthur's control to Nimitz's, and Lieutenant General Robert Richardson's US Army Forces in the Pacific Ocean Areas (USAFPOA) command was transferred from Nimitz to MacArthur's AFPAC. Created under USAFPOA, and now part of MacArthur's command, was the new US Tenth Army, led by Lieutenant General Simon Bolivar Buckner.

USAAF assets in the Pacific were also realigned. The Seventh Air Force, commanded by Major General Robert Douglass, which had units scattered throughout the POA, was transferred from Nimitz's CINCPAC control to join the Fifth and Thirteenth Air Forces in Kenney's FEAF. Based in Hawaii for most of the war, its headquarters had relocated to Saipan in December 1944. An exception to the Seventh Air Force reassignment was the VII Fighter Command, which had been moved to Iwo Jima in March 1945 with three fighter groups of P-51D Mustangs to serve as fighter escorts for Twentieth Air Force B-29s. It would continue in this role under the operational control of the Twentieth.

As for the Twentieth Air Force, it would remain under Hap Arnold's control, but with another level inserted into the chain of command effective in July 1945. Arnold anticipated the creation of an entity called the US Army Strategic Air Forces in the Pacific (USASTAF); this would be based on Guam and contain both the Twentieth Air Force and the Eighth Air Force, which was to be relocated from England after the defeat of Germany. The "Mighty Eighth" had grown to the point where it was capable of routinely launching thousand-bomber attacks against the Third Reich, and this level of firepower was seen as an important addition to the growing strength of the Twentieth.

The organization of the USASTAF would parallel that of the US Strategic Air Forces in Europe (USSTAF); this had been created in 1944 as an umbrella organization for the Eighth and the Fifteenth Air Forces, which were conducting the strategic campaign against Germany. General Carl "Tooey" Spaatz commanded the USSTAF. Arnold planned to have him come to the Pacific in July to take over the USASTAF, though when Arnold visited Manila on his Pacific inspection tour in June 1945, MacArthur personally lobbied him to put George Kenney in that post. Arnold declined. He had worked closely with Spaatz since before the war, and believed that his experience in Europe made him uniquely qualified.

The Eighth Air Force would continue to be commanded by General Jimmy Doolittle – who had led the first bombing raid on Japan in April 1942, and who had assumed command of the Eighth in January 1944. General Nathan Twining, who commanded the Fifteenth, would relocate to the Pacific as the field commander of the Twentieth.

The organizational changes initiated by the Joint Chiefs directive of April 3, 1945 occurred two days after the invasion of Okinawa. The importance of this 466-square-mile island to the overall strategic plan was as a staging base for the planned invasion of Kyushu, the southernmost of Japan's four main islands. It would also provide the basing from which the heavy bombers of Kenney's FEAF and Doolittle's Eighth Air Force could operate against Japan in concert with the B-29s of the Twentieth Air Force.

Located in the Ryukyu Islands about 350 miles south of the southern main Japanese island of Kyushu, Okinawa had been a prefecture of Japan proper since 1879 and was the first such territory upon which the Allies would conduct a major landing. For this reason, Japanese resistance was ferocious, despite overwhelming American superiority.

The 180,000 combat troops in the new Tenth Army would take the lead in the Okinawa invasion, known as Operation *Iceberg*. Though it was a new entity, the Tenth was comprised of seven veteran combat divisions with experience in the Pacific. These included four US Army infantry divisions as well as three Marine divisions. Ashore on Okinawa, the troops would be opposed by around 70,000 enemy troops, mainly from the IJA Thirty-Second Army, but also including more than 20,000 Okinawan conscripts, many in their early teens or younger.

The American troops on Okinawa were supported by 1,200 ships, and overhead mainly by the naval airpower of two dozen American and British aircraft carriers. Kenney's Fifth Air Force, meanwhile, was deployed mainly in a continuation of previous campaigns. This included very extensive tactical operations against Japanese holdouts in the islands of the Philippines, and against Japanese shipping throughout the South China Sea. They also went after strategic targets in Formosa and Japanese-occupied China, from Canton (now Guangzhou) to Hong Kong to Shanghai. The synthetic fuel plants on Formosa continued to be important targets and were the focus of operations by Kenney's B-32 very heavy bombers.

Japanese airpower focused on the invasion fleet off Okinawa. They launched conventional bombing strikes as well as around 1,500 *kamikaze* sorties against Allied shipping. The success rate for the *kamikazes* was estimated at one hit per nine aircraft deployed, but each hit was potentially devastating. Most of these missions originated from Kyushu, but some were launched from Formosa. More than 30 Allied ships would be sunk, including a dozen destroyers, and more than 300 were damaged. IJN warships that intervened fared poorly. These included the new super battleship *Yamato*, which was sunk by US Navy carrier airpower.

In 82 days of fighting on Okinawa, which culminated on June 22, American ground forces suffered more than 50,000 casualties, including around 14,000 KIA and MIA, the latter being roughly the same number lost in the Philippines and four times the number lost in the New Guinea campaign. Among the Okinawa dead was General Buckner, killed in an artillery barrage on June 18. He was the highest-ranking American officer killed by enemy action during World War II, though three other lieutenant generals died accidentally. Buckner was temporarily replaced by Marine Major General Roy Geiger, and later by US Army General Joe Stilwell, previously commander of American forces in China.

The Japanese, who routinely fought to the death rather than endure the humiliation of being captured, were doubly motivated to do so when fighting for what they perceived as Japanese soil. Around 110,000 were killed, and only about 7,000 captured. Most horrifically, they used Okinawan civilians as human shields and convinced or forced many to commit suicide rather than surrender. At least 40,000 died.

As George Kenney summarized the situation, the Japanese "realized that the next jump would probably be to Japan proper. Okinawa, with plenty of room for staging troops and with airdrome sites which we could develop extensively enough to handle up to 5,000 airplanes, was so important strategically that the Japanese garrison died almost to a man before our occupation was completed."

In contrast to his very hands-on approach to the battles in New Guinea and the landings in the Philippines, Douglas MacArthur did not personally participate in the Okinawa operations. Indeed, Okinawa is mentioned only cursorily in his memoirs. Nor does Okinawa rate more than a passing mention in George Kenney's recollections.

For nearly two months, from March 6, when his wife arrived from Australia, until June 3, MacArthur had left Manila only once, and that was to make a brief visit to the battlefront northeast of the city where his Sixth Army was mopping up Japanese holdouts.

On June 3, with the fierce and climactic battle raging a thousand miles to the north, MacArthur boarded the cruiser USS *Boise*, his flagship for the Luzon invasion in January, and headed south. He set sail, not for Okinawa, but for Borneo.

In contrast to MacArthur's previous operations in what had been the SWPA, the Borneo operations included no American ground troops. Operation *Oboe*, which began on May 1, involved the Australian I Corps under the command of Lieutenant General Leslie Morshead, which was within MacArthur's Allied chain of command.

Americans were overhead and offshore, though. Bill Streett's Thirteenth Air Force and Admiral Thomas Kinkaid's Seventh Fleet supported Australian air and naval units.

While naval airpower was engaged at Okinawa and the Fifth Air Force was active from the Philippines to Formosa to China, the Thirteenth was engaged in the Dutch East Indies and Indochina. From Morotai, the 307th Bomb Group attacked targets ashore and patrolled the sea lanes of the Dutch East Indies the way that the Fifth Air Force patrolled the South China Sea. Because the antishipping missions had been so successful, the Japanese shifted their transport operations in Indochina to the railroads, so the Thirteenth began targeting rail junctions and marshaling yards in Vietnam, such as those at Phan Rang. On April 9, H2X-equipped B-24s from the 43rd Bomb Group began flying the occasional 2,400-mile mission as far south as Surabaya on Java.

B-24s, as well as B-25s of the 42nd Bomb Group, based on the western Philippine island of Palawan, ran missions against Tarakan, Celebes, and Borneo, especially ahead of and during Operation *Oboe*. As Japanese airpower had largely dissipated across the Dutch East Indies, the P-38s supporting these actions were used mainly in strafing and ground attack operations.

While not venturing near Okinawa, MacArthur himself was up close to the action on Borneo, with Kenney at his side. As he wrote in his memoirs, "at Brunei, I personally supervised the initial landing, and, with General Morshead and General Kenney, went ashore with the assault waves. Resistance was negligible. Rarely was such a prize obtained at such low cost."

On July 1, MacArthur landed at Balikpapan with Morshead from the heavy cruiser USS *Cleveland*, telling him that "today I think we settled the score of that Macassar Strait affair of three and a half years ago [when the ABDA fleet was badly mauled by Japanese airpower and forced into retreat]."

Ironically, just as MacArthur was remarking about the light opposition, he and the Australian general came under Japanese machine gun fire. As MacArthur recalled in his memoirs, some of their group had to "hit the dirt."

21

Operation *Downfall*

I n the trajectory of MacArthur's operations from Port Moresby to Hollandia to Luzon, and from that of US Navy and Marine Corps operations in the Pacific from Guadalcanal to the Marianas to Iwo Jima, it was apparent that the lines of action would converge on Japan itself. It was no secret that Okinawa was seized as a staging base for such an operation. The obvious question was "when?"

It was not until earlier in 1945 that Allied leaders began to seriously consider timing for the invasion of Japan. Prior to that, such a move had been discussed only in notional terms. At the Roosevelt–Churchill Quadrant Conference in Quebec in August 1943, a planning document circulated that envisioned the Japan operation as late as 1948.

Though tremendous progress had been made, no one was certain when the Japanese forces outside their home islands might be degraded to the point where the Allies could focus on the invasion. Most had assumed it would not be soon. As late as its June 4, 1945 issue, *Time* ran a piece relating:

> ... the men who are fighting the Pacific war cut their slogans to fit their hopes. The most optimistic have clung to "Home alive by '45." A few have made it; more will make it before this year's end, but for most it is only a mirage. Those who stay may take their choice from among the following: "Out of the sticks in '46;" "From hell to heaven in '47" and the old standby, "Golden Gate by '48."

As the prolonging of the war was considered to be a morale issue, the Allied leaders decided that the final blow upon Japan should be struck as soon as possible after the defeat of Germany. It will be recalled that the Arcadia Conference, convened in December 1941, had called for the defeat of "Germany first."

On their way to the infamous Argonaut Conference with Josef Stalin at Yalta in February 1945, Roosevelt and Churchill had met at Malta in the Mediterranean, where they discussed the Japan operations, and the American Joint Chiefs of Staff began work on a concrete plan, operating on the assumption that the war in Europe would be over by July 1.

On March 29, the Joint Chiefs rolled out highly classified plans for the appropriately named Operation *Downfall*. It consisted of two parts. The first, called Operation *Olympic*, called for the invasion of Kyushu, the southernmost and third largest of Japan's four main islands. The primary objective here, as with the Okinawa operation, was to seize bases to support the climactic operation. The second phase and climax of Operation *Downfall* was Operation *Coronet*, which targeted Honshu, Japan's largest and most populous island. *Coronet* would center upon a series of amphibious landings within a 60-mile radius of Tokyo itself. Some consideration was given to *Coronet* without *Olympic*, but MacArthur, among others, felt the need for Kyushu as a staging base for bombers, but especially for fighters.

In an April 20 memo to the War Department, MacArthur wrote about the benefits of occupying Kyushu:

> [It would establish] airpower at the closest practicable distance from the final objective in the Japanese islands; would permit application of full power of our combined resources, ground, naval, and air, on the decisive objective; would deliver an attack against an area which probably will be more lightly defended this year than next; would continue the offensive methods which have proved so successful in Pacific campaigns; would place maximum pressure of our combined forces upon the enemy, which might well force his surrender earlier than anticipated; and would place us in the best favorable position for delivery of the decisive assault early in 1946.

The timetable for *Downfall* called for the X-Day of *Olympic* to be December 1, 1945 and for *Coronet* to follow on Y-Day, March 1,

1946. Some had advocated postponement, arguing that Japan needed more "softening up," involving a naval blockade and continued B-29 attacks. Others, including MacArthur, advocated accelerating the timetable because of winter weather. Admiral Chester Nimitz, as the naval commander for *Downfall*, readily agreed and the JCS moved the schedule for *Olympic*'s X-Day forward to November 1.

Still others, notably Curtis LeMay and Hap Arnold of the USAAF, believed that strategic airpower could defeat Japan *without* an invasion. In a memo that he wrote to the JCS and quoted in his memoirs, Arnold said:

> ... estimates of the Joint Target Group indicate that the military and economic capacity of the Japanese nation can be destroyed by an effective dropping, on Japan, of 1,600,000 tons of bombs. This tonnage should disrupt industry, paralyze transportation and seriously strain the production and distribution of foods and other essentials of life. These effects might cause a capitulation of the enemy, and, in any event, will assure the success of the land campaign in Japan, and reduce the loss of American lives to a minimum.

On June 13, 1945, when Arnold visited LeMay in the Marianas, he got an earful in support of the use of strategic airpower alone to end the war. As LeMay later told this author:

> We gave him a briefing on what we had done to date, what we were doing, and what we planned to do. We also gave him a list of targets that we were going to hit. My staff and I were convinced, when we came up with this plan, that this was the best that could be done at the time, and that we had a good chance of defeating Japan before the invasion. I believe that General Arnold always thought airpower could do the job, but he was more convinced than ever after we gave our briefing ... I think Arnold realized, when he visited us, that our strategic air offensive might be the one chance of stopping [the ground invasion].

When Arnold had asked LeMay when the war was going to end, he reviewed the target lists, did some calculations, and picked a date six months after the initial Tokyo incendiary attack and three months after the beginning of routine 400-plane raids. The date was September 1.

With this, Arnold ordered LeMay to fly to Washington immediately to brief the JCS and "to prevent the American bloodshed we knew would come with the invasion."

LeMay and his briefing team flew into Washington National Airport in a B-29 just before midnight on June 16, and were at the Pentagon the following morning. His recollections of the presentation to the JCS and their staff officers are far from complimentary, as he explained in our conversation:

Throughout the briefing, each of them had completely blank expressions on their faces. They paid absolutely no attention to us. Marshall was sleeping or dozing through most of it. Admiral Ernest King, the Chief of Naval Operations, reacted with disbelief and a complete lack of interest, just as the Navy brass always had. General Arnold, the other member of the Joint Chiefs, wasn't there, of course. I don't blame Marshall for dozing off, though. He was probably whipped down to a nub by then, and needed the sleep. In any case, they had already approved the decision to go ahead with an invasion.

However, MacArthur did not agree with LeMay. He had already issued his scathing rebuttal of the use of strategic airpower alone in an April 20 memo to the JCS. He may have long been one of the most outspoken advocates of airpower among members of his generation of ground commanders, but he refused to believe that airpower could defeat Japan without ground troops.

In this document, he had written that such a course:

... would fail to utilize our resources for amphibious offensive movement [and] assumes success of airpower alone to conquer a people in spite of its demonstrated failure in Europe, where Germany was subject to more intensive bombardment than can be brought to bear against Japan, and where all the available resources in ground troops of the United States, the United Kingdom, and Russia had to be committed in order to force a decision.

Even before LeMay's briefing, the JCS had already given the green light to the operation, and had issued their directive for Operation *Downfall* on May 25. Lieutenant General Richard Sutherland, MacArthur's chief of staff at AFPAC, had followed three days later with *Downfall: Strategic Plan for Operations in the Japanese Archipelago*. Only 42 copies of the plan were circulated, with 14 retained by AFPAC and nine sent to the JCS. Nimitz received five and Kenney received three at FEAF. LeMay had already gotten his copy when he made his Washington trip. The others went to the commanders of other commands involved and the field armies upon whose shoulders the heavy lifting of the ground campaign would lie.

The Sixth Army, under General Walter Krueger – MacArthur's original field army, having proven itself from Buna to Luzon – would be the centerpiece of Operation *Olympic*. For Operation *Coronet*, Lieutenant General Robert Eichelberger's Eighth Army would go ashore west of Tokyo, while General Courtney Hodges's First Army, relocated from Europe, would land east of Tokyo. It would then advance across the open area known as the Kanto Plain. The Eighth would take Yokohama and the two armies would converge on the capital.

The Tenth Army, having wrested Okinawa from Japanese control, would be rested and readied as a follow-up force for Operation *Coronet*. The force landed during *Olympic* would have been somewhat larger than that which the Allies landed at Normandy on June 6, 1944 in Operation *Overlord*. *Coronet* was planned to have been three times the size of *Overlord*, with as many as 1.2 million Allied personnel involved in various roles.

The Sixth Army, with nearly 450,000 soldiers and Marines, was organized into three corps and several independent units that were to conduct simultaneous landings on X-Day. These landings were to be presaged by the most massive air bombardment yet seen in the Pacific, utilizing both FEAF and Twentieth Air Force bombers.

For Operation *Coronet*, which the May 28 AFPAC plan colorfully described as the "knockout blow to the enemy's heart," Eichelberger's Eighth Army was tentatively assigned three corps containing eight divisions, two of them armored divisions. The First Army was to have one Army and one Marine Corps, each with three divisions. Commanded by Lieutenant General Charles Keightley, a British Commonwealth Corps was also assigned. An additional 12 American infantry divisions, as well as the 11th Airborne Division and Australian 104th Division, were held in reserve.

To support these operations, Nimitz would contribute the largest naval force ever assembled. It included the Third Fleet under Admiral William Halsey, the Fifth Fleet, commanded by Admiral Raymond Spruance, and the Seventh Fleet under Admiral Thomas Kinkaid. Also present was the British Pacific Fleet operating as part of Halsey's Third Fleet. Between them, they would have around 50 aircraft carriers, including escort carriers, two dozen battleships, nearly 50 cruisers, more than 400 destroyers and destroyer escorts, more than 400 support ships, and around a thousand landing craft.

Overhead, the invasion forces could count on the support from the aircraft aboard Nimitz's carriers. Of the roughly 50 carriers that would have been available, around 20 were fleet carriers with a complement of around 90 aircraft. The remainder were escort carriers with approximately 20 aircraft each, so the total naval carrier aircraft would have been in excess of 2400. This is not to mention the more than 100 US Marine Corps squadrons which were mainly in the Pacific, nor the US Navy's long-range patrol aircraft.

Under MacArthur's AFPAC command, Kenney's FEAF, the Fifth, Seventh, and Thirteenth Air Forces, consisted of 14 bombardment groups and ten fighter groups. By August 1945, three months ahead of X-Day, they possessed a total of 5,588 aircraft, including 4,004 combat aircraft, with virtually all American aircraft production now devoted to FEAF needs. Of the August inventory, there were 689 B-24 heavy bombers, 366 B-25 medium bombers, 295 A-20 light bombers, and a handful of B-32 very heavy bombers. Among the FEAF fighter force, there were 808 P-38s, 307 P-47s, and 502 P-51s.

The nexus of FEAF and other USAAF operations on Okinawa was a facility that came into American hands as a 4,600-foot crushed coral landing field badly damaged in the fighting. It was quickly transformed and expanded by US Army engineers into one of the largest operating bases in the Pacific. Known as Kadena Air Base (AB), the 12,000-acre base was to be an important American military facility throughout the Cold War and into the 21st century. Today it is the largest US Air Force facility in the Asia-Pacific region.

The Twentieth Air Force, meanwhile, had 1,042 B-29s on hand by August 1945 with more in the pipeline, and its VII Fighter Command possessed 349 P-51s. The Eighth Air Force, which was being relocated to the Pacific to aid in the strategic bombing campaign, had possessed more than 2,000 B-17s and 1,000 B-24s at its peak, but it is unclear how many of these would have been shifted halfway around the world from England to Okinawa. By August the ADVON on the Eighth was starting to receive B-29s. The Eighth was also operating more than 2,000 P-47s and 1,800 P-51s when the war ended in Europe.

To the strategic bomber contingent arrayed for Operation *Downfall*, the British Royal Air Force was relocating around 500 Avro Lancasters from its Bomber Command to a new organization called Tiger Force. About half of these aircraft would be configured to conduct aerial refueling. Australia was to have contributed the 12 squadrons of its First Tactical Air Force.

The Allied plan was to build toward at least 80 air groups based from the Marianas to Okinawa, with a goal of delivering 100,000 tons of bombs monthly by September 1945, and 170,000 tons by January 1946. By March 1946, when Operation *Coronet* was launched, the total was expected to have reached at least 220,000 tons to be used against Japan's home islands, mainly Honshu. The latter was equal to roughly a quarter of the total tonnage dropped on Germany through all of 1944.

As late as January 1945, the Japanese had no fully articulated defense strategy and formulating one was complicated by extensive ongoing losses of ships, aircraft, and experienced crews. Most of the numerical strength of the Imperial Japanese Navy had been sunk by the end of the Okinawa campaign, and most of the numerical strength of the Imperial Japanese Army was overseas, either completely isolated in the Pacific or on the Asian mainland from where it could not be brought home because of a lack of shipping.

Through the spring, a hasty mobilization more than quintupled the strength of the IJA on the four main islands from just 11 divisions in January 1945. As John Toland wrote in *Rising Sun*, "in the face of the bloody lessons of Tarawa and Saipan, the plan was to crush the Americans on the beaches with 53 infantry divisions and 25 brigades – a total of 2,350,000 troops."

The JCS meanwhile estimated 3.5 million troops. After the war, US Military Government data summarized that 6,465,435 Japanese military personnel were formally demobilized in Japan proper, meaning that both Toland and the JCS underestimated the potential opposition.

Plans were made for rapid redeployment of these forces to meet the Allies at probable landing sites, while maintaining troops throughout the islands. The Kanto Plain, in which the Tokyo–Yokohama metro area lies, is one of the few flat areas within mountainous Japan that is conducive to a conventional massed offensive. Special preparations were made to reinforce and defend this gateway to Japan's capital.

Based on factors such as the relative intensity of American tactical air strikes, the Japanese correctly deduced that the Americans would invade Kyushu in the fall of 1945 and Honshu in the spring of 1946, estimating that the US would employ ten or 12 divisions, which was close to accurate considering the Sixth Army reserve. However, they incorrectly predicted an invasion of Shikoku at the same time as the Kyushu operation. The Allies had no plans to land on Shikoku, but did anticipate a diversion there.

In any case, the Japanese wanted to be prepared for multiple contingencies by developing a means of movement within Japan. Much of the Japanese road system was unpaved, so the shuffling of troops depended on rail and boat transportation. However, because the Americans had achieved air superiority over Japan, such modes of transport were greatly compromised. The defensive doctrine finally embraced the idea of making troop movements by foot and at night.

Under Operation *Ketsu-Go* (Operation *Decision*), the Japanese organized for the final defense of their four main islands from an Allied attack. As the American air superiority made air operations suicidal under any circumstances, most aircraft were now earmarked for suicide missions. IJAAF and IJNAF aircraft of all types, from first-line fighters and bombers to rickety biplane trainers, were set aside and hidden at secret camouflaged airfields in preparation for the American invasion.

A postwar Demobilization Bureau Report in the *Homeland Air Operations Record* was compiled by the US Far East Command (FEC) in December 1946. It notes:

> … to conserve air strength for employment against the landing forces, carrier task forces supporting the invasion would be attacked by only a few hundred planes and then only when it became unmistakable that a full-scale invasion was in progress. The bulk of the air fleet of 10,500 planes, mostly of the small special-attack [*kamikaze*] type, would be launched against the warships and transports in the crucial

invasion area. Japanese plans called for these planes to be completely expended within a ten-day period in a supreme effort to repel the invasion forces. By the end of June 1945, 8,000 of the necessary craft were already available; the other 2,500 were expected to be finished by fall.

The IJN was also preparing fast attack boats, nearly 400 midget submarines, and around 200 *kaiten* ("human torpedoes") for use against the American invasion ships. Their conventional strength included nearly two dozen operational destroyers and around three dozen fleet submarines that were deployed at sea and among the islands of the Inland Sea. Their role would be to harass Allied supply lines. A half dozen IJN battleships and cruisers survived in home waters, but they would remain in port, functioning as fixed antiaircraft platforms.

As late as May 1945, there was no fully organized civil defense plan. With Japan having experienced the worst rice harvest since 1905 and transportation other than by foot at a virtual standstill, the civilian population was suffering. Against the backdrop of potential civil unrest, Japan's military government reached for its ace in the hole, the virtually universal devotion to Emperor Hirohito and the prevalent belief that he was a Shinto *arahitogami*, or living deity.

Throughout the war, Japanese troops had fought to the death on behalf of the Emperor, and now it was time to energize the Japanese population likewise. As noted by historians Williamson Murray and Allan Reed Millett in *A War To Be Won*, under the Volunteer Military Service Law of June 1945, "the Japanese Cabinet [Toland wrote that it was the Diet, or legislature] essentially called the entire population into military service, while propagandists began 'The Glorious Death of One Hundred Million' program to whip up enthusiasm for dying for the emperor." Japan's actual 1945 population was around 70 million.

Toland wrote that the 2.35 million IJA troops – or up to 6.5 million based on postwar data – were augmented by nearly 4 million IJA and IJN civilian employees, while the Volunteer Military Service Law potentially added 28 million civilians to the total. He went on to say that the law conscripted men from the ages of 15 to 60, and women from 17 to 45, adding that "the military spokesmen, whose impressive testimony had ensured passage of the bill [in the Diet], later showed [Prime Minister Kantaro] Suzuki and his cabinet a display of the weapons that would be used by the volunteers: muzzle-loading rifles and bamboo sticks cut into spears stacked beside bows and arrows from feudal times."

The Americans were aware of these developments. An AFPAC intelligence report *Estimate of the Enemy Situation with Respect to Kyushu* dated July 29 spoke of "Volunteer Home Defense Units composed largely of partially trained reservists" and estimated that "approximately 125,000 of these are available in Southern Kyushu and approximately 450,000 in Northern Kyushu."

It was further noted that:

> ...since April 1945, enemy strength in Southern Kyushu has grown from approximately 80,000 troops including in mobile combat the equivalent of about two Infantry Divisions to an estimated 206,000 including seven divisions and two to three brigades, plus naval, air, ground, and base and service troops [assigned to three corps under the 16th Area Army headquartered at Fukuoka]. This rapid expansion within a few weeks' time, supply of this large concentration of troops, and the movement of defensive material has undoubtedly so strained the capacity of all existing lines of communication that any major interruption thereof would seriously reduce the effectiveness of the enemy's preparations.

This was a prescription for rough going for the Sixth Army in Kyushu. Even as MacArthur and Nimitz were mustering the largest American force ever assembled, the Japanese were preparing to counter them with a force which, while being comprised largely of untrained volunteers and conscripts, was far larger and more passionately motivated.

With this understanding of the immense scale of Japanese defenses, the Joint Chiefs of Staff had been looking at casualty projections, of which there were many variations based on many different criteria. Beginning in the summer of 1944, the Joint Planning Staff (JPS) of the JCS had been studying the matter using the ratio of the number of Japanese combat troops to actual American casualties based on the experience at Saipan, where that ratio of defenders to American battle deaths had been seven to one for a 24-day campaign on a 1,400-square-mile island.

The JCS concluded in their August 30, 1944 report that "in our Saipan operation, it cost approximately one American killed and several wounded to exterminate seven Japanese soldiers. On this basis it might cost us half a million American lives and many times that number wounded … in the home islands."

After operations on Luzon, but before Okinawa, the "Saipan ratio" was adjusted, and in April 1945, using a projection of 766,700 personnel in combat for 90 days in Operation *Olympic*, the JCS calculated 514,072 casualties, including 134,556 KIA and MIA.

In the 82 days of the Okinawa campaign, which came to be considered as a template for what was to come as the Japanese defended their home islands, the Americans had landed around 180,000 combat troops and had suffered more than 50,000 casualties, including 14,000 dead or missing, but not including those who died later of their injuries. Based on 76,000 IJA defenders, and excluding the conscripts thrown into the fight, the ratio on Okinawa was around five to one.

On Luzon, the ratio was six to one, and this was the comparison that US Army Chief of Staff General George Marshall used in a June 18 meeting with President Harry Truman. He said that he anticipated 31,000 total casualties in the first 30 days of Operation *Olympic*, basing his estimate on the Japanese having 350,000 troops in Kyushu. In fact, they had more than 900,000 by that time and might have had more than a million by X-Day. Based on these numbers and the Okinawa ratio, the numbers of casualties could have been astronomical, with more than 160,000 Allied battle deaths on Kyushu.

Citing the July 26–27 *Daily Summary of Enemy Intelligence* from the Military Intelligence Service, D.M. Giangreco in his article "Casualty Projections for the US Invasions of Japan, 1945–1946," in the July 1997 issue of *The Journal of Military History*, wrote:

> … in the first half of June [1945, Secretary of War Henry Lewis] Stimson twice asked the Army planners to comment on outside estimates that the number of Americans killed could extend from 500,000 to 1,000,000, figures that imply total casualties running in the area of 2,000,000 to 4,000,000. While these numbers were not, in themselves, unimaginable if the intent had been to conquer all Japanese forces on the Home Islands by force of arms, such had never been the intent or desire of planners who firmly believed that effective "military control" of all Japan could be "obtained by the securing of a relatively few vital coastal areas" on Honshu.

In July 1945, the War Department commissioned an analysis of the data from William Bradford Shockley. An American physicist working at Bell Laboratory, Shockley shared the 1956 Nobel Prize in Physics for the development of transistors and pioneering work in the field of semiconductors.

In his July 21 memo to Stimson aide Edward Bowles summarizing his conclusions, Shockley wrote:

> ... if the study shows that the behavior of nations in all historical cases comparable to Japan's has in fact been invariably consistent with the behavior of the troops in battle, then it means that the Japanese dead and ineffectives at the time of the defeat will exceed the corresponding number for the Germans. In other words, we shall probably have to kill at least 5 to 10 million Japanese. This might cost us between 1.7 and 4 million casualties including 400,000 to 800,000 killed.

Meanwhile, the Army Service Forces, commanded by Lieutenant General Brehon Somervell, was charged with projecting the number of US Army and USAAF personnel needed through the end of 1946 to replace the "dead and evacuated wounded." The number that Somervell's people used in their calculations, which excludes US Navy and Marine Corps casualties, was 720,000.

At the same time, the War Department ordered Purple Heart medals to be awarded to combat casualties from Operation *Downfall*. The number that were minted was half a million.

22

Ultimate Downfall

During the second week of July 1945, Douglas MacArthur was in Manila and more consumed with the ongoing mopping up operations in the Philippines and with Borneo than he was with Operation *Downfall*, which was still nearly four months off. Kenney was still in Manila, but he already was looking ahead to Operation *Olympic*. He had been up to Okinawa on July 6 to pick out a location for his new FEAF headquarters, into which he planned to move on August 1. He met with General Joe Stilwell of the Tenth Army and asked for "unloading priority" at the docks for the bombs that would soon be arriving for the FEAF dumps – en route to targets in Kyushu.

Admiral Slew McCain's Task Force 38 from Halsey's Third Fleet was now in Japanese waters, and had launched more than 1,000 carrier-based aircraft against Tokyo on July 10, while LeMay continued his incendiary attacks on Japanese cities with 466 Superfortresses on July 16 and 470 on July 19. On July 24, he sent 570 B-29s with high-explosive ordnance against industrial targets from Nagoya to Osaka. In that same space of time, his Superfortresses ran five smaller missions, including mine-laying operations in Japanese inland waterways.

Kenney was anxious for his "boys" to have a piece of the action over Japan proper. The first FEAF group to move into Okinawa, the veteran 35th Fighter Group, had arrived from Clark Field at the end of June. They had run a 48-plane sweep up the Kyushu coast as far as the big IJN base at Sasebo on July 3, and had shot down three floatplanes. These were the only aircraft they had seen.

Across the world in Potsdam, just outside Berlin, the second week of July 1945 saw the beginning of the Terminal Conference, the last of the Big Three conferences. The Big Three had changed. Harry Truman had succeeded Franklin Roosevelt, and before the conference was finished, British Prime Minister Winston Churchill had suffered a stunning defeat at the ballot box and was replaced by Clement Atlee. Josef Stalin was there as he had been at Tehran and Yalta. The only ballots ever cast in the Soviet Union offered no surprising results.

On July 16, Truman arrived, dashed off a cheerful note to his wife, and looked through the messages that had just arrived. Of utmost urgency was the news that, on that very morning, a new weapon had been detonated in the New Mexico desert which had the power to change the course of the war.

Almost nobody knew that the US Army's Manhattan Project was developing nuclear weapons. Even Truman, as Vice President, had not been told. He wasn't briefed on the program until General George Marshall came to see him on the morning that he was sworn in as President. Winston Churchill knew, and Atlee would know, because the British had been involved in the Manhattan Project. Stalin knew because there were Soviet agents surreptitiously embedded in the project staff – but the other two of the Big Three did not know that he knew. Even Douglas MacArthur, Chester Nimitz, and George Kenney had not been briefed on the secret until July. Within Japan, the IJA and IJN each had its own top-secret nuclear weapons program, but neither of these was far advanced by the time the war ended.

Picking up on the decisions made at Yalta, the Terminal Conference both finalized the plans for the military occupation of Germany and solidified the Soviet sphere of influence in Eastern Europe that would stand for more than four decades.

On July 26, Britain, the United States, and Nationalist China issued the Potsdam Declaration, which called for the immediate and unconditional surrender of the Empire of Japan. The Soviets, who had not yet declared war on Japan, were not signatories. In part it read:

The might that now converges on Japan is immeasurably greater than that which, when applied to the resisting Nazis, necessarily laid waste the lands, the industry and the method of life of the whole German people. The full application of our military powers, backed by our resolve, will mean the inevitable and complete destruction of the Japanese armed forces and just as inevitably the utter destruction of the Japanese homeland. The time has come for Japan to decide whether she will continue to be controlled by those self-willed militaristic advisers whose unintelligent calculations have brought the Empire of Japan to the threshold of annihilation, or whether she will follow the path of reason.

In conclusion, the Allies called upon Japan to "proclaim now the unconditional surrender of all Japanese armed forces, and to provide proper and adequate assurances of their good faith in such action. The alternative for Japan is prompt and utter destruction."

Stalin read the phrase "prompt and utter destruction," and knew what Truman had in mind.

The Japanese read the phrase "prompt and utter destruction," and called Truman's bluff.

He had made the decision to play the nuclear card. The specter of a million American casualties, or even half that number, led him to attempt to end the war with a weapon that had been developed, at least in the beginning, to checkmate Adolf Hitler's nuclear ambitions. Hitler was gone now, but Hirohito remained.

The 509th Composite Group of the 313th Bombardment Wing of the Twentieth Air Force had been training for nuclear strike missions since the first of the year. They had assembled on the Mariana Island of Tinian in June and had trained by flying several missions to Japan with high-explosive bombs matching the size and weight of atomic bombs. The nuclear weapons themselves were delivered to Tinian on July 26 aboard the USS *Indianapolis*. One was a uranium-235 weapon named "Little Boy," the other a plutonium-239 weapon called "Fat Man."

"I was told about it because of the preparations that had to be made on Tinian for it," LeMay told this author. He continued:

Of course the bomb was so secret that almost no one else in the Marianas knew it was there. Even most of the people in the 509th Composite Group who were supposed to drop it didn't know what was going on. They knew they were going to drop a special bomb, but that's about all ... When the bomb arrived, I made no change in the course of operations because I didn't know what this thing was going to do, or what it was supposed to do. The Twentieth Air Force really didn't make any plans for the atomic bomb, because it was the Engineer Corps' baby all along. Even when it was ready to use, the Engineer Corps wouldn't let go of the thing.

On August 4, a top-secret cable reached Manila explaining that the "gadget" – as those in the know called it – was going to be used against the port city of Hiroshima on the main Japanese island of Honshu. MacArthur was briefed on the target and so was Kenney, who was just as mystified as LeMay.

"No one really knew what this new weapon would do," he wrote in his memoirs, "so the whole area, for 50 miles around the target city, was declared off limits for all aircraft on that day, except, of course the one doing the bombing."

On August 5, Kenney flew up to Okinawa to brief Lieutenant General Ennis Whitehead, who had just moved his Fifth Air Force headquarters to the hard-won island. It turned out that Whitehead had several missions to the Hiroshima area planned for August 6, and these had to be rearranged without causing any undue rumors.

"These newfangled gadgets are certainly raising hell with my operations," Whitehead complained.

As Kenney reflected, "Whitehead had a job to do, and this new earth-shaking development, which some people said would cause an explosion that would be felt halfway around the world, didn't cause him anything but annoyance if it interfered with carrying out his mission."

He went on to describe the events of the next day, August 6:

[Kenney and Whitehead] held our breaths and waited for the big event. The first news came from the Japanese radio, which reported that they were out of communication with Hiroshima, following a tremendous shock from some new type of explosive. The crew of the B-29 that had dropped the bomb reported a successful strike, with the cloud of smoke and dust rising to over 20,000 feet. Much to our gratification we felt no shock at Okinawa. The Japanese got it all and later radio reports began to tell the story.

More a topic of conversation in Fifth Air Force circles that day than the nuclear strike was "something else had happened that somehow touched them more intimately and more deeply." This was the news that Major Richard Bong, the top-scoring ace of the Fifth, and indeed of the whole USAAF, had been killed that same day in Burbank, California. He had crashed on takeoff from Lockheed's home airfield in a Lockheed P-80 jet fighter that he was test flying. Ironically, two of the principal artifacts of postwar military aviation – nuclear weapons and jet propulsion – had been intertwined in the day's dispatches.

In the meantime, it was business as usual for Whitehead's Fifth Air Force. On the same day as the nuclear strike, more than 170 B-24s, B-25s, and P-47s attacked Kagoshima, while more than 60 B-25s and P-51s were raking Japanese shipping in the Tsushima Strait and off Kyushu's southern coast. Another strike package sent 150 A-26s and P-47s against Miyakonojo.

On August 7 and 8, the FEAF assault on Kyushu continued, while LeMay sent B-29s to continue sowing mines in the Shimonoseki Strait, which separates Japan from Korea, and across which reinforcements from Japan's armies in Asia would travel to join the defense of Kyushu. August 7 also saw 124 Superfortresses bomb the IJN arsenal at Toyokawa on Honshu, and the next day, LeMay put a 221-plane incendiary raid on Yawata.

On August 8, the Soviet Union declared war on Japan and followed up immediately with a full-scale invasion of Japanese-occupied Manchuria – which Japan had conquered in 1931 and repurposed as the puppet kingdom of Manchukuo. Stalin's Red Army deployed 12 field armies and 1.5 million troops against the 700,000-man Kwantung Army, one of Japan's most capable fighting units. Ironically, throughout the war, the crack Kwantung Army, which could have made a difference on the Pacific battlefields, had remained tied down in Manchuria watching for the Soviet invasion that had finally come. The Soviets overwhelmed the defenders and proceeded to pillage on a scale that matched the Japanese treatment of China and the Philippines.

Much has been written about the reaction to Hiroshima within the halls of power in Tokyo that week, but suffice to say that despite much debate, the Japanese government did nothing. Perhaps it was because the damage had been literally incomprehensible. Three days later, on August 9, with the Japanese government having not responded favorably, the 509th was ordered to drop Fat Man on Kokura. That city was clouded over and therefore dodged a nuclear bullet as the bomber diverted to the secondary target, Nagasaki.

The intention of two nuclear strikes in three days was to suggest to the Japanese that the Americans had the capability to use nuclear weapons every few days – although there were no more, at least for the time being.

Nor did the conventional campaign subside. On the same day that Nagasaki was struck, Whitehead sent a 200-plane fighter sweep, backed by B-25s, across Kyushu while his B-24s were attacking Iwakuni on Honshu.

Emperor Hirohito, who had rejected the Potsdam Declaration in July, and who had dithered after Hiroshima, reacted to Nagasaki under the belief that continued nuclear strikes were the embodiment of the "prompt and utter destruction" that had been promised at Potsdam two weeks earlier.

On August 10, Hirohito asked the cabinet to draft an "Imperial Rescript ending the war," even as Japanese negotiators were trying to confirm through Swiss intermediaries that the Allies did not plan to topple the Emperor and eliminate the monarchy.

On August 12, the official American reply stated their terms:

[While the Potsdam Declaration] does not comprise any demand which prejudices the prerogatives of His Majesty as a sovereign ruler, our position is as follows: From the moment of surrender the authority of the Emperor and the Japanese Government to rule the state shall be subject to the Supreme Commander of the Allied Powers who will take such steps as he deems proper to effectuate the surrender terms. The Emperor will be required to authorize and ensure the signature by the Government of Japan and the Japanese Imperial General Headquarters of the surrender terms necessary to carry out the provisions of the Potsdam Declaration, and shall issue his commands to all the Japanese military, naval and air authorities and to all the forces under their control wherever located to cease active operations and to surrender their arms, and to issue such other orders as the Supreme Commander may require to give effect to the surrender terms.

And who was to be this "Supreme Commander" of whom the diplomatic cables spoke?

In Manila on August 13, Douglas MacArthur received a radiogram from General Marshall at the War Department granting him this new title, though most accounts have him assuming the new post on August 15. Initially, the title read "Supreme Commander *of the* Allied Powers," but it was later revised subtly as "Supreme Commander *for the* Allied Powers," with the same acronym, SCAP.

At Potsdam, the Big Three had discussed the notion of "a supreme commander" for the Japanese operations. Stalin wanted to have a Soviet marshal involved, perhaps on an equal footing with an American, but Truman essentially ignored him. As Truman wrote in *1945: Year of Decision*, "as I reflected on the situation during my trip home [from Potsdam], I made up my mind that General MacArthur would be given complete command and control after victory in Japan. We were not going to be disturbed by Russian tactics in the Pacific."

Even as Hirohito sat down to record his Imperial Rescript for radio broadcast, Whitehead continued his relentless assault from his new base on Okinawa. He sent 198 bombers against Kumamoto, while his other aircraft were attacking shipping in Japan's Inland Sea and targets of opportunity as far north as Honshu. On August 14, in the last Twentieth Air Force combat operations of World War II, LeMay sent 741 Superfortresses to Japan, including 302 against the IJN facilities at Osaka and Hikari.

Among Japan's ruling elite, the idea of surrender did not meet with universal acceptance. A coup was attempted by disgruntled officers wishing to prevent Hirohito's message from being broadcast, and the recording had to be smuggled out of the Imperial Palace with a batch of laundry. Ultimately, the coup failed, but all across Tokyo, officers who could not accept surrender chose ritual suicide.

Across the Far East – from Singapore to Shanghai – millions of Japanese troops who had vowed to fight to the death and who had not been defeated struggled to accept the fact of the surrender. William Manchester's description of the long isolated defenders of Rabaul summarizes the mood of dismay and despair that prevailed.

"Their loss of face was incalculable," he wrote. "When they finally received Hirohito's Imperial Rescript, ordering them to surrender, many of them, unable to bear the humiliation, faded into New Britain's rain forests to live out the rest of their wretched days as tropical animals."

At noon on August 15, Japanese time, Hirohito's message to his people was broadcast by Nippon Hoso Kyokai (NHK), Japan's public radio. He explained:

> ... the enemy has begun to employ a new and most cruel bomb, the power of which to do damage is, indeed, incalculable, taking the toll of many innocent lives. Should We continue to fight, not only would it result in an ultimate collapse and obliteration of the Japanese nation, but also it would lead to the total extinction of human civilization. Such being the case, how are We to save the millions of Our subjects, or to atone Ourselves before the hallowed spirits of Our Imperial Ancestors? This is the reason why We have ordered the acceptance of the provisions of the Joint Declaration of the Powers.

It was the first time most Japanese people had ever heard his voice. His words, in the stilted classical form of the language spoken in the Imperial court, were hard to understand, but the message was clear. The broadcast was also picked up via shortwave in the United States, translated, and handed to Truman, who immediately ordered American forces to halt offensive operations.

"As soon as the radio flash came in I got in touch with all my commanders and told them to call off the attack," Kenney recalled in his memoirs. He continued:

> If any aircraft were already in the air they were to be recalled by radio at once. Whitehead had his whole force in motion, in the air or getting ready to take off. He got in touch with all of them except about 20 strafers, who were on the way to sweep the Tsushima Straits for shipping. They found no targets and returned that afternoon to their base with their bombs. [Major General Paul] Wurtsmith's Thirteenth, [Major General Thomas] White's Seventh, and [Air Vice Marshal William] Bostock's Australians were in about the same position but managed to get everyone back without getting involved in attack or combat. The shooting part of the war was over.

The Fifth Air Force and other FEAF organizations would continue to patrol the skies over Japan in the ensuing weeks, under orders to attack noticeable Japanese troop movements and to respond to hostile fire, but they encountered nothing untoward. For the first time in years, their patrols encountered only quiet skies.

Kenney, Whitehead, and their staffs celebrated, but only a little, as "everyone seemed a bit tired and wanted to get some sleep. The 49th Fighter Group opened the magnum of brandy. They said the next day that it was not bad." Kenney went on to say:

> [He and his pilots] added up the scores of the fighter groups to see what the kids were to brag about for the rest of their lives. The 49th Group led the field with a final total of 677 confirmed air victories. The 47th with 545, the 8th with 443, the 35th with 397, and the 348th with 356 followed in order as the Fifth Air Force's contribution. The two fighter groups of the Thirteenth Air Force, the 18th and 347th, finished in that order with scores of 274 and 246.

Dick Bong and Tommy McGuire, with 40 and 38, respectively, were the highest-scoring aces of the Fifth Air Force and the highest of any American aces before or since. Neither survived to see the war end. In the next echelon of the hierarchy of aces, Charles MacDonald had 27, while Jerry Johnson, Neel Kearby, and Jay Robbins each had 22. Robert Westbrook and Tommy Lynch rounded out the list of, as Kenney described it, "those who had scored a score or more confirmed victories in the war against Japan." Kearby, Westbrook, and Lynch had all been killed.

One of Douglas MacArthur's first actions as SCAP was to order the Japanese to send a 16-man delegation to Manila to discuss a formal surrender ceremony. They were to fly in an aircraft painted white and marked with green crosses. They were to land at the Fifth Air Force fighter base on Ie Shima, an island off the northwest tip of Okinawa, on August 19. They were to use the call sign "B-A-T-A-A-N." MacArthur, always high on symbolism, wanted to give them a reminder of their brutality to Americans and Filipinos on Bataan in 1942. The Japanese replied that they would use the call sign "J-N-P." MacArthur sternly ordered a reply that the call sign would be "B-A-T-A-A-N." And so it was. MacArthur was now in charge.

Escorted by Fifth Air Force fighters on their flight to Ie Shima in a Mitsubishi G4M, the delegation was transferred to a USAAF Air Transport Command C-54 and flown on to Manila. It seems that no one in Japan had wanted the humiliating duty of being on the delegation, but 16 men had finally been found. Katsuo Okazaki represented the Foreign Ministry and Lieutenant General Torashiro Kawabe, deputy chief of the IJN General Staff and a former IJAAF officer, was the senior military man. After a drive from the airport with Filipinos throwing things at their cars, they were received by Major General Charles Willoughby, MacArthur's intelligence chief, and sat down with Lieutenant General Richard Sutherland, MacArthur's chief of staff. MacArthur himself remained dramatically aloof and unseen.

Sutherland handed them General Order No. 1, which detailed the surrender and military occupation process. After some heated debate over semantics, the Japanese left with a draft of the *Instrument of Surrender* for the signature of Hirohito himself.

23

Americans in Japan

At Manila, the Japanese delegation had been told that their county should prepare for the beginning of military occupation. Across the globe, everyone from Harry Truman to the Joint Chiefs of Staff were anxious for this to begin as soon as possible. An August 14 radiogram (TSWX-49042) from Marshall at the War Department had told MacArthur to "effectuate the surrender terms with the least practicable delay." This was in part to curb any possible dissension that might arise in Japan if the Americans did not move quickly and with decisiveness – and in part to counter the growing concern that the Soviets, having been handed Sakhalin and the Kurile Islands at Yalta, might decide to send troops into Hokkaido, Japan's northernmost main island.

A contingency plan for the occupation, assuming Japan surrendered ahead of Operation *Olympic*, had been drawn up in July and had been constantly updated. Codenamed Operation *Blacklist*, the plan called for an incremental occupation of 14 major areas in Japan and at least three in Korea in which Allied forces would exert undisputed military, economic, and political control. The Eighth Army, under General Robert Eichelberger, was to occupy Hokkaido and northern Honshu, while Walter Krueger's Sixth Army would occupy Kyushu, as it was to have done under Operation *Olympic*, as well as Shikoku and southern Honshu. The Eighth was to go in first, but its advance was delayed two days by a series of typhoons.

Finally, August 28 was set for the arrival of the first American troops, who would be flown into Atsugi airfield, 10 miles west of Yokohama.

The 11th Airborne Division would be the first, followed by the arrival on August 30 of General Douglas MacArthur himself.

George Kenney's FEAF transport fleet consisted mainly of twin-engine C-47s, such as his command had been using since the early days in New Guinea. However, since Atsugi lies some 950 miles from Okinawa, these aircraft would have to lay over in Japan until fuel was delivered. Kenney wanted to be able to fly as many missions as possible as round trips without the necessity of being on the ground inside Japan without fuel. With this in mind, Kenney contacted USAAF Commanding General Hap Arnold and asked him for the use of some of the Douglas C-54 Skymaster four-engine transports that were being operated in the Pacific by the USAAF Air Transport Command (ATC). At the time, the USAAF possessed 852 of these transports and they were assigned to routine flight schedules around the globe, something that no airline had yet accomplished. Based on the Douglas DC-4 airliner, they had a range of around 4,000 miles, more than double that of the C-47, which was based on the Douglas DC-3.

Kenney explained to Arnold that they "could carry over double the load of my transports and had enough fuel capacity to make the round trip without taking on gas at Yokohama. I was quite sure that the Japanese could not furnish us any aviation gasoline or that, if they did have any, it would not be good enough to use in our engines."

Arnold ordered the ATC to furnish Kenney whatever Kenney needed and ordered them to start concentrating in Okinawa to await instructions. One of the C-54s had been earmarked for MacArthur's use and given the name *Bataan*, the name that had previously adorned the B-17 that he used as an executive transport during the New Guinea campaign.

However, it was not the ATC, nor a C-54, that was first into defeated Japan. It was a pair of P-38s piloted by Lieutenant Colonel Clay Tice, who had succeeded Jerry Johnson as commander of the 49th Fighter Group, and his wingman, Flight Officer Douglas Hall. As Tice wrote in his after-action report and as George Kenney related in his memoirs, it all happened as the two men were conducting a routine patrol over Kyushu on August 25, three days ahead of the official arrival of the occupation force.

They had taken off at 08:05hrs and had flown over Nagasaki before heading northeast toward Nakatsu. It was there, around 11:00hrs, that Hall discovered that he did not have enough fuel to get back to Okinawa.

Routine practice in such situations was for pilots to rendezvous with a B-17 search and rescue airplane, then bail out as the B-17 dropped a lifeboat, and hope to be picked up by the Navy. However, as Hall was a new pilot, Tice had no confidence that he could bail out safely, so he came up with an alternate plan – landing at an airfield in Japan!

Tice checked his map and picked a small field on Kyushu's east coast. After a couple of low passes, Tice landed and told Hall to come in and park beside him. At first Tice thought of squeezing Hall into his own P-38, but he then decided to invite the B-17 to come pick him up. To break the monotony of circling over open ocean, Lieutenant Edwin Hawkins agreed.

The fighter pilots explored the immediate area on foot and found it deserted – until a man rode by on a bicycle about an hour later. He hurried off to a building in the distance and soon two IJA officers and several soldiers walked out to the Americans. Tice recalled having been in New Guinea when the Japanese had chopped the head off an American pilot, and had heard nothing but horror stories about situations such as they were now in.

However, the Japanese officers saluted and Tice hesitantly returned the salute. The two officers began to smile and spoke to the Americans in Japanese. Finally, one of them produced a phrase book and Tice was able to tell the Japanese why the Americans had landed.

One of the officers shouted an order to a soldier who ran off and returned 15 minutes later with a fuel truck. Because of shortages, Japanese aviation fuel was now laced with castor oil, and Tice refused to put it into the P-38s. By this time, Hawkins's B-17 had arrived, and so had a large group of Japanese civilians, apparently awed by the size of the B-17. A party atmosphere now prevailed. The B-17 crew broke out their emergency rations and gave candy to the swarms of Japanese children, whose parents shared homemade candy with the Americans. A Shinto priest arrived on his bicycle, apparently to bless the American airplanes.

Tice decided to try to transfer fuel from the bomber to Hall's fighter, but had no pump. A Japanese officer understood the dilemma. Soon a hand-operated pump with long hoses appeared and the Japanese soldiers helped the Americans transfer 300 gallons of fuel.

Before the Americans took off, one of the Japanese officers handed his samurai sword to Clay Tice. He wasn't sure whether the man thought he was surrendering all of Japan to the Americans.

Tice later read that there were still renegade IJA troops in Kyushu at the time who threatened to kill any Americans. He had made a lucky pick of a landing site.

The *official* first American plane to land in Japan touched down at Atsugi airfield three days later. Colonel Charles Tench of MacArthur's GHQ operations staff was greeted by Lieutenant General Seizo Arisue, late of the IJN 23rd Army and now on the IJN General Staff. They were surrounded by Japanese aircraft, all of which had their propellers removed per MacArthur's instructions.

After the 15 transports accompanying Tench had landed, two further waves of 15 C-54s, C-46s, and C-47s arrived, escorted by Grumman F6F Hellcats from Seventh Fleet carriers.

The official US Army history of this aspect of MacArthur's campaigns noted that the "Japanese were impressed by the speed with which the Americans motorized themselves and invested the entire field area. Their amazement was outspoken when within 45 minutes after the leading planes had touched down, portable Signal Corps transmitters were on the air establishing communications with Okinawa. The last planes of the party brought fuel, lubricants, and maintenance equipment to make the intrepid little unit compact and self-sustaining."

The C-54s also brought the advance guard of the 11th Airborne Division, commanded by Major General Joseph Swing, to begin the occupation. Over the course of the next 48 hours, more C-54s were shuttling back and forth from Okinawa. By the end of the day on August 30, 4,200 troops and 123 aircraft had been deployed to Atsugi. General Eichelberger landed that morning, with MacArthur himself due in the afternoon.

As MacArthur recalled in dramatic prose, "at two o'clock in the afternoon my C-54, *Bataan* emblazoned on its nose, soared above Kamakura's giant bronze Buddha, past beautiful Mount Fuji, and swung down toward Atsugi."

As they approached, General Courtney Whitney, acting as MacArthur's military secretary, was sure that the end was near. Though the C-54 was escorted by P-38s flown by veterans of the 49th Fighter Group, he wrung his hands as he gazed out at the Kanto Plain, noting that "nearly everywhere Japanese soldiers had refused to give up until killed; the usual laws of war had not been complied with; deadly traps had frequently been set. Here was the greatest opportunity for a final and climactic act. The antiaircraft guns could not possibly miss at this range. Had death, the insatiable monster of the battle, passed MacArthur by on a thousand fields only to murder him at the end?"

MacArthur recalled in his memoirs that everyone from his own staff to the Japanese delegation who flew to Manila had feared for his life if he landed at Atsugi so soon. They had worried that for "the supreme commander, a handful of his staff, and a small advance party to land unarmed and unescorted where they would be outnumbered by thousands to one was foolhardy."

Through the hindsight of his memoirs, MacArthur was unafraid. As he wrote, "years of overseas duty had schooled me well in the lessons of the Orient and, what was probably more important, had taught the Far East that I was its friend."

Apparently the "Far East" had gotten the message. The gamble paid off. As Whitney recalled, "I held my breath. I think the whole world was holding its breath. But as usual, he had been right. He knew the Orient."

First out of the C-54, MacArthur greeted Eichelberger and Swing, making the comment that "Melbourne to Tokyo was a long road but this looks like the payoff."

Official photographers and GIs with personal cameras documented the arrival and watched as the SCAP and his entourage boarded a gaggle of Japanese automobiles for their short drive to the New Grand Hotel in Yokohama, which was to be MacArthur's interim headquarters.

Kenney recalled MacArthur's advice as they were preparing to get into the cars:

> MacArthur had noticed that most of us were carrying pistols in shoulder holsters. It had become a habit during the past three years. He said we had better leave the pistols behind. There were fifteen fully armed Japanese divisions within 10 miles of us. If they decided to start anything, those toy cannon of ours wouldn't do any good. We left our weapons in the airplanes. I found out afterward that it was excellent psychology and made a tremendous impression on the Japanese to see us walking around in their country unarmed and seemingly with utter disregard of danger from the nation of

70,000,000 people we had defeated. To them it meant that there was no doubt about it. They had lost.

Kenney also recalled that "all along both sides of the road to Yokohama, stationed about a hundred yards apart, were Japanese soldiers, fully armed and with their backs to the line of automobiles as we passed. It was partly a token of submission but was also meant to insure against any possibility of sniping by any Jap who didn't agree with the imperial edict calling the war off."

On September 2, MacArthur and Kenney were taken in a destroyer to the USS *Missouri*, anchored in Tokyo Bay for the formal surrender. They were joined by all the senior air commanders in the Pacific. Ennis Whitehead of the Fifth Air Force was there, along with Thomas White of the Seventh and Paul Wurtsmith of the Thirteenth. Air Vice Marshal Bill Bostock of the RAAF and Air Vice Marshal Leonard Isitt of the Royal New Zealand Air Force (RNZAF), both in Kenney's chain of command, were also on hand. Even Tooey Spaatz of the USASTAF had flown up to be with MacArthur.

The Japanese arrived, their military men in formal uniform, their civilians in top hats and tails. MacArthur greeted them across the surrender table in khakis and an open-collared shirt. He made a short speech that was broadcast around the world.

"Today the guns are silent," he began. "A great tragedy has ended. A great victory has been won. The skies no longer rain death – the seas bear only commerce – men everywhere walk upright in the sunlight. The entire world lies quietly at peace."

When MacArthur concluded by saying that "unshackled peoples are tasting the full sweetness of liberty, the relief from fear," Foreign Minister Mamoru Shigemitsu stepped forward to sign on behalf of Emperor Hirohito.

Kenney recalled:

[He] took off his silk hat, laid it on the table, took off his white gloves, put his hat back on his head, and finally put both the hat and gloves down. He was quite visibly nervous about something. It was the first time he had done anything like that and he was probably afflicted with stage fright. He looked from one paper to another and seemed to be puzzled as to which one he should look at first.

"Sutherland," MacArthur said impatiently, breaking the absolute silence of the occasion. "Show him where to sign."

General Richard Sutherland, the SCAP's chief of staff, stepped forward and pointed to the line where Shigemitsu was supposed to sign. General Yoshijiro Umezu signed next, and when the Japanese were finished, MacArthur sat down.

He signed as the Supreme Commander using several pens, two of which were handed to Lieutenant General Jonathan Wainwright and British Lieutenant General Arthur Percival. Captured respectively at Corregidor and Singapore, they were the highest-ranking officers of their respective nations to have been captured during the war. Gaunt and grossly underweight from the effects of malnutrition, they had been released from prisoner of war camps in Manchuria only a few days before.

Flanked by Admirals Halsey and Sherman, Admiral Chester Nimitz then signed for the United States, followed by representatives of the other Allied powers. General Sir Thomas Blamey, the Allied Land Forces commander in MacArthur's chain of command since New Guinea, signed for Australia. Lieutenant Admiral Conrad Helfrich, who had briefly led the naval forces of the ill-fated ABDA command, signed for the Netherlands. Among the others, General Hsu Yung-chang signed for China, Admiral Sir Bruce Fraser for the United Kingdom, Colonel Lawrence Moore Cosgrave for Canada, General Philippe Leclerc for France, Air Vice Marshal Leonard Isitt for New Zealand, and Lieutenant General Kuzma Derevyanko for the Soviet Union, which had fought against Japan for less than a month.

When MacArthur was finished, and as the Japanese delegation rose to depart, he turned to Admiral Halsey and asked, "Bill, where the hell are those airplanes?"

Almost as though on cue, a drumming, humming sound in the sky above exploded into rolling thunder as wave upon wave of white-starred airplanes clouded the sky. Most, in fairness to Halsey's contribution, were US Navy carrier aircraft – around 1,500 of them. However, the USAAF was not to be outshown. From the Marianas, Curtis LeMay had sent about 500 B-29 Superfortresses, the sound of whose Wright R-3350 engines was deafening in both the literal and metaphorical sense.

As World War II ended – with MacArthur on the deck of the USS *Missouri* – his air forces now constituted the second-largest component within the USAAF. The three FEAF numbered air forces commanded by Kenney were comprised of 216,616 personnel, or 26 percent of all overseas deployed USAAF airmen, and possessed more than 5,500 aircraft. By comparison, the air forces in the European Theater of Operations, the Eighth and Ninth, had about 272,000 personnel at war's end, down from a March 1945 peak of around 457,000. The highest personnel total ever reached by the third-place Mediterranean Theater air forces (the Twelfth and Fifteenth) was 178,800 in August 1944.

For the Japanese leaders on the *Missouri* that day, in their uniforms or top hats, there was no doubt who had won and lost the war they had begun, and whose airpower was responsible.

As George Kenney recalled, the vast aerial armada merged into "a long sweeping majestic turn as they disappeared toward the mists hiding the sacred mountain of Fujiyama."

24

The Shogun and his Air Force

W hen Douglas MacArthur finally made his entrance into the city of Tokyo on September 8, 1945, it was more businesslike than triumphant, but it was clear that dramatic changes were coming. Surrounded by an honor guard of the 1st Cavalry Division and accompanied by Eighth Army commander Robert Eichelberger and Admiral Bill Halsey, MacArthur drove directly to the United States Embassy compound, abandoned since 1941 and largely untouched by intrusion or by the bombing of the city, and raised the American flag.

Six days had passed since the surrender ceremony aboard the USS *Missouri*, and the Japanese people were beginning to grasp the reality of occupation, but MacArthur was greeted with more curiosity than animosity.

Each side entered into the occupation in stark contrast to what the other side had expected. The domineering brutality that had accompanied the Japanese subjugation of lands from China to the Philippines to Southeast Asia, and which the Japanese expected now to endure as *they* were now under occupation, never materialized. Meanwhile, the Americans, who had a few weeks earlier expected to meet more than 70 million people ready to fight to their death, were greeted with a reception so far from hostile that it bordered on cordial.

The victors exacted no mass retribution from the defeated. Even the roundup of those to be charged as war criminals targeted dozens, rather than hundreds or thousands. As had been the case after the fall of Nazi Germany four months earlier, the Allies had clearly stated that those guilty of mass crimes against innocent civilians, prisoners of war, and others would be arrested. As an Allied military tribunal would sit in judgment at Nürnberg, so too would tribunals be empaneled in Tokyo and Manila.

There was considerable support among the Allies for heading the war criminal list with the Emperor's name. He was, in the minds of many, the man ultimately responsible for all of the atrocities, crimes, and aggression perpetrated by the Empire of Japan. Indeed, the war had been waged in his name and with his acquiescence.

As a student of the history and culture of the Far East, though, MacArthur understood that the continuity of the monarchy was an integral part of the Japanese national identity, and an integral part of his ability to rule occupied Japan. The Supreme Commander had arrived in Japan with the power to institute a military government, but instead he chose to rule Japan through its existing instructions, rather than imposing an American political hierarchy to manage the country's towns and prefectures – a course of action not always popular in the United States. One of his first acts was to allow the Imperial Japanese Army to disarm itself rather than to task his occupation army with doing so.

This is not to say that MacArthur accepted imperial rule as it had been, nor the Emperor as an absolute monarch. Those days were over. When the Emperor finally sent word to MacArthur on September 27, inviting him to come to the Imperial Palace, MacArthur refused. Under the surrender terms, the "authority of the Emperor and the Japanese Government to rule the state shall be subject to the Supreme Commander of the Allied Powers." Hirohito would have to come to him.

When the Emperor arrived at MacArthur's residence in the embassy compound, he was still not sure that he was not headed for the gallows. He left their meeting having been assured that he would keep his life, but knowing that the rest of it would be spent as a constitutional monarch, not as a living god.

MacArthur would rule Japan, not as its emperor, but more as a shogun, the Japanese term for a military dictator who wields true power though an emperor is on the throne.

The Japanese referred to him as their "Gaijin Shogun," or foreign ruler. As Supreme Commander, MacArthur set up his headquarters in the Dai-Ichi Insurance Company building, a seven-story steel and concrete edifice that had survived the Superfortress bombing raids. Located in central Tokyo, it overlooked the Imperial Plaza where Japanese troops once paraded.

The Shogun's own occupation army arrived across uncontested beachheads in the days and weeks following the surrender. They reached their objectives without the carnage and bloodshed anticipated by the Allied planners of Operation *Downfall*. The Allies now executed Operation *Blacklist*, the contingency plan that had been drafted for implementation in the event – considered unlikely as late as July – that Japan surrendered without a full-scale invasion.

Within about six weeks of the surrender, American occupation troops in Japan numbered about 460,000, equally divided between Eichelberger's Eighth Army in Tokyo, and Walter Krueger's Sixth Army, headquartered in Kyoto. The bulk of the British Commonwealth Occupation Force (BCOF), including Australians, New Zealanders, and Indians, as well as British troops, arrived early in 1946 and accounted for around 36,000 personnel at their peak.

So smoothly had the initial phase of the occupation gone that by October, MacArthur surprised many by predicting that the overall total could be drawn down to 200,000 by July 1946. Indeed, on December 31, 1945, the Sixth Army was relieved of occupation duty and sent home. In turn, the personnel strength of the Eighth Army, which took over all occupation duties, was reduced from 241,506 at the end of December to 194,061 at the end of January 1946.

The Shogun's air force had begun to arrive in Japan even before the surrender. Armed patrols over Japan by Fifth and Seventh Air Force aircraft out of Okinawa continued through the early days of the occupation, but these patrols were uneventful. LeMay's Twentieth Air Force B-29s, meanwhile, had shifted from offensive operations to dropping supplies into prisoner of war camps on August 27. As prisoners of war and civilian internees were located and liberated by ground troops, those requiring hospitalization were airlifted to Okinawa and the Philippines by FEAF troop carrier aircraft, as well as Air Transport Command C-54s.

Of the three air forces in General George Kenney's FEAF, Lieutenant General Ennis Whitehead's Fifth Air Force was designated as the American occupation air force. The Thirteenth remained in the

Philippines and the Seventh moved from Okinawa to Hawaii at the end of the year.

On September 25, 1945, two weeks after MacArthur set up shop at the Dai-Ichi building, Whitehead established his Fifth Air Force and V Bomber Command headquarters at the Irumagawa Air Base, 20 miles west of central Tokyo. They would later be relocated to Nagoya.

Irumagawa had opened in 1938 as the airfield for the IJAAF Academy. It was used mainly for training, but toward the end of the war it became a base for Yokosuka MXY7 Okha manned, rocket-propelled suicide aircraft. The facility was later renamed as Johnson Air Base after Lieutenant Colonel Jerry Johnson, the 49th Fighter Group commander and 22-victory ace. On October 7, only two weeks after Irumagawa was taken over, Johnson was piloting a B-25 out of the base when the aircraft became lost in a typhoon. He gave up his parachute so that the entire crew could bail out while he and his copilot attempted unsuccessfully to return to Irumagawa. In praise of Johnson, Kenney said that he was "the bravest man I ever knew and the bravest thing he ever did was the last thing, when he did not need to be brave."

Near Johnson were two other bases, Yokota and Tachikawa, which became important hubs for American air activity. On the south side of the city, Haneda, Tokyo's major commercial airport, was taken over for US military transport flights, though in 1947, the commercial carriers Northwest Orient and Pan American began sharing Haneda. In 1951, it was turned back to Japanese control as Tokyo International Airport.

The air base at Atsugi, which had been the first major aerial port of entry into Japan by American forces in September 1945, was utilized by the Fifth Air Force for a time, but the US Navy assumed control of the base because of its proximity to the big naval base at Yokosuka, 20 miles to the southeast.

On Kyushu, the two fields taken over by the Fifth Air Force were the former IJAAF interceptor base at Ashiya, and Itazuke (previously called Mushiroda) near the city of Fukuoka. Itazuke was also designated as the headquarters of V Fighter Command. In southern Honshu, the Fifth maintained facilities at Itami, near Osaka, and Komaki, near Nagoya. In northern Honshu, across the Tsugaru Strait from the northern main Island of Hokkaido, the American airmen took over the air base at Misawa, which had been used by both the IJAAF and the IJNAF during the war. It was on Lake Ogawara, near Misawa, that Japanese pilots trained for the Pearl Harbor attack. On Hokkaido, the Fifth Air Force took over the IJNAF base at Chitose, near Hokkaido.

Of all these bases, the US Air Force continued its operations at Itazuke, Yokota, and Misawa into the 21st century, as did the US Navy at Atsugi and Yokosuka. Today, Yokota remains as the headquarters of the Fifth Air Force and of the US Forces, Japan (USFJ) joint command.

Soon after the surrender, many Fifth Air Force units were deactivated, while others moved into Japan. The 49th Fighter Group moved first to Atsugi, but in February 1946, having converted from P-38s to P-51s, it relocated to Chitose. In March 1948, now equipped with F-80 jets, the 49th moved to Misawa, where it became the 49th Fighter Bomber Group. The 35th Fighter Group arrived at Irumagawa in October 1945, but converted to F-80s and moved to Yokota as the 35th Fighter Interceptor Group in January 1950. The 475th Fighter Group, with which Tommy McGuire had become America's penultimate ace, was sent to Korea. It established its headquarters at the Japanese air base at Kimpo on the edge of Seoul in September 1945, but it moved to Itazuke in Japan in August 1948, and later to Ashiya before being inactivated in April 1949.

Among the Fifth Air Force bomb groups to move into Japan, the veteran 3rd was first, being based at Atsugi and Yokota before landing at Johnson AB in March 1950. The 38th Bomb Group moved first to Itazuke, and then to Itami in October 1946, where it remained until April 1949.

During the earlier redeployment from the Philippines to Okinawa, the Fifth's bomb groups equipped with A-20s and B-25s were in the process of converting to the Douglas A-26 Invader, a fast twin-engine attack bomber, and it was with this aircraft that they deployed into Japan. Redesignated as B-26 after the retirement of wartime Martin B-26 Marauders, the Invaders would remain in operational combat service until 1965.

Flying the photoreconnaissance variants of the P-38 and P-51, the 6th and 71st Reconnaissance Groups moved to Japan, where they used a broad range of aircraft, including RF-51s, RB-17s, RB-29s, RF-61s, and RF-80 jets, to map the damage done by the strategic air offensive against targets in Honshu.

None of the Fifth Air Force heavy bomb groups were moved to Japan. Rather they were inactivated in Okinawa or in the Philippines, though many were later reactivated with new, more advanced, aircraft for service with the Strategic Air Command.

Meanwhile, based on agreements reached in late 1945, the British contribution to the occupation air operations arrived in the form of the British Commonwealth Air Group (BCAir), an element of BCOF. The BCAir commander, RAF Air Vice Marshal Cecil Bouchier, established his headquarters at Iwakuni under Fifth Air Force operational control on March 1, 1946. It was comprised of No. 14 Squadron of the Royal New Zealand Air Force and No. 4 Squadron of the Royal Indian Air Force, as well as three units of the Royal Australian Air Force, Nos. 11 and 17 Squadrons, and No. 81 Wing. The latter wing was equipped with P-51 Mustangs and de Havilland Mosquitoes, while the New Zealanders flew Vought Corsairs and the other units operated Supermarine Spitfires. After 1948, only No. 77 Squadron of No. 81 Wing remained in Japan.

Transport groups that were involved in the initial deployment of troops into Japan in September 1945 included the 2nd Combat Cargo Group and the 434th Troop Carrier Group, which had been with the Fifth Air Force since 1944 and 1943, respectively. The Fifth Air Force would continue to conduct routine airlift activities throughout Japan. Longer and higher density routes, such as routine scheduled service from the United States via the Philippines and Okinawa, were maintained by the Central Pacific Wing (later Western Pacific Wing) of the USAAF Air Transport Command, operating C-54s.

Not to be overlooked in the routine FEAF operations in Japan was the work done by the Far East Air Service Command (FEASC). Responsible for logistical and maintenance infrastructure, as well as the routine flow of supplies, FEASC arrived in Japan with, or ahead of, the first waves of Fifth Air Force combat units and continued to expand their facilities at all of the Fifth Air Force bases throughout Japan.

FEAF itself continued to exist during the postwar years, though between December 6, 1945 and January 1, 1947 it was superseded by an entity known as the Pacific Air Command, US Army (PACUSA). In May 1946, under its brief guise as PACUSA, the headquarters of the once and future FEAF were relocated from Fort McKinley, near Manila, to offices in central Tokyo.

The air forces under the umbrella of PACUSA/FEAF included the Fifth, Seventh, and Thirteenth from the wartime FEAF, as well as the Eighth Air Force, which had moved to Okinawa in anticipation of Operation *Downfall*, and the Twentieth Air Force, which no longer needed to be under Joint Chiefs of Staff control now that the strategic air campaign against Japan had concluded.

Reestablishment of FEAF was only one part of a new command structure that was introduced by the Joint Chiefs of Staff on January 1, 1947. A Far East Command (FECOM) was created to encompass the region from the Marianas through the Philippines to Japan and Korea. In addition to his role as SCAP, Douglas MacArthur became FECOM's commander in chief (CINCFE).

Meanwhile, a Pacific Command (PACOM), roughly analogous to the wartime Pacific Ocean Areas (POA), was introduced for the rest of the Pacific. Admiral John Towers, who had succeeded Admiral Chester Nimitz as Commander in Chief, Pacific (CINCPAC), now commanded PACOM with the CINCPAC title. Under the January 1947 realignment, the Seventh Air Force, now in Hawaii, was transferred to PACOM from the new FEAF. However, Naval Forces Far East (NAVFE) were placed under the FECOM chain of command, with their commander, the COMNAVFE, answering to MacArthur rather than CINCPAC. This would be important during the upcoming Korean War.

In September 1947, the National Defense Act completely reorganized the armed forces, combining them into what would be the Department of Defense and transforming the US Army Air Forces, an autonomous component of the US Army since 1941, into the fully independent US Air Force.

General Tooey Spaatz's US Army Strategic Air Forces in the Pacific (USASTAF), which had been created in 1945 to contain both the Eighth and the Twentieth, was dissolved and Spaatz himself returned to Washington, where he succeeded Hap Arnold as commanding general of the USAAF in February 1946. With the creation of the US Air Force in September 1947, Spaatz became its first chief of staff.

General George Kenney, who had commanded FEAF through the end of the war and beyond, left the Pacific on December 30, 1945, and returned to the United States, where he would assume command of the new Strategic Air Command (SAC) in March 1946.

Ennis Whitehead moved up from the Fifth Air Force to command PACUSA, and remained in this post as it became FEAF again. On April 25, 1949, he traded places with Lieutenant General George Stratemeyer as commander of the Continental Air Command back in the United States. During World War II, Stratemeyer had served in various command roles in the China–Burma–India Theater, and as the first commander of the Air Defense Command when it was created in March 1946. He now took over the new iteration of FEAF.

In October 1945, during the immediate postwar command shuffle at FEAF, Whitehead's place at the head of Fifth Air Force was taken over by Major General Kenneth B. Wolfe, who had commanded the XX Bomber Command of the Twentieth Air Force briefly in 1944. Since then, Wolfe had been back in the States with the Air Materiel Command and at USAAF headquarters. In 1948, command of the Fifth was assumed by Major General Earle "Pat" Partridge, who had served on the staffs of the Eighth and Fifteenth Air Forces during the war, and who was to have commanded the Eighth's 3rd Air Division during Operation *Downfall*.

As the USAAF became the US Air Force, the command structure also changed. Units at the previous "group" level in the hierarchy were redesignated as "wings," with existing groups becoming their wing's combat component. The former 49th Fighter Group, for example, was now the 49th Fighter Bomber Wing. World War II wings, which were very large administrative and operational organizations that usually controlled several combat groups, were redesignated as air divisions.

Aircraft designations also changed, including the letter "F" superseding "P" (for "pursuit") in the nomenclature for fighter aircraft. For instance, the well-known P-51 Mustang was now the F-51 Mustang. The "F" prefix for reconnaissance aircraft was eliminated and the F-6 Mustang became the RF-51 Mustang.

In the years following World War II, the mission of the Shogun's PACUSA/FEAF gradually changed. Initially, it was the combat role of maintaining air supremacy over a defeated and occupied Japan and providing air protection for naval forces and shipping. However, as the collapse of Japanese hostility had been so quick and so far-reaching, the mission became a routine one of operating radar and air traffic control, as well as air-sea rescue services in Japanese and Korean air space and surrounding waters, and on the air routes coming in from Okinawa, the Philippines, and elsewhere.

As the elements of the Fifth Air Force were gradually consolidated, inactivated, or sent home, Americans of the occupation forces, from MacArthur on down, came to realize that any threat to the peace and stability of the Far East was *not* going to be coming from the Japanese. However, there would be plenty of other sources of concern.

25

Land of Morning Surprises

The news came abruptly and unexpectedly in the wee-hour darkness. Douglas MacArthur likened it to his learning of Pearl Harbor nine long years earlier. In his memoirs, he called it a nightmare.

On June 25, 1950, ten divisions of the North's Korean People's Army (KPA), armed with Soviet tanks and Soviet artillery, swept easily across the 38th Parallel that separated the two Koreas, overwhelmed the South Korean troops who were posted there with little more than rifles, and quickly captured their initial objectives.

The "Land of Morning Calm," as Korea was known, had abruptly become the "Land of Morning Surprises." Suddenly, after nearly a half decade of observing war clouds only on distant horizons, such as in the Chinese civil war that brought the Communists to power in 1949, the Shogun found himself at war.

During and immediately after World War II, Korea had been a strategic afterthought for the Allies, a place that had rated little more than a footnote in planning documents. Korea had been occupied by Japan since 1910, and at the wartime conference at Yalta in February 1945, Allied leaders agreed that it should be freed from Japanese rule and granted its independence after an unspecified period of "trusteeship." In August 1945, when the Soviet Union entered the war against Japan, an agreement was quickly drawn up that called for a "temporary" division of Korea at the line of 38 degrees north latitude, the "38th Parallel." Soviet trusteeship would be imposed to the north, with American trusteeship to the south.

Having occupied Manchuria, the Soviet Twenty-Fifth Army swept into the Korean Peninsula, accepting the surrender of Japanese forces on August 19, 1945 and reaching Pyongyang, near the 38th Parallel, on August 24. As would be the case in Eastern Europe, Soviet leader Josef Stalin wished to establish a pro-Soviet Communist state in northern Korea, and he ultimately hoped to unite all of Korea under such a government.

To get things rolling, Stalin sent in political commissar Colonel General Terentii Shtykov, who interviewed a number of Korean Communists to find a suitable front man. His choice, bypassing Cho Man-sik, leader of a People's Republic of Korea (PRK) that had already been proclaimed in the wake of the Japanese withdrawal, was 33-year-old Kim Il-sung (born Kim Song-ju). A revolutionary who had fought alongside the Chinese Communists, Kim had not actually been in Korea since he was seven years old, but he was vetted by Lavrentiy Beria, head of the Soviet secret police, the NKVD (predecessor to the KGB), who recommended him to Stalin. Cho, meanwhile, was jailed in Pyongyang, where he later died. Kim arrived in northern Korea in September 1945, where Shtykov installed him as chairman of a "Provisional People's Committee for North Korea."

South of the 38th Parallel, Lieutenant General John Hodge and his XXIV Corps force arrived on September 8, and accepted the surrender of the Japanese in Seoul the next day. He then established the US Army Military Government in Korea (USAMGIK) within MacArthur's SCAP chain of command. In contrast to MacArthur's experience in Japan, however, he was greeted by civil unrest as Koreans vented their frustration after two generations of Japanese rule. He found southern Korea in chaos, with tens of thousands of Korean and Japanese refugees fleeing from the Soviets and like numbers of surrendered Japanese troops awaiting repatriation to Japan. Unlike MacArthur, Hodge was compelled to declare martial law.

Just as Kim Il-sung in the north had been out of Korea for 26 years, the heir apparent to the political leadership of the south had been gone for most of his 70 years. Syngman Rhee had been a life-long crusader for Korean independence who had spent most of his life abroad. In October 1945, he was flown into Seoul aboard Douglas MacArthur's own C-54. Like Stalin and Kim, Rhee championed the cause of Korean unification, but he was a staunch anti-Communist and wanted a unified Korea on *his* terms.

The military occupation ended in 1948, but with no progress having been made toward unification. Two new countries were born. The Republic of Korea was proclaimed in the south, with Rhee having been elected as president. In the north, the Democratic People's Republic of Korea came into being with Kim as premier, and Shtykov exchanging the cap of Soviet administrator for that of Soviet ambassador.

Over the coming months, Shtykov and Kim discussed strategies for unifying Korea under Communist rule. After the Communist victory in China in 1949, they decided that it could be done by force – using the tanks, artillery, and other arms that the Soviets had flooded into North Korea. They predicted that they could defeat the Republic of Korea quickly and easily – *and* that the United States would not find it in their interest to intervene. It seemed obvious to Shtykov and Kim – and to Stalin as well – that if the United States had not intervened to stop a Communist takeover of China a year earlier, they certainly would not stand in the way of a Communist takeover of the smaller and less significant Korean Peninsula.

Much has been made of Secretary of State Dean Acheson's January 12, 1950 speech at the National Press Club where he gave a detailed overview of his view of the American defense perimeter in the Far East, which he said ran from the Aleutians to Japan to the Ryukyu Islands, especially to Okinawa and south to the Philippines. This line expressly excluded Korea. Five months later, and for the rest of Acheson's life, critics piled onto him, blaming him for encouraging North Korean aggression.

In fact, it was just an oversight. Acheson omitted Korea simply because it did not seem important in the grander scheme of things. Douglas MacArthur himself had drawn much the same line during a *New York Times* interview in March 1949. In Washington, meanwhile, Congress had consciously declined to appropriate money for military aid to South Korea, though the US Army had deployed a small Korean Military Advisory Group (KMAG).

The June 25, 1950 invasion, which so startled MacArthur, pitted 200,000 KPA troops against the Republic of Korea (ROK) Army, with fewer than 100,000 troops and no tanks. The North's air force consisted of nearly 200 Russian-made combat aircraft, including Yakovlev Yak-9 fighters, many of which were flown by Soviet pilots with World War II experience. The South had fewer than two dozen trainers and light aircraft.

The United States had no contingency plan for such an invasion. "What is the United States policy in Asia?" MacArthur asked rhetorically in his memoirs, answering that "the United States has no definite policy in Asia."

MacArthur's first action, on the day of the invasion, was to send FEAF transport aircraft, under fighter escort, to evacuate roughly 2,000 Americans from South Korea.

President Harry Truman, meanwhile, moved to authorize the use of American troops and combat aircraft to secure the airfields at Kimpo on the edge of Seoul – South Korea's largest airport – as well as Suwon, 20 miles to the south, both of which were being used by FEAF evacuation flights. Because of inconsistencies in place names on Japanese and Korean maps, FEAF adopted the convention of numerically designating airfields in Korea. Suwon was K-13 and Kimpo was K-14, but we use the Korean place names in this narrative.

Resisting North Korea hastily became US policy. Truman, and Secretary of State Acheson – for whom Korea was *now* a priority – concluded, according to National Security Council Report 68, that "if South Korea was allowed to fall, Communist leaders would be emboldened to override nations closer to our own shores. If the Communists were permitted to force their way into the Republic of Korea without opposition from the free world, no small nation would have the courage to resist threat and aggression by stronger Communist neighbors."

On June 25, the United Nations Security Council passed Resolution 82, condemning North Korean aggression and demanding that it stop. Two days later, Resolution 83 recommended that UN members do as Truman was willing to do, to "furnish such assistance to the Republic of Korea as may be necessary to repel the armed attack and to restore international peace and security in the area."

The Soviet Union could have and would have vetoed the resolutions, but they were then boycotting the Security Council because the United Nations continued to recognize (as they would for another two decades) that the Nationalist government on Taiwan, rather than the Communists on the mainland, was the legitimate government of China.

In what was about to become a combat theater, the air assets under MacArthur's chain of command were within FEAF, now commanded by Lieutenant General George Stratemeyer. As a deputy, Stratemeyer was soon assigned Major General Otto Weyland. During World War II, Weyland had commanded the highly successful XIX Tactical Air Command, the ground support organization attached to General George Patton's Third Army. He had just been assigned to head the Tactical Air Command, but he was rerouted to the Far East.

The air forces within FEAF included Major General Earle "Pat" Partridge's Fifth Air Force in Japan, Major General Howard Turner's Thirteenth in the Philippines, and Major General Alvan Kincaid's Twentieth on Okinawa. It was Partridge's Fifth, though, that was immediately on the front lines of the air war and tasked with establishing air superiority over South Korea. This included protecting Kimpo and Suwon as well as aiding the ROK Army in its admittedly futile efforts to halt the invasion.

The 8th Fighter Bomber Wing was forward deployed to Taegu, aka K-2, in South Korea, about 150 air miles south of Seoul, and its commander, Colonel Jack Price, became Partridge's de facto ADVON commander.

Among the first units deployed with the 8th were the 68th and 339th Fighter All-Weather Squadrons (FAWS) flying North American F-82 Twin Mustangs, the double-fuselage adaptation of the F-51 Mustang. Here, these units would be joined by the 18th Fighter Bomber Group flying F-51s. These propeller aircraft proved to be more valuable at this stage of the war than the fast new F-80s because they had greater endurance than the jets, whose fuel consumption did not allow them to linger so long in the combat zone. The F-51s and F-82s were more than a match for the piston-engined Yak-9s.

The Fifth Air Force's first air-to-air combat action of the war came on June 27, as five F-82s engaged five Yaks that had come to attack American airlifters at Kimpo. Lieutenant William Hudson of the 68th scored the first aerial victory, while Major James Little and Lieutenant Charles Moran each also claimed a Yak. The other Yaks escaped.

Partridge established his ADVON Fifth Air Force headquarters at Itazuke AB in Japan, and moved F-80s to Itazuke and B-26 bombers to Ashiya AB for missions in Korea. The latter, from the 3rd Bomb Group, launched the first air strikes of the Korean War on June 28, attacking rail and road traffic between the 38th Parallel and Seoul. The first armed F-80 patrols were underway, and RF-80 reconnaissance flights had begun. Two days later, 18 B-26s struck north of the 38th for the first time in an attack against Heijo airfield near Pyongyang.

On June 28, the fast-moving KPA forces occupied Seoul and captured Kimpo. The following day, Douglas MacArthur flew into Suwon through a driving rainstorm in his C-54 *Bataan* on his first of 17 inspection trips to Korea. As his C-54 was on final approach, a Yak made a firing pass at the aircraft, but it was shot down by an escorting F-51.

As Partridge was pressing his Fifth Air Force into the fight, Stratemeyer called up his other assets, including the B-29 Superfortresses of the Twentieth Air Force, then based at Kadena AB on Okinawa. Even as MacArthur was on the ground at Suwon, eight B-29s of the Twentieth's 19th Bomb Group were striking Kimpo and Seoul, both now in KPA hands. Within two days, Suwon also fell to the KPA, and the bombers were striking its runways.

Meanwhile, US Navy assets in the Far East commanded by Vice Admiral C. Turner Joy also fell under MacArthur's chain of command in his role as FECOM. The US Navy contributed its Task Force 77, which included a growing number of fleet carriers, while Britain's Royal Navy also supplied carriers. The USS *Valley Forge* and the British carrier HMS *Triumph* were both in action on July 3, on which day Lieutenant (junior grade) Leonard Plog and Ensign Eldon Brown, flying F9F Panthers, became the first US naval aviators to down enemy aircraft over Korea. These carriers were soon joined by the USS *Philippine Sea* and the USS *Boxer*. The USS *Leyte* arrived by early September. The 1st Marine Aircraft Wing (1st MAW) was formally committed on July 2 and its assets were shipped from the United States.

Joy and Stratemeyer, who occupied parallel slots in the chain of command, were tasked with coordinating the efforts of their strike aircraft, a process that would not always go smoothly, especially with regard to forward air controllers, who would be vital in coordinating ground support operations. For the time being, their intramural wrangling would be the least of their worries.

26

Korean Disaster, Korean Deliverance

T he scene that MacArthur witnessed during the eight hours of his first visit to the Korean battlefront on June 29, 1950 was appalling. Four days into the Korean War, huge columns of smoke rose from Seoul, now in enemy hands, and waves of southbound refugees clogged the roads.

Having seen with his own eyes that the ROK Army was now essentially nonexistent, MacArthur informed US Army Chief of Staff General J. Lawton Collins that the only way to stem the tide and have any chance of pushing the North Koreans back was to introduce American combat troops to fight the KPA. He was confident that the US Navy could control the seas around Korea, and that his Fifth Air Force could achieve air superiority, but on the ground, nothing then stood in the way of the KPA.

On June 30, Truman authorized the introduction of ground troops and MacArthur ordered Lieutenant General Walton Walker, commander of the Eighth Army, to send the 24th Infantry Division and elements of the 25th and 1st Cavalry Divisions into Korea from Japan. However, these understrength units were just a shadow of what they had been five years before. The experienced and battle-hardened troops that had taken World War II to Japan's doorstep had long ago been discharged, and their places taken by young, inexperienced troops who had been trained and equipped for little more than occupation duty. Few officers who had seen combat remained to lead them, and they lacked the heavy weapons needed for sustained combat.

As might have been expected, things did not go as well for American ground troops as they had for the airmen. Airlifted into Korea by the 374th Troop Carrier Wing, the 24th's Task Force Smith worked their way north to Osan, 20 miles south of Suwon, where on July 4, they met KPA troops in the first US Army combat action of the war. The outnumbered and outgunned Americans were defeated and sent reeling.

Nevertheless, the United Nations Security Council seemed to have great confidence in these soldiers. On July 7, they issued Resolution 84, in which they "recommended" that member states answering the call of Resolution 83 to "furnish assistance" to the Republic of Korea should "make such forces and other assistance available to a unified command under the United States." The Security Council requested "the United States to designate a commander of such forces."

In his role as commander of the US Far East Command, the task of repelling the attack had already been assumed by Douglas MacArthur, though after Resolution 84, there was some second guessing in the United States that someone with more experience in coalition warfare, such as Dwight Eisenhower, would be chosen.

On July 24, the "United Nations Command" (UNC or UNCOM) was formally created, with MacArthur as its commander in chief (CINCUNC). Though he was authorized to fly the UN flag concurrently with national flags, the UN could not allow itself to be considered a belligerent and it exercised no control, operational or otherwise, over MacArthur or any troops involved.

While the Security Council resolutions clearly envisioned a grand international coalition, and 17 countries eventually did contribute troops, the UNC was essentially a joint American and South Korean organization. Recovering from their pitiful opening performance, the South Koreans would account for 62 percent of the UNC at its peak, and the Americans 32 percent. Australia and the United Kingdom each contributed around 2 percent. In the air, Australia was first to arrive, placing the Mustangs of the RAAF No. 77 Squadron under Fifth Air Force command on June 30, 1950.

Though the ROK Army would later shoulder the heaviest load, on the ground in the summer of 1950 the US Army was the only viable force, and it was swimming upstream against a powerful KPA current.

The 24th Division, under Major General William Dean, which had hoped and expected to halt the KPA advance, established itself at

Taejon (now Daejeon), aka K-5, about 60 miles south of Osan. Both the Eighth Army and the Fifth Air Force, meanwhile, set up their respective advance headquarters at Taegu, 75 air miles southeast of Taejon. Various Fifth Air Force combat units also relocated their headquarters to Taegu during the summer of 1950.

The North Korean onslaught continued unabated, and by July 14, the KPA had reached Taejon. Here, after a week of bloody combat, the 24th Division was roundly defeated. General Dean became separated from his command and was taken prisoner.

By the first week of August, the Americans were dug into a defensive position around Pusan (now Busan) on the southeastern corner of the Korean Peninsula. The KPA had conquered the entire peninsula except for this slim salient south of the Naktong (now Nakdong) River. The Pusan Perimeter, as it was known, was barely 140 miles in length and included the city of Taegu, as well as Pusan.

Troops and supplies, especially ammunition, were brought into Pusan by ship. Materiel coming from the United States by ship, especially tanks, was being sent directly to Pusan, bypassing staging depots in the Pacific or Japan. Because of the urgency of resupply, FEAF had established an air bridge with its terminus at airfields around Pusan (K-1 and K-9). C-46s and C-47s, marshaled from throughout the Pacific, were coming and going at a frantic pace. The new Fairchild C-119 Flying Boxcar, capable of carrying larger-diameter cargo than other transports, made its combat debut in July.

In late August, FEAF established the 1st Troop Carrier Task Force as the nucleus of a new FEAF Combat Cargo Command. Major General William Tunner, the operational architect of the trans-Himalaya Hump airlift of World War II and the Berlin Airlift of 1948–49, was brought in to command it. The situation was reminiscent of George Kenney's use of airlift to supply and transport troops in New Guinea in 1942. However, back then, combat airlift was still a new concept, and it was done on a much smaller scale.

Though American airpower – both that of the US Air Force and that of US Navy carriers offshore – had virtually annihilated the North Korean air force, the airmen were unable to curb the advance of the KPA. On July 8, Stratemeyer organized a provisional FEAF Bomber Command (BomCom) to manage the bombing campaign. To run it, he brought in Major General Emmett "Rosey" O'Donnell, who had commanded the 73rd Bomb Wing under LeMay in World War II, and who now commanded the Fifteenth Air Force under LeMay at the Strategic Air Command. Five days later, 49 FEAF B-29s from the 22nd and 92nd Bomb Groups struck targets at Wonsan, about 100 miles into North Korea. In August, the 98th Bomb Group flew its own first mission over Korea shortly after its B-29s landed at Yokota, and the 307th Bomb Group began operations from Okinawa. Over the coming weeks, B-29s ranged as far north as the port of Rason in northeastern North Korea, near the Soviet border, through which Soviet war materiel flowed.

While MacArthur favored the use of all of his aerial firepower, including B-29s, against the KPA on the battlefield, after a meeting with Air Force Chief of Staff Hoyt Vandenberg, who flew out to Tokyo to meet him, he did permit Stratemeyer to begin striking strategic targets in North Korea. These ranged from ports to railroad marshaling yards, but also included chemical plants and oil refineries.

Throughout August, the assault on the Pusan Perimeter was relentless and fierce. Walker's Eighth Army held on as best they could – waiting for reinforcements and resupply with their backs to the Korea Strait. The KPA, whose advance from the 38th Parallel had been literally unstoppable, clearly wanted to finish the job and push the defenders into the sea before reinforcements could arrive in substantial numbers.

The first Medal of Honor awarded to a member of the US Air Force was for an action on the Pusan Perimeter on August 5. Major Louis Sebille was the commander of the 67th Fighter Bomber Squadron of the 18th Fighter Wing, a Fifth Air Force unit that had forward deployed to Taegu from Clark Air Base in the Philippines. He was leading a trio of F-51s in a ground support mission against a KPA column when one of his two bombs hung up on his aircraft. Realizing that his aircraft was too badly damaged by ground fire to get back to Taegu, Sebille opted to crash his F-51 into the enemy, creating considerable damage, but costing his life.

A few weeks later, on September 14, Captain John Wamsley of the Fifth earned a posthumous Medal of Honor on a mission over North Korea. He was flying a B-26 of the 8th Bomb Squadron of the 3rd Bomb Wing on a night mission against an enemy supply train. Such traffic was run at night to avoid American bombers, but Wamsley used an arc light on his aircraft to illuminate the train while another bomber attacked it. Wamsley took no evasive action so that the train would remain visible, but in so doing, his aircraft suffered so much antiaircraft damage that it crashed.

Gradually, Walker's reinforcements began to reach the embattled enclave within the Pusan Perimeter. The 1st Provisional Marine Brigade and the British Commonwealth 27th Infantry Brigade joined the American divisions under Walker's command. Somehow, the battered ROK troops caught their breath and rallied. Five divisions had reformed and managed to join the Americans.

In August, the B-29s began, as MacArthur had wanted, to attack enemy troop concentrations. The threat against the Pusan Perimeter by the KPA was considered so dangerous that on August 16, FEAF Bomber Command sent nearly 100 B-29s to blast enemy troops northwest of Taegu with 1.6 million pounds of bombs. This was the biggest ground support operation since the Normandy campaign in 1944.

Nevertheless, the Fifth Air Force Joint Operations Center itself came under threat, with the KPA only 8 miles away, and it had to be pulled back from Taegu to Pusan at the end of August, with the Eighth Army headquarters relocated on September 6. As the enemy launched a major offensive against the entire Pusan Perimeter on August 31, MacArthur saw his ground forces in a situation more precarious than anything he had experienced since New Guinea. He ordered Stratemeyer to use all available FEAF airpower, including B-29s, to help the Eighth Army save the perimeter.

MacArthur noted in his memoirs that "the pattern and density of the enemy's supply and reinforcement movement showed that heavy tonnage was coming from Chinese Manchuria and Russian Siberia, through Seoul, in spite of our bombing and strafing. It moved habitually by night. The ingenuity and tenacity in repair of bridges and tracks was of the highest order."

With this, he decided that it was time for strategy so bold that it bordered upon foolhardy:

… a turning movement deep into the flank and rear of the enemy that would sever his supply lines and encircle all his forces south of Seoul. I had made similar decisions in past campaigns, but none more fraught with danger, none that promised to be more vitally conclusive if successful. The target I selected was Inchon [now Incheon], 20 miles west of Seoul and the second largest port in South Korea. The target date, because of the great tides at Inchon, had to be the middle of September. This meant that the staging for the landing at Inchon would have to be accomplished more rapidly than that of any other large amphibious operation in modern warfare.

In Washington, the plan was greeted by skepticism. Both Lawton Collins and Admiral Forrest Sherman, the Chief of Naval Operations, flew out to Tokyo to discuss the plan with MacArthur. They argued that Inchon and Seoul were too heavily defended for such an attack – never mind Inchon's notoriously treacherous tides. MacArthur countered that the North Koreans would not expect such a move and it would therefore achieve the element of surprise. In this, he would be proven right.

On the early morning of September 15, 1950, with MacArthur observing from aboard the USS *Mount McKinley* offshore, the 40,000 troops of Major General Edward Almond's X Corps, spearheaded by the 1st Marine Division, landed at Inchon, secured their beachhead, and moved toward Seoul, barely 20 miles away.

The Marines captured the airport at Kimpo two days later, and on September 18, the FEAF Combat Cargo Command began an airlift into Kimpo, landing nine C-54s and 23 C-119s loaded with 208 tons of equipment and supplies for the ground troops. Within three days, Suwon was recaptured and was also becoming an airlift hub. The C-119s even airlifted a pontoon bridge that would be used for X Corps to cross the Han River near Seoul. On September 22, X Corps entered Seoul, where the KPA held on tenaciously until finally being subdued in house-to-house fighting that lasted nearly a week.

In the meantime, I Corps of the Eighth Army, along with ROK units, had broken out of the Pusan Perimeter and had begun a sustained offensive against the enemy, whose lines began to crumble. The once unstoppable KPA, which had scored a continuous series of victories throughout the summer, had been so degraded by the relentless assaults by the FEAF Bomber Command that its effectiveness collapsed.

As the Eighth Army pushed north, reversing the momentum that had taken it to Pusan in July, the KPA disintegrated as a fighting force. Equipment was abandoned and unit cohesiveness, once maintained by iron discipline, evaporated. Throughout the contested area, B-29s were dropping flares, so that B-26s and other strike aircraft could run ground attack missions at night as well as by day. By September 26, when the troops advancing out of the Pusan Perimeter linked up with those who had come ashore at Inchon to retake Seoul, the number of KPA troops who surrendered had exceeded 120,000.

On September 29, MacArthur flew into Seoul aboard his new executive transport aircraft, a Lockheed VC-121A Constellation marked with his title as *SCAP*. Some sources claim that *SCAP* was a Lockheed C-69 Constellation, but the early model C-69s were of 1943 vintage, while his VC-121A, ordered in 1948, was the equivalent of the latest Constellation Model 749A commercial airliners. Syngman Rhee followed in MacArthur's earlier personal airplane, the C-54 Skymaster named *Bataan*. The general awarded Distinguished Service Crosses to Almond and Walker, restored Rhee to his presidency, and flew back to Japan.

With South Korea no longer occupied, and with ROK Army units having advanced to – and in some cases *across* – the 38th Parallel, the mandate of Resolution 83 to "repel the armed attack" had been achieved. However, the part of Resolution 83 about restoring "peace and security in the area," seemed unmet by the fact that a repeat of the June 25 invasion was still possible. There were 30,000 KPA troops that had escaped from South Korea and another 30,000 were still in training camps in North Korea.

The question of what MacArthur was to do next in Korea – a topic of interest from street corners to editorial pages around the world – was clarified in a top-secret directive to MacArthur that was approved by President Truman on September 27. It originated with Secretary of Defense George Marshall (formerly Secretary of State, and Chief of Staff of the US Army during World War II) and was shared with the State Department, who shared it in turn with the United States Mission at the United Nations in their message 357.AD/9-2650 of September 26. Approved by Truman, the directive went from Marshall to MacArthur the next day as Joint Chiefs of Staff message 92895, and marked "personal."

In this, Marshall told MacArthur:

... your military objective is the destruction of the North Korean armed forces. In attaining this objective you are authorized to conduct military operations, including amphibious and airborne landings or ground operations north of the 38th Parallel in Korea, provided that at the time of such operation there has been no entry into North Korea by major Soviet or Chinese Communist forces, no announcement of intended entry, nor a threat to counter our operations militarily in North Korea.

What happened next would mark a turning point in the Korean War, in the career of Douglas MacArthur, and in the history of the 20th century.

27

From a Position of Strength

At the beginning of October 1950, Douglas MacArthur was at the apogee of his career, something rarely said of a man who had turned 70 a few months earlier. Since World War II, he had transformed Japan, a once and future major world power, from a feudal society into a modern democracy. His daring, even reckless, Inchon landing two weeks earlier had not only succeeded in spectacular fashion, it had reversed the disastrous course of the war. Through this bold stroke, he had triumphantly achieved the goals set for him in Korea, and after Inchon – and he had accomplished this in less than two weeks.

What he was about to do was controversial at the time, and has been the subject of extensive discussion and debate ever since. Having ejected the KPA from South Korea, he moved his UNC forces north, across the 38th Parallel, with the objective of destroying the KPA. In so doing, he ignored or dismissed statements, both public and through diplomatic channels, by both China and the Soviet Union, that they would consider intervening in Korea to prevent the elimination of a Communist state on the Korean Peninsula. In the directive approved by President Truman on September 27, George Marshall had cautioned MacArthur about provoking just such an intervention.

On October 1, MacArthur advised Washington:

… under the provisions of the United Nations Security Council Resolution of 27 June, the field of our military operations is limited only by military exigencies and the international boundaries of Korea. The so-called 38th Parallel, accordingly, is not a factor in the military employment of our forces ... our forces, in due process of campaign will seek out and destroy the enemy's armed forces in whatever part of Korea they may be located.

MacArthur, as well as the governments of the United States and other countries, took UN General Assembly Resolution 376 of October 7 as an endorsement of his actions, when it stated that the "essential objective" of previous resolutions had been "the establishment of a unified, independent and democratic Government of Korea, [that] all appropriate steps be taken to ensure conditions of stability throughout Korea." MacArthur therefore operated under the assumption that the UN had authorized him to use the UNC to unify Korea under a non-Communist government.

On October 12, MacArthur received a surprising cable from Marshall telling him that Truman would like to arrange a face-to-face meeting somewhere in the Pacific. Marshall said that the President preferred Hawaii, 5,000 miles from Washington, but "if the situation in Korea is such that you feel you should not absent yourself for the time involved in such a long trip," Truman would travel an additional 2,300 miles to Wake Island. MacArthur readily picked Wake Island, 2,100 miles from Tokyo.

The reason for this meeting, like many other elements in the relationship between Truman and MacArthur, was sufficiently unclear as to foster many decades of discussion, debate, and the innuendo of deep political motives.

William Manchester, MacArthur's biographer, discussed and rejected the popular notion that Truman wanted to be seen with the larger-than-life general to burnish his fading political popularity ahead of the midterm elections, but acknowledged the confusion that still swirls about the President's purpose.

Manchester wrote:

Harry Truman was a forthright man, but his motive in flying two-thirds of the way around the world for less than two hours with MacArthur was mysterious then and is still [circa 1978] puzzling. The UN cause was approaching a crisis, but neither he nor his Supreme Commander saw it at the time. In his memoirs the President would write simply that "I wanted to have a personal talk with the General."

The two men met for half an hour alone, and were then joined by others, including Admiral Arthur Radford, the CINCPAC; as well as Ambassador to South Korea John Muccio; Secretary of the Army Frank Pace; Chairman of the JCS General Omar Bradley; and Dean Rusk and Averell Harriman of the Diplomatic Corps.

Much of the conversation had to do with the details of rebuilding Korea *after* the war, which the conferees seemed – in the meeting transcript – to assume was all but over.

"It is my hope to be able to withdraw the Eighth Army to Japan by Christmas," MacArthur said confidently. "I hope the United Nations will hold elections by the first of the year."

Later, Truman asked pointedly, "What are the chances for Chinese or Soviet interference?"

"Very little," MacArthur replied. "Had they interfered in the first or second months it would have been decisive. We are no longer fearful of their intervention."

Finally, after 90 minutes, an amazingly short time, considering the hours that everyone had spent in transit, Truman quipped, "no one who was not here would believe we have covered so much ground as we have been actually able to cover. We might break up to have luncheon."

"If it's all right," MacArthur said, "I am anxious to get back as soon as possible and would like to leave before luncheon if that is convenient."

"I believe this covers the main topics," Truman replied, and they were done.

During the week that the conferees were commuting to Wake, the Eighth Army that MacArthur hoped to withdraw by Christmas was on the move. The American I Corps, spearheading the Eighth Army advance, pushed up the western side of the Korean Peninsula toward Pyongyang, North Korea's capital, while X Corps and the ROK Army I Corps moved up the east coast toward Wonsan, North Korea's major port – both about 90 miles north of the 38th Parallel. The two ground contingents were compelled to operate independently, separated by the steep and rugged Taebaek Mountains that form the spine of the peninsula.

While the terrain precluded mutual support between the two contingents, both were supported by the aircraft of Pat Partridge's Fifth Air Force. During the first week of October, Partridge had relocated the headquarters of several Fifth Air Force units back to South Korea. This included the 8th Fighter Bomber Wing to Suwon and the 35th Fighter Interceptor Wing to Pohang (K-3). The 51st Fighter Interceptor Wing, one of the units that deployed overseas at the start of the war, moved into Kimpo.

Joining the RAAF No. 77 Squadron, No. 2 Fighter Squadron of the South African Air Force (SAAF) also arrived that week and was assigned to the Fifth Air Force 18th Fighter Bomber Wing. This SAAF squadron was one of only a few integral combat squadrons from a nation other than the United States or South Korea to serve in the war, though Greece's Hellenic Air Force supplied a transport squadron. Canadian pilots served under Fifth Air Force command, but with American squadrons. Britain's Royal Navy deployed five aircraft carriers, at least one of which was on station at any given time throughout the Korean War, and Australia deployed two carriers.

On the ground, the UNC was augmented in 1950 by the 27th British Commonwealth Brigade and the British Army 29th Infantry Brigade, and in 1951 by the British 28th Infantry Brigade and the 1st Commonwealth Division, which included the Canadian 25th Brigade. Turkey also supplied a brigade-strength force in 1950, and other countries supplied smaller contingents.

While there had been a massive effort to reinforce the American ground forces available to MacArthur in Korea, there was a parallel reinforcement of FEAF. The total number of personnel increased from 54,477 in June to 82,887 in November, while the number of combat squadrons increased from 36 to 49, including light bombardment (B-26) squadrons and troop carrier squadrons, along with 18 fighter squadrons.

Through October, the number of B-29 squadrons had increased from nine to 15, but this number soon dropped back to the June levels as the strategic air campaign against North Korea had reached a point where most objectives had been neutralized.

The B-29s had spent September reaching into North Korea to strike industrial sites, power plants, and troop training centers in Chonjin, Hungnam, Pyongyang, Songjin, and Wonsan. By October, though, the industrial infrastructure of the North had been so degraded that General George Stratemeyer had returned the 22nd and 92nd Bomb Groups to SAC and sent their B-29s back to the United States. Rosey O'Donnell's FEAF Bomber Command continued interdiction operations, including strikes against bridges and airfields. In attacking bridges, the bombers had begun employing the 1,000-pound VB-3 Razon (Range and Azimuth) radio-controlled guided bomb first used in 1945.

X Corps, spearheaded by the ROK Army I Corps on the east side of the Korean Peninsula, captured Wonsan and its airport (K-25) on October 10. In the west, I Corps, spearheaded by the US 1st Cavalry Division and the ROK 1st Infantry Division, entered Pyongyang on October 19. With Pyongyang no longer his, Kim Il-sung went into hiding, while Stalin fired Terentii Shtykov, his man behind a throne that had now been lost.

The following day, the FEAF Combat Cargo Command dropped more than 2,800 troops of the US 187th Airborne Regimental Combat Team 30 miles north of Pyongyang, to complete the envelopment of the capital. The Combat Cargo Command then began airlifting Eighth Army supplies into Pyongyang's airfields, which were designated as K-23 and K-24.

On October 24, American and ROK troops pressed on to the Chongchon River, just 50 miles south of the Yalu River, which forms the border with China. MacArthur had given them a green light to go all the way to the Yalu. By now, MacArthur's United Nations Command had occupied most of North Korea and he wanted to finish the job before winter set in. The phrase "Home for Christmas," mentioned at the Wake Island meeting, was now widely used among American troops on the ground and the media at home. Much of the

US Navy's Task Force 77 was being withdrawn, assuming that their job was finished.

Two days later, the first ROK Army units reached the Yalu, with American troops soon to follow. As the first snowflakes of the winter began to swirl, the troops of the UNC were in the cities of Chosan and Hyesan, from which they could gaze across the ice-covered river at the snow-capped mountains of Manchuria.

28

Reversal of Fortune

By the beginning of November, American and ROK troops in the vanguard of the UNC northward advance toward the Yalu River had encountered numerous Chinese soldiers. However, it was not yet apparent – or at least not admitted by the UNC – until the last week of the month, that Chinese troops had begun moving south of the Yalu in great strength.

The Chinese presence was clouded by semantics. Neither side wanted to acknowledge that the Chinese had "officially" entered the war. MacArthur had been authorized by Marshall to "conduct military operations ... provided that at the time of such operation there has been no entry into North Korea by major Soviet or Chinese Communist forces, no announcement of intended entry." Therefore, the Chinese soldiers were described as being "volunteers," not regular troops, so that MacArthur would not have to curtail his operations now that he was so close to his goal of occupying all of North Korea.

The Chinese, meanwhile, had organized their personnel into an entity called the People's Volunteer Army (PVA). It was comprised of units of the regular Chinese People's Liberation Army (PLA) that had been transferred and reconstituted in order that China's regular army would technically not be entering into combat against American troops.

There had also been numerous border incidents along the Yalu by this time, as shots were being exchanged on the ground between the PVA and the ROK Army. An F-51 was shot down by Chinese antiaircraft artillery over the Yalu on the same day that MacArthur was meeting Truman. Arguably the most serious cross-border incident occurred on October 8. It involved two Fifth Air Force F-80s that accidentally strafed a Soviet airfield near Vladivostok. Because those in Washington – especially Truman and Marshall – feared Soviet intervention more than that of the Chinese, this incident resulted in Stratemeyer court martialing the pilots involved.

By November 1, the situation south of the Yalu had fundamentally changed. The 1st Cavalry Division fought its first major engagement with the PVA, and, overhead, enemy Yak fighters engaged American Fifth Air Force aircraft for the first time since July. F-51s claimed two Yaks and one was downed by a B-26 gunner. In turn, F-80s attacked the Sinuiju airfield, overlooking the Yalu in northernmost Korea, and destroyed several Yaks on the ground. However, antiaircraft fire from the Chinese side of the river took out one of the F-80s. Under rules of engagement stipulated by the Joint Chiefs of Staff, enemy positions inside China could not be attacked.

With Chinese troops crossing into China, these rules of engagement became problematic when Stratemeyer requested permission to bomb the bridges across the Yalu River that the PVA was using to bring troops down from China. On November 6, Undersecretary of Defense Robert Lovett brought Stratemeyer's urgent request to Dean Rusk at the State Department. According to transcripts now in the Truman Presidential Library, they phoned President Truman, who said that he would "approve the action if it was necessary because of an immediate and serious threat to the security of our own troops."

The decision seems to have fallen to Marshall, who initially forbade strikes within 5 miles of the Yalu. Those in the field, from MacArthur to Stratemeyer to Rosey O'Donnell, found this distressing.

"The only way to stop this reinforcement of the enemy is the destruction of the bridges by air attack and air destruction of installations in North Korea which would facilitate the movement," MacArthur wired Marshall. "I feel that the operation is within the scope of the rules of war and the resolutions and directives which I have received. And I can accept the instructions rescinding my orders only under the greatest protest. [I] urgently request reconsideration of your decision."

Marshall eventually approved attacks on the Korean end of the bridges using Razon bombs – as Stratemeyer had originally requested.

Meanwhile, FEAF reconnaissance aircraft observed a buildup of aircraft at Antung (now Dandong), a large air base just across the Yalu River in China, and this included Soviet-built MiG-15 jet fighters.

On November 3, Stratemeyer complained to MacArthur that "hostile aircraft have been sighted flying from Korean territory across the border into Manchuria. Current directives prohibit UN aircraft from continuing pursuit of such enemy aircraft beyond the border ... It is requested that clearance be obtained for UN aircraft to pursue enemy aircraft across the North Korean border to destroy them in the air or on the ground and to determine the location of their bases."

Three days later, MacArthur issued a press release complaining that the Chinese were meddling in a war that had already been won. He asserted that "the Korean War was brought to a practical end with the closing of the trap on enemy elements north of Pyongyang and seizure of the east coastal area ... In the face of this victory for United Nations arms, the Communists, without any notice of belligerency, moved elements of Chinese Communist forces across the Yalu River into North Korea and massed a great concentration of possible reinforcing divisions."

On November 7, MacArthur sent a message (CX68411) to Marshall in Washington, saying that "hostile planes are operating from bases west of the Yalu River against our forces in North Korea. These planes are appearing in increasing numbers ... The present restrictions imposed on my area of operation provide a complete sanctuary for hostile air immediately upon their crossing the Manchuria–North Korean border. The effect of this abnormal condition upon the morale and combat efficiency of both air and ground troops is major."

In his reply (JCS 95949), Marshall reiterated what he had been saying for the past two months, writing that "it is vital in the national interest of the US to localize the fighting in Korea. It is important that extreme care be taken to avoid violation [of] Manchurian territory and airspace."

Over the coming months, MacArthur and Stratemeyer would make this case again and again, but the answer would remain the same.

By November, the Soviets had agreed to supply materiel to the Chinese, especially with aircraft and advanced weapons. Though not publicly acknowledged or recognized at the time, a very large number of Soviet pilots also joined the conflict, destined to take part in aerial combat. The 64th Fighter Aviation Corps of the Soviet Air Force operated covertly in Korea under PLA Air Force command throughout the war, flying MiGs with Chinese markings. The pilots were also briefed to speak Chinese in their radio transmissions, but they and their controllers often slipped into Russian.

On November 8, the FEAF Bomber Command launched the biggest incendiary raid of the war against Sinuiju, while B-29s made their first strikes on the Yalu bridges. On that day, when MiG-15s in Chinese markings intervened to intercept FEAF aircraft over Sinuiju, the first ever air-to-air combat between jet fighters occurred. One of the MiGs engaged an F-80C flown by Lieutenant Russell Brown of the 16th Fighter Interceptor Squadron of the 51st Fighter Interceptor Wing.

Media reports at the time, and subsequent retellings of the story, credit Brown with being the first jet pilot to down another jet aircraft. However, since the turn of the century, Soviet records cited by aviation historian Robert Dorr and others have come to light which tell of Lieutenant Vladimir Kharitonov of the 72nd Guards Fighter Aviation Regiment – covertly flying under Chinese cover – engaging an F-80C that day, but escaping after having been damaged.

The following day, Lieutenant Commander William Amen, flying a Grumman F9F Panther jet fighter from the carrier USS *Philippine Sea*, shot down a MiG-15 while escorting ground support aircraft over Korea. Its crash was witnessed by many. If not Brown, then Amen was the first victor in a jet-on-jet dogfight. Soon there were more as intense jet aerial combat immediately filled Korean skies.

At the same time, the MiG-15s were challenging the B-29s over the Yalu bridges. One of World War II's ultimate warplanes, the B-29, had met its match in jet fighters. The first Superfortress lost to a MiG went down on November 10, and 15 MiGs challenged 18 B-29s four days later.

Elsewhere, the Fifth Air Force fighters and attack bombers continued to support the still steadily advancing UNC troops, and on November 18, the 35th Fighter Interceptor Wing relocated its combat group headquarters to Yonpo Air Base (K-27) at Hungnam, 150 miles north of the 38th Parallel.

On November 24, MacArthur launched a major ground offensive, which in the words of the communiqué he issued, "should for all practical purposes, end the war."

That day, as B-29s struck the Yalu bridges and enemy supply depots that had been identified by aerial reconnaissance, MacArthur was also in Korean skies himself, having ordered Lieutenant Colonel Anthony Story, his pilot, to fly him and Stratemeyer, along with members of their staffs, up to the Yalu in his VC-121A, *SCAP*. As the aircraft followed the course of the river at 5,000 feet, the men sipped champagne and snacked on Stratemeyer's birthday cake, baked before the flight at the US Embassy in Tokyo. Luckily, no MiGs appeared.

By this time, only three relatively small areas of North Korea were outside UNC's control. The objective was to capture these inside 30 days, and based on recent experience it seemed doable.

However, a surprise was in store.

The American commanders had greatly underestimated the number of PVA troops that had crossed into North Korea. Led by Peng Dehuai as field commander, under the close supervision of Communist Chinese leaders Mao Zedong and Zhou Enlai, the Chinese infiltration into Korea had grown to a scale much larger than MacArthur and his commanders imagined. Because the Chinese troops traveled mainly by night to avoid detection by FEAF reconnaissance aircraft, they were able to infiltrate more than 300,000 troops at a time when UNC estimates put their number at around 70,000.

As the main force of Walton Walker's Eighth Army, including ROK units and the Turkish Brigade, jumped off from their line along the Chongchon River on the west coast of North Korea, they walked into a massive trap set for them by the PVA. Across the Taebaek Mountains to the east, the PVA launched a similar attack on Edward Almond's X Corps, including the 1st Marine Division, cornering them at the Chosin Reservoir (now called Changjin Lake). As the troops found themselves surrounded, William Tunner's FEAF Combat Cargo Command undertook to supply them by air. While the encircled Marines and soldiers began to fight their way south toward Hungnam on the coast, from which they could be evacuated by sea, B-26s of the 3rd Bomb Group led the way in flying ground support missions.

The UNC ground contingents, geographically separated on the east and west coasts by the barrier of the Taebaeks, were overwhelmed and badly battered by both the enemy and bitter winter weather. As the men on the east side fought to escape encirclement, the Eighth Army in the west fell back in the face of the PVA onslaught. As the Turkish

Brigade fought a costly rearguard action, Walker's force evacuated their positions in northwestern Korea.

On November 27, Stratemeyer wrote in his diary that he "had a call from Partridge at 1700 hours and he reported that the ground situation on the right flank of the Eighth Army was bad. He personally flew out over the lines at 1240 hours and arrived at this estimate of the situation from the radio chatter that he listened to. Calls were coming in for fighter support from all over the front."

The collapse of the Eighth Army, spread across the front pages at home, was rightly perceived as a disaster. How could it be, wondered pundits and public alike, that a victorious army, due home for Christmas in less than a month, could have been defeated and forced into a headlong retreat?

Said MacArthur to George Marshall in a radiogram on November 28, "we face an entirely new war."

Desperate measures were being discussed – behind closed doors, as well as in public forums. The use of nuclear weapons in Korea was first publicly mentioned by the President, who had signed off on the Hiroshima and Nagasaki strikes five years earlier. On December 1, the headline in the *New York Times* read, "Truman Gives Aim: Truman Repeats Statement To Press ... President Warns Bomb May Be Used [by] Supreme Command." The article by Anthony Leviero and Bruce Hoertel went on to say that "Truman declared today that ... 'we would use the atomic bomb, if necessary, to assure victory.'" Another article in the paper by A.M. Rosenthal added that UN delegates were "startled ... after learning of Truman's statement on Atom Bomb." Sensing great propaganda value, the Soviet government was outspoken in its condemnation of nuclear weapons in Korea.

The following day, the Associated Press reported that MacArthur "has not asked for the Atomic Bomb," while adding in a headline that MacArthur had complained publicly that "Orders Barring Attacks on Manchuria Aid Chinese Invaders."

On December 4, General Lawton Collins, the US Army Chief of Staff, arrived in Tokyo to confer with MacArthur, Stratemeyer, and Admiral Joy. As Stratemeyer noted in his diary, they discussed "retrograde movements" (retreats), and a hope of holding a beachhead at Inchon. They also discussed the fear that permeated all discussions of the Korean front that winter – the fear of *Soviet* intervention. He added that "there were other subject matters discussed that were of such a high classification that I dare not even put them in this document [his diary]." Presumably these involved nuclear weapons, and perhaps their potential use against the Soviets, who the American leadership feared would enter the war at any moment.

Collins then flew to Korea to see Walker and Partridge. On December 6, after these talks, Partridge phoned Stratemeyer to say that Walker had told Collins that "he could not guarantee to hold Seoul ... I'm going to save the Eighth Army and I can do that by orderly withdrawals [back] to Pusan."

Partridge had told Collins that "we are killing Communists by the thousands and will continue but we can't do anything unless the Army finds someplace to stop and fight and push [the enemy] in the open. We'll have to find a place where the Army can make a stand."

On the topic of the Soviets entering the war, Partridge told Stratemeyer that "we have enough Air Force to fight the Soviet Air Force unless they commit their entire force. We can defeat them if they come down and fight in our own backyards."

On December 9, after all of these gloomy conversations under the shadow of nuclear warfare, Stratemeyer wrote in his diary that "the A-bomb is our ultimate weapon and we should surely keep it in reserve as a deterrent, or for use in event of Russia launching a third world war."

The Soviet nuclear arsenal of 1950 was small compared to that of the United States, but Truman's remarks notwithstanding, no one really wanted to test Stalin by making the first move in a nuclear war.

In a confidential report a month later, Stratemeyer was told by Brigadier General Charles Banfill, his deputy for intelligence, that "the Soviet Union will continue both to decry use of the atomic bomb, and to lure us into using it in Asia in order that worldwide opinion may be turned against us, while giving the USSR an opportunity to assess the degree of success we are able to achieve with our 'ultimate weapon.'"

On the battlefront, Pyongyang was captured by the PVA on December 6 after seven weeks under UNC management, and Wonsan came under Chinese control three days later. The men of X Corps who had extricated themselves from the Chosin River encirclement were boarding evacuation ships at Hungnam by December 11.

The Eighth Army, which was to have extended its line to the Yalu River in time to be home for Christmas, had its back pushed all the way down the Korean Peninsula to – and past – the 38th Parallel in less time than it had taken to advance northward from that landmark.

Adding insult to injury for the badly outnumbered Eighth, its commander, General Walton Walker, was killed in a head-on collision with a retreating ROK Army vehicle on the north side of Seoul on December 23. The evacuation by sea of the last of 100,000 UNC troops and a like number of civilians from encircled Hungnam was completed the next day. The incursion into, and occupation of, North Korea by the UNC, which was considered nearly complete a month earlier, had now been rolled back 250 miles and erased by the PVA.

Walker's successor arrived on the day after Christmas. Lieutenant General Matthew Ridgway, who had commanded the XVIII Airborne Corps in Europe during World War II, was tasked with halting the Chinese tidal wave, though he knew that doing so at the 38th Parallel was impossible.

A major Chinese encirclement of Seoul began on New Year's Eve, and Ridgway had the ignoble distinction of ordering the Eighth Army to abandon the city on January 3, 1951. As the PVA crossed the frozen Han River, the air bases at Kimpo and Suwon were once again in enemy hands. This meant that American jet fighters had to withdraw to Taegu, 400 miles from the contested skies of northwestern Korea.

The entire UNC front was collapsing as the new year began, leaving numerous pockets of surrounded troops who would become prisoners of war. As had been the case six months earlier, American troops found themselves in retreat on the roads between Seoul and Pusan, and MacArthur was considering the abandonment of the Korean Peninsula, nearly all of which he had controlled six weeks before.

Around the world, media reports were accompanied by editorials condemning MacArthur for the debacle. As William Manchester recalled, MacArthur lashed out, blaming those whom he called "irresponsible correspondents at the front, aided and abetted by other such unpatriotic elements at home." He went on to condemn China and to state his intention to roll back the PVA as he had the KPA.

MacArthur's fiery rhetoric, in turn, ignited more fires on the editorial pages. As military officers engaging in such discourse is considered out of line by their civilian leaders, President Truman took action.

On December 6, Truman ordered Marshall to issue a top-secret directive to MacArthur and all other military commanders stipulating that "no speech, press release or other public statement concerning military policy should be released until it has received clearance from the Department of Defense," adding that "the purpose of this memorandum is not to curtail the flow of information to the American people, but rather to insure that the information made public is accurate and fully in accord with the policies of the United States Government."

As we know with historic hindsight, this exchange put Truman and MacArthur on a collision course.

On the Korean Peninsula, the great reversal of fortune that had begun with MacArthur's bold landing at Inchon in September had been reversed again.

29

The Final Act

As the curtain rose with the first light of 1951, Douglas MacArthur was in the unexpected opening scene of his final act upon the stage of the 20th century's momentous events.

The phrase "pushed into the sea," widely used by the media around the world in connection with the Pusan debacle of July, was dusted off for reuse in January. Secretary of State Dean Acheson later wrote in his memoirs of the "stench of spiritless defeat, of death of high hopes and broad purposes," that permeated the conversation in Washington.

On December 29, Marshall sent MacArthur a top-secret memo (JCS 99935) in which he observed that "it appears from all estimates available that the Chinese Communists possess the capability of forcing United Nations forces out of Korea if they choose to exercise it ... We believe that Korea is not the place to fight a major war."

Marshall cautioned MacArthur that it was now "our last reasonable opportunity for an orderly evacuation."

In his reply the next day, MacArthur wrote that "if we are forced to evacuate Korea without taking military measures against China proper as suggested in your message, it would have the most adverse effect upon the peoples of Asia, not excepting the Japanese."

In December, the PVA had swept south to the 38th Parallel just as the UNC had moved north to the Yalu in October and November. As the curtain rose on the final act on the first day of 1951, the PVA and their KPA allies launched a major offensive southward from the 38th Parallel. On January 4, Seoul fell into enemy hands for the second time in half a year.

Two days later, Pat Partridge of the Fifth Air Force wrote pessimistically to George Stratemeyer of FEAF that "even the Pusan perimeter is ill-equipped to stop the determined onslaught."

As 1951 began with the UNC in retreat, there was no FEAF buildup as there had been during their similar retreat in the summer of 1950. The number of operational combat squadrons within FEAF, which stood at 36 when the war started, peaked at 58 in December 1950 and remained constant at 57 or 58 for the next six months. The reason had nothing to do with the PVA offensive.

On January 15, 1951, when Air Force Chief of Staff General Hoyt Vandenberg came out to call on FEAF, Stratemeyer had asked for three additional fighter groups. To this, Vandenberg had answered that "they just did not exist."

Stratemeyer recalled that Vandenberg had admitted that "he didn't have sufficient fighters to defend his bases in Europe, and to my great surprise, he informed me that the best the British had was about four squadrons of fighters. He further indicated that I had here in the Far East, except for [the long-range bombers of the Strategic Air Command], the fighting units of the US Air Force."

Two days later, when Stratemeyer was in Korea, the beleaguered Matthew Ridgway said, "I would appreciate very much your letting me know how much air support I could expect from our Air Forces in support of the Eighth Army if the Russians came into the war."

Knowing that Vandenberg had just told him that FEAF had all that it would get, the Soviet specter was especially chilling.

Stratemeyer answered Ridgway, telling him on January 21 that in the event of Soviet intervention, continuing FEAF's "present all-out support ... would leave the initiative in the air to the enemy, and would probably result in our complete attrition by the Russian Air Force and subsequent great casualties in your command."

Stratemeyer then said he would *attempt* to stretch FEAF both to fight the Soviets and to support the UNC on the ground.

As it turned out, the Soviets never intervened on the ground, nor in the air – except covertly. This meant that Stratemeyer could and would focus the lion's share of FEAF's attention on the relentless interdiction campaign.

Finally, this began to pay off. In his memoirs, MacArthur wrote of the PVA's "stretched supply lines," involving difficult and damaged roads over which goods traveled by foot and only at night, and the enemy's susceptibility to "widespread epidemics."

Just as similar issues had helped halt the KPA at the Pusan Perimeter in 1950, these factors brought the Chinese advance to a gradual halt less than 100 miles south of Seoul.

MacArthur was at last able to order Ridgway "to start north again."

As the prediction of the Eighth Army going home in December never materialized, neither did the prediction of its being pushed into the sea in January. The UNC evacuation from Korea, which Marshall and others were willing to accept, would not come to pass.

On January 25, after a week of heavy ground attack operations by American strike aircraft, General Ridgway and his rested and rebuilt Eighth Army "started north again." MacArthur and Stratemeyer flew into recaptured Suwon three days later on an inspection tour.

On February 1, with the tide having turned, the United Nations General Assembly felt empowered to look ahead. They passed Resolution 498, finally condemning Chinese aggression and calling for the withdrawal of Chinese troops from Korea.

In addition to tactical ground support operations, FEAF resumed tactical airlift support, with the Combat Cargo Command, a provisional organization, superseded by the 315th Air Division – reconstituted as a transport unit from its earlier incarnation as the Composite Wing – with air logistics genius William Tunner still in command. In February, they would fly 15,000 tons, more than the Cargo Command had airlifted in all of 1950. (Throughout the war, FEAF airlifted 296,316 tons of cargo into Korea, 149,039 tons out, and 133,755 within Korea.)

In the north, B-26s and fighter-bombers continued their extensive interdiction campaign across the Korean Peninsula, now using MPQ-2 radar and flares to allow them to attack at night. A practice was initiated whereby the same crews attacked the same infiltration routes repeatedly, with their familiarity allowing them to spot camouflaged enemy vehicles in the landscape.

Meanwhile, B-29s continued their attacks across North Korea, striking railroads, bridges, and airfields using traditional ordnance and new weapons. On January 13, one of the big bombers attacked the bridge across the Changja River at Kanggye, 30 miles south of the Yalu, using an ASM-A-1 Tarzon, a 6.5-ton bomb that used a guidance system similar to that of the Razon.

Largely overlooked beyond Korean skies amid the winter's pessimism – in part because it remained secret until late December – was another important qualitative development for FEAF. The 4th Fighter Interceptor Wing had arrived at Johnson AB in Japan with its North American Aviation F-86 Sabres, destined to be the harbingers of a turning point in air combat. Such was the promise of the new fighters that Stratemeyer initially kept their arrival secret.

The wing itself had a promising pedigree. During World War II, the 4th Fighter Group, the 4th FIW's predecessor, had been one of the highest-scoring fighter groups in the European Theater.

Sabre operations over Korea began on December 15. Two days later, when they were first challenged by MiGs, Colonel Bruce Hinton of the 4th shot down one piloted by Yakov Efromeenko to score the first F-86 aerial victory of the war.

Withdrawn through January as the PVA overran Kimpo and Suwon, the 4th FIW resumed F-86 operations from Suwon in March, escorting B-29 strike missions into northwestern Korea. Because these missions were contested so often by MiG-15s, the skies south of the Yalu around Sinuiju came to be known as "MiG Alley." This would be the scene of intense aerial combat between MiGs and Sabres for the remainder of the Korean War.

Through the war, Sabre pilots shot down 792 MiG-15s, with only 78 F-86s lost to MiGs, achieving a remarkable ten to one victory ratio. The highest-scoring of 38 US Air Force aces – all of whom flew the F-86 – were Captain Joe McConnell with 16 victories and Major James Jabara with 15.

The first scene of MacArthur's final act had begun with the Chinese in Seoul and UNC troops on the run. It ended on March 15 with Seoul having been restored to the Republic of Korea as its capital.

The next scene opened, as MacArthur described in his memoirs, with him formulating his "long-range plans for destroying the Chinese forces in Korea." William Manchester recalled MacArthur's February 11 radiogram to George Marshall in which he outlined his strategy, the text of which he repeated in his memoirs:

My decisive objective would be their supply lines. I would then clear the enemy rear all across the top of North Korea by massive air attacks. If I were still not permitted to attack the massed enemy reinforcements across the Yalu, or to destroy its bridges, I would sever Korea from Manchuria by laying a field of radioactive wastes, the byproducts of atomic manufacture, across all the major lines of enemy supply. The destruction in North Korea had left it bereft of supplies. Everything the Chinese used in the way of food or munitions had to come across the border. The Reds had only ten days' supply of food in their North Korean dumps to feed nearly a million troops, and their ammunition was equally limited.

As strange and unnerving as this scheme may seem today, it was also advocated by Congressman Albert Gore of Tennessee, father of the future Vice President. On April 17, 1951, the *New York Times* wrote that Gore "had suggested to President Truman that United States forces 'dehumanize' a belt across the entire peninsula of Korea by radiological contamination." In its headline, the paper used the term "Atomic Death Belt."

Though the scheme was enshrined in MacArthur's memoirs, the suggestion of sowing a 900-mile strip of nuclear waste was probably more a means of getting Marshall's attention and inducing him to allow attacks against the air bases inside China than it was a serious tactical plan.

MacArthur also told Marshall that he wanted to bring substantial numbers of Nationalist Chinese troops into Korea to fight the PVA in concert with his UNC in a sort of rematch of the civil war that the Communists had won in 1949.

"I would make simultaneous amphibious and airborne landings at the upper end of both coasts of North Korea, and close a gigantic trap," he said. "The [PVA] would soon starve or surrender. Without food and ammunition, they would become helpless. It would be something like Inchon, but on a much larger scale."

However, in Washington, at the United Nations, and around the world, there was no serious momentum, or *will*, to support an offensive to reoccupy North Korea. As Marshall had told MacArthur in December when the PVA had sent the UNC into retreat, "we believe that Korea is not the place to fight a major war."

In his biography of MacArthur, William Manchester quoted Secretary of State Dean Acheson, who said, "what lost the confidence of our Allies were MacArthur's costly defeat, his open advocacy of widening the war at what they rightly considered as unacceptable risks, and the hesitance of the [Truman] administration in asserting firm control over him."

Of course, MacArthur must be understood as a soldier, not as a politician. Manchester went on to explain that "having withdrawn from North Korea, he insisted that he be permitted to retake it. He hadn't challenged the administration's prewar policy of abandoning South Korea, but once he had been sent into battle, he contended, he must be allowed to win. If a nation wasn't willing to make that total military commitment, he said, it shouldn't fight at all."

Indeed, MacArthur continued the war as though he *intended* to win. While the Fifth Air Force and the FEAF Bomber Command hammered the PVA in North Korea, Ridgway's Eighth Army once again pushed north of the 38th Parallel.

On March 24, MacArthur issued a press release in which he spoke enthusiastically of UNC operations continuing "according to schedule and plan," adding that "of even greater significance than our tactical success has been the clear revelation that this new enemy, Red China, of such exaggerated and vaunted military power, lacks the industrial capacity to provide adequately many critical items essential to the conduct of modern war."

As his renewed battlefield successes continued, it was to MacArthur's detriment that he allowed himself to drift too far into dangerous political waters, and once again to speak out as he had before Truman's December 6 directive *not to* make any unvetted "public statement concerning military policy."

He assumed that his perception of the Korean situation was the correct one, and that by stating his position, Truman, Acheson, Marshall, and the others in Washington would see the light. This only accelerated him on his collision course with Truman.

In his diary, Stratemeyer wrote of a dinner conversation on April 3 that turned to Marshall's continued reluctance to support MacArthur's strategic suggestions. MacArthur looked up at the FEAF commander, shook his head, and quipped, "Why, Strat, that old man has gone nuts."

The straw that broke the camel's back was probably a letter that MacArthur wrote to Congressman Joseph Martin of Massachusetts on March 20, which Martin read into the *Congressional Record* on April 5. MacArthur said that "if we lose the war to communism in Asia the fall of Europe is inevitable, win it and Europe most probably would avoid war and yet preserve freedom. As you pointed out [in a February 12 letter], we must win. There is no substitute for victory."

On April 6, Truman met with Acheson and Marshall, as well as Averell Harriman and General Omar Bradley, Chairman of the Joint Chiefs of Staff, to discuss MacArthur. The consensus was that he should be relieved of duty for insubordination.

According to the Office of the Historian at the Department of State, "although Truman and Acheson accused MacArthur of insubordination, the Joint Chiefs avoided any suggestion of this … Insubordination was a military offense, and MacArthur could have requested a public court martial similar to that of Billy Mitchell in the 1920s … and it might well have found him not guilty and ordered his reinstatement."

Bradley said that "MacArthur had stretched but not legally violated any JCS directives. He had violated the President's December directive [not to make public statements on policy matters], relayed to him by the JCS, but this did not constitute violation of a JCS order."

As for what MacArthur had proposed for the Korean battlefront, Bradley said, "Red China is not the powerful nation seeking to dominate the world. Frankly, in the opinion of the Joint Chiefs of Staff, this strategy would involve us in the wrong war, at the wrong place, at the wrong time, and with the wrong enemy."

Supported by those around him, Truman decided to go ahead with relieving MacArthur of duty. He planned to appoint Ridgway to succeed MacArthur in all of his posts – as SCAP, as CINCFE, and as CINCUNC. Truman signed the appropriate orders on April 10, with plans for Secretary of the Army Frank Pace, then in Korea, to hand deliver them to MacArthur in Tokyo on April 11 (April 12 in Japan). When Pace was delayed, and Bradley could not get a message through because of a radio glitch, Truman called a 01:00hrs White House press conference and told the world.

The curtain of the final scene of the final act in Douglas MacArthur's role as a prominent figure upon the global stage rose at 15:03hrs on

April 12 in Tokyo when he learned – from a commercial radio news bulletin – of Truman's announcement that he had been fired.

"To say that I was stunned and shocked expresses it lightly," George Stratemeyer of the FEAF wrote in his diary the following day. "Even this morning, after an almost sleepless night, I cannot understand why our President could be so wrongly influenced as to remove General MacArthur. To me, it means capitulation of our government and all that it has stood for ... Every Red, regardless of his place in the world, was gleeful at this drastic order."

In Japan, which he had helped guide to preeminence as the most prosperous country in Asia, they mourned his departure, but he did not linger. His VC-121A, which had been named *SCAP* when he was the Supreme Commander, was rechristened as *Bataan III*, and made ready. Manchester wrote that a quarter million people lined the dozen miles between his Tokyo residence and the airport at Haneda on April 16, 1951, waving American flags and calling out "*sayonara*." Stratemeyer wrote that he arranged a flyover by F-80s, B-29s, and F-86s.

Similar crowds greeted MacArthur, his wife, and his son in Honolulu and in San Francisco – where he received a confetti-showered welcome. His son had never seen the United States and MacArthur had not set foot in the country since 1935 except for a brief visit in 1937.

The global media, critical of MacArthur in December and January, now rallied to him as though Inchon had been just yesterday. The people of the United States were greeting the conquering hero of World War II – whom they had not yet had a chance to welcome – rather than the controversial figure of 1951. In his being fired for standing up for his beliefs, MacArthur was once again a hero. Truman's approval ratings would sink lower than Richard Nixon's during Watergate.

Douglas MacArthur arrived in Washington, DC just after midnight on April 19, and at Joseph Martin's invitation, he was at the Capitol addressing a Joint Session of Congress 12 hours later.

It was his most memorable speech, though the theme was familiar:

Efforts have been made to distort my position. It has been said in effect that I was a warmonger. Nothing could be further from the truth. I know war as few other men now living know it, and nothing to me – and nothing to me is more revolting. I have long advocated its complete abolition, as its very destructiveness on both friend and foe has rendered it useless as a means of settling international disputes … But once war is forced upon us, there is no other alternative than to apply every available means to bring it to a swift end. War's very object is victory, not prolonged indecision. In war there can be no substitute for victory.

Most memorable were the closing lines, when, quoting an old "barracks ballad," he said, "old soldiers never die; they just fade away … I now close my career and just fade away, an old soldier who tried to do his duty as God gave him the light to see that duty."

Epilogue
Not Fade Away

G eneral of the Army Douglas MacArthur descended the air stairs as he had done on countless occasions through the years, but on May 7, 1951, it was for the last time. He turned and looked back up at the big Lockheed VC-121A Constellation in which he had flown over the Yalu River, across the Pacific, and across the United States.

"It's a great plane, a great crew, and a great pilot," he said, bidding farewell to Lieutenant Colonel Anthony Story, his pilot, on the ramp at New York's Idlewild Airport. "As it flies out of my life I feel I am losing something of inestimable value – an old friend."

As a general of the army with five-star rank, MacArthur could not be formally retired, and he would have been entitled to continue using a military aircraft. However, from now on, with no further active duty command responsibilities, he would choose to travel only on commercial flights.

As MacArthur walked away from the VC-121A that day, mechanic Eddie Miller had already climbed a ladder to begin removing the word *Bataan* from the nose of the aircraft under the watchful eye of an armed military policeman. That done, the aircraft was turned back to the US Air Force and the final iteration of "MacArthur's Air Force" faded away.

After his famous speech on April 19, most people had not expected MacArthur himself to fade away, and for the moment, they were right. On May 3, he returned to Washington for three days of testimony before the Senate Foreign Relations and Armed Forces Committees at the invitation of Senator Richard Russell of Georgia. It was an opportunity for Congress to investigate his sacking, and for MacArthur to state his views on the unification of Korea and his opposition to Communism in Asia.

Millions turned out for his ticker tape parade in New York, and he spent about a year on the lecture circuit reiterating his demands for decisive action to thwart Chinese Communism in Asia and advancing his contention that there could be "no substitute for victory" in Korea.

Less than a week after MacArthur had left Japan, the Chinese and North Koreans launched another major offensive to gain a victory for themselves, but Ridgway met them with a counterattack which reestablished the front line about 40 miles north of the 38th Parallel in the east, though he had relinquished the Ongjin Peninsula in the west to North Korea. It was roughly along this line that a stalemate would rest for the next two years.

Over that line and through MiG Alley, however, the air forces assigned to FEAF – including Marine Corps Aviation and other UN forces as well as US Air Force units – continued to maintain air superiority through those two long years.

General George Stratemeyer, who commanded FEAF, taped an address that was broadcast on Armed Forces Day, May 19, one month after MacArthur addressed Congress. In it, he said:

> ... in the Far East, the skyfilling throb of airpower overhead, the constant snarl of machine guns in forward positions on the ground, and the majestic roar of naval gunfire speak in unison to say that the three armed services of the United States are in concerted action against the foe ... United Nations forces under the leadership of General Ridgway who are fighting so valiantly in the unified effort against Communism, the common enemy of all free peoples of the world.

The following afternoon, Stratemeyer was toppled by a heart attack so severe that he had to be hospitalized in Japan for several months before he could be evacuated to the United States. He left the service early in 1952 and lived until 1969.

With the unexpected departure of Stratemeyer on the heels of the unexpected – though perhaps predictable – departure of MacArthur, there was a reshuffling within the FEAF command structure. Pat Partridge of the Fifth Air Force was named as FEAF's interim commander, but Otto Weyland, Stratemeyer's deputy, assumed permanent command three weeks later on June 10. Partridge returned to the United States, where he would head the Air Research and Development Command. At the Fifth, he was succeeded briefly by his deputy, Major General Ted Timberlake, and then by Major General Frank Everest. Weyland remained in command of FEAF through the end of the Korean War, and was succeeded by Partridge, who returned to the Far East in 1954.

Matthew Ridgway remained as Supreme Commander in Tokyo until the Japanese government was reconstituted in April 1952. A month later, he handed the leadership of the United Nations Command in Korea to General Mark Clark and went to Europe to succeed Dwight Eisenhower as Supreme Allied Commander, Europe (SACEUR) and as head of NATO. Eisenhower was on his way back to the United States, where he would be persuaded to run for President.

Douglas MacArthur was also widely and seriously discussed for the Republican presidential nomination in 1952, but he showed only modest enthusiasm. He did address the Republican Convention that year, but it was in support of Robert Taft, and the party nominated Eisenhower instead. After Eisenhower was elected as President, he and John Foster Dulles, his future secretary of state, met with MacArthur, who recommended that the new President give Josef Stalin an ultimatum demanding unification of Germany and Korea under peril of a nuclear strike. Dulles explained that this might be overly ambitious for Eisenhower's first year in office.

The Korean War still raged when Eisenhower was inaugurated – 21 months after MacArthur had left. In his campaign, Eisenhower had promised to visit Korea and to negotiate an armistice to end the war. He did the former as President elect, and accomplished the latter after six months in office. Technically, the Korean War did not end, but the peninsula fell under a ceasefire. The two Koreas that existed before the war would remain, separated by a demilitarized zone which conforms closely to the place where the front lines ran when MacArthur left the battlefield.

Kim Il-sung not only remained in power in North Korea, but founded a dynasty that would see the impoverished nation ruled by both his son and grandson, while South Korea emerged as one of Asia's most prosperous nations.

During the three years and a month of the Korean War, the air forces assigned to FEAF flew 864,011 missions, 80 percent of them after MacArthur and Stratemeyer departed. Of these, the US Air Force flew 82 percent and the US Marine Corps 13 percent. Other UN air forces assigned to FEAF command accounted for the rest. The number of operational FEAF combat squadrons, which stood at 36 when the war started and remained at around 57 through the first half of 1951, increased in 1952, peaking at 70 in the third quarter. Personnel strength, which stood at 54,477 when the war started, had reached 82,887 in November 1950, and peaked at 143,175 in May 1953.

The average number of active aircraft in the FEAF arsenal increased from around 1,800 when MacArthur departed to about 2,400 in the spring of 1953. By the end of the war, these numbers included more than 500 F-84s and a like number of F-86s. During the war, 976 enemy aircraft were downed and 1,218 damaged in aerial combat by FEAF pilots. Of the number shot down, 81 percent were MiG-15s shot down by F-86s. FEAF lost 1,986 aircraft, half to enemy action, but only 139 in air-to-air combat.

FEAF continued to exist until July 1957, when all US Air Force assets in the Pacific region were consolidated into the Pacific Air Forces (PACAF) command, based at Hickam Air Force Base (AFB) in Hawaii. PACAF still exists to this day. The Fifth Air Force, which was the cornerstone of MacArthur's air forces during World War II and over Korea, still exists as a PACAF component and as of this writing is still headquartered in Japan.

The Seventh Air Force, which was part of FEAF from 1944 to 1947, briefly became the Pacific Air Command, but ceased to exist from 1949 to 1955, when it was reactivated in Hawaii. From 1966 to 1975, it led USAF operations in Southeast Asia, based in South Vietnam until 1973 and Thailand thereafter. Inactivated from 1975 to 1986, it was then reactivated as a PACAF component at Osan AB in South Korea, where it remains.

The Thirteenth Air Force, which joined FEAF in 1944, became part of PACAF in 1955. The Thirteenth remained based in the Philippines from 1944 until 1991, when the eruption of Mount Pinatubo buried Clark AB under volcanic ash. It has since gone in and out of deactivation, being operational with PACAF at Andersen AFB on Guam (1991–2005) and Hickam AFB (2006–2012).

The Twentieth Air Force, commanded by Hap Arnold and led by Curtis LeMay during World War II, was part of FEAF from the end of that war through the end of the Korean War, when its bomber assets were reassigned to the Strategic Air Command (SAC). The Twentieth was reactivated in 1991, and served successively with the SAC for one year, with Air Combat Command for a year, with Air Force Space Command until 2006, and with Air Force Global Strike Command thereafter.

Of the men who were part of MacArthur's air team during World War II, Ennis Whitehead commanded FEAF until he turned it over to Stratemeyer in 1949. He then went home to help create the Air Defense Command and the Tactical Air Command, though he never commanded either. Disillusioned by being passed over as deputy chief of staff of the Air Force, he retired in 1951 having never earned his fourth star as general. He died in 1964.

Paul Wurtsmith, who commanded the V Fighter Command and later the Thirteenth Air Force, took over the Eighth Air Force after World War II, but died in 1946 in the crash of a B-25 during a storm in North Carolina.

Paul Irvin "Pappy" Gunn, the irrepressible engineering genius of the Fifth Air Force, was reunited with his family after their having been imprisoned by the Japanese in Manila through World War II, left the service, and returned to helping shape Philippine Air Lines. In 1957, like Wurtsmith in 1946, his life ended prematurely in a plane crash during a storm.

George Kenney, who more than anyone else filled the role of "MacArthur's airman," went home to take charge of the new Strategic Air Command, but he left the work of the command to his deputy while he devoted his own time and attention to the Military Staff Committee of the UN Security Council, an entity that proved to have little power and in which other member countries showed little interest. Kenney earned low marks from Congress and others within his own service for allowing the SAC to deteriorate, with poor readiness and low morale.

Kenney had hoped to succeed Tooey Spaatz as Air Force Chief of Staff, but in 1948, that job went instead to General Hoyt Vandenberg, the wartime commander of the Ninth Air Force who had served for a year as director of the CIA. One of Vandenberg's first moves was to replace Kenney with Curtis LeMay, who would turn the SAC into one of the most exemplary organizations in the Air Force. Kenney was sent to Alabama to head the Air University at Maxwell AFB. Here he remained until 1951, when he retired to Florida, where he died in 1977.

Meanwhile, the spotlight on MacArthur gradually dimmed. He had taken up residence at the Waldorf Astoria Hotel in New York and resided there for the rest of his life. His views on nuclear warfare evolved. Though it was Truman, not MacArthur, who first publicly suggested the use of nuclear weapons in Korea, he had suggested nuclear contamination as a weapon. By 1955, he was outspoken in his opposition to nuclear war. As noted in *Life* magazine, at his 75th birthday commemoration in Los Angeles in January 1955, he asserted that given the "triumph of scientific annihilation," war on a global scale should be abolished. He added that "science has clearly outmoded [war] as a feasible arbiter."

In 1961, upon his return from his last trip to the Far East, he found that his counsel was sought by John F. Kennedy, who had just come to office and who was a MacArthur admirer. It was Kennedy who convinced MacArthur that his funeral should be a "suitable national tribute." Ironically, it took place in April 1964, more than four months after Kennedy's own untimely funeral.

Today, MacArthur is one of a handful of American generals from World War II whose name is still a household word. As controversial in death as he was in life, he is remembered for his mistakes and his failures, but mostly for his victories, certainly made possible through airpower, and for his having invented modern Japan. Douglas MacArthur has never faded away.

Acronyms

AB	Air Base
ABDA	American–British–Dutch–Australian Command
ABDACOM	Alternate form of ABDA incorporating the word "Command"
ADVON	Advanced Echelon
AF	Air Force
AFB	Air Force Base (US Air Force in United States territory only)
AFPAC	Army Forces in the Pacific (US)
AIF	Australian Imperial Force
ATC	Air Transport Command (of the USAAF)
AVG	American Volunteer Group (the "Flying Tigers")
AWPD	Air War Plans Division (of the USAAF)
BCAir	British Commonwealth Air Group
BCOF	British Commonwealth Occupation Force
CATF	China Air Task Force (of the USAAF)
CENPAC	Central Pacific Area
CIA	Central Intelligence Agency
CINCFE	Commander in Chief, Far East

CINCPAC	Commander in Chief, Pacific
CINCUNC	Commander in Chief, United Nations Command
COMNAVFE	Commander, Naval Forces Far East
ETO	European Theater of Operations
FAWS	Fighter All-Weather Squadron
FEAF	Far East Air Force (of the USAAF), 1941–43
FEAF	Far East Air Forces (of the USAAF/USAF, 1944–45, 1947–57)
FEASC	Far East Air Service Command
FEC	Far East Command (US; alternate of FECOM)
FECOM	Far East Command (US; alternate of FEC)
GHQ	General Headquarters
GHQAF	General Headquarters Air Force
HMS	His Majesty's Ship
IJA	Imperial Japanese Army
IJAAF	Imperial Japanese Army Air Force
IJN	Imperial Japanese Navy
IJNAF	Imperial Japanese Navy Air Force
JCS	Joint Chiefs of Staff
JPS	Joint Planning Staff
KGB	Soviet Committee for State Security
KIA	Killed in Action
KMAG	Korean Military Advisory Group
KNIL	Koninklijk Nederlands Indisch Leger (Royal Netherlands East Indies Army)
KPA	Korean People's Army (North Korea)
LAB	Low Altitude Bombing
MAW	Marine Aircraft Wing

MIA	Missing in Action
ML-KNIL	Militaire Luchtvaart van het Koninklijk Nederlands-Indisch Leger (Military Aviation of the Royal Netherlands East Indies Army)
MTO	Mediterranean Theater of Operations
NATO	North Atlantic Treaty Organization
NAVFE	Naval Forces Far East
NKVD	Soviet People's Commissariat for Internal Affairs (predecessor to the KGB)
NORPAC	North Pacific Area
OSP	Offshore Patrol
OSS	Office of Strategic Services
PAAC	Philippine Army Air Corps
PACAF	Pacific Air Forces
PACOM	Pacific Command
PACUSA	Pacific Air Command, United States Army
PDAF	Philippine Department Air Force
PLA	People's Liberation Army (China)
POA	Pacific Ocean Areas
PRK	People's Republic of Korea (North Korea)
PVA	People's Volunteer Army (China)
RAAF	Royal Australian Air Force
RNZAF	Royal New Zealand Air Force
ROK	Republic of Korea (South Korea)
SAAF	South African Air Force
SAC	Strategic Air Command
SACEUR	Supreme Allied Commander, Europe
SCAP	Supreme Commander of [later *for*] the Allied Powers

SEAC	South East Asia Command
SHAEF	Supreme Headquarters Allied Expeditionary Force (Europe)
SOPAC	South Pacific Area
SWPA	South West Pacific Area
UNC	United Nations Command (alternate of UNCOM)
UNCOM	United Nations Command (alternate of UNC)
USAAF	United States Army Air Forces
USAFFE	United States Army Forces in the Far East
USAFPOA	United States Army Forces in the Pacific Ocean Areas
USAMGIK	United States Army Military Government in Korea
USASTAF	United States Army Strategic Air Forces in the Pacific
USFIA	United States Forces in Australia
USFJ	United States Forces, Japan (a modern joint command)
USMC	United States Marine Corps
USS	United States Ship
USSTAF	United States Strategic Air Forces in Europe
WPO	War Plan Orange

Bibliography

Acheson, Dean. *Present At The Creation: My Years in the State Department.* New York: W. W. Norton & Company, 1969.

Appleman, Roy E. *South to the Naktong, North to the Yalu: United States Army in the Korean War.* Washington, DC: Department of the Army, 1998.

Arnold, Henry H., General of the Air Force. *Global Mission.* New York: Harper & Brothers, 1949.

Arnold, Henry Harley (edited by John W. Huston). *American Airpower Comes of Age: General Henry H. "Hap" Arnold's World War II Diaries, Volume 1.* Collingdale, Pennsylvania: Diane Publishing, 2002.

Arnold, Henry Harley (edited by John W. Huston). *American Airpower Comes of Age: General Henry H. "Hap" Arnold's World War II Diaries, Volume 2.* Collingdale, Pennsylvania: Diane Publishing, 2002.

Bergerud, Eric M. *Fire in the Sky: The Air War in the South Pacific.* Boulder, Colorado: Westview Press, 2000.

Borneman, Walter. *MacArthur at War.* Boston: Little, Brown and Company, 2016.

Brereton, Lewis H. *The Brereton Diaries: The War in the Air in the Pacific, Middle East, and Europe, 3 October 1941 – 8 May 1945.* New York: William Morrow, 1946.

Bunnell, John G. *Knockout Blow? The Army Air Force's Operations against Ploesti and Balikpapan.* Maxwell Air Force Base, Alabama: Air University School of Advanced Air And Space Studies, 2005

Carter, Kit and Mueller, Robert. *The Army Air Forces in World War II: Combat Chronology.* Washington, DC: Office of Air Force History, 1973.

Churchill, Winston. *The Second World War, Volume 3. The Grand Alliance.* Boston: Houghton Mifflin Company, 1950.

Churchill, Winston. *The Second World War, Volume 4. The Hinge of Fate*. Boston: Houghton Mifflin Company, 1950.

Churchill, Winston. *The Second World War, Volume 5. Closing the Ring*. Boston: Houghton Mifflin Company, 1951.

Churchill, Winston. *The Second World War, Volume 6. Triumph and Tragedy*. Boston: Houghton Mifflin Company, 1953.

Craven, Wesley Frank and Cate, James Lea. *The Army Air Forces in World War II, Volume 1. Plans and Early Operations, January 1939 to August 1942*. Washington, DC: Office of Air Force History; Chicago: University of Chicago Press, 1948.

Craven, Wesley Frank and Cate, James Lea. *The Army Air Forces in World War II, Volume 2. Europe: Torch to Pointblank, August 1942 to December 1943*. Washington, DC: Office of Air Force History; Chicago: University of Chicago Press, 1949.

Craven, Wesley Frank and Cate, James Lea. *The Army Air Forces in World War II, Volume 3. Europe: Argument to VE Day, January 1944 to May 1945*. Washington, DC: Office of Air Force History; Chicago: University of Chicago Press, 1951.

Craven, Wesley Frank and Cate, James Lea. *The Army Air Forces in World War II, Volume 4. The Pacific: Guadalcanal to Saipan, August 1942 to July 1944*. Washington, DC: Office of Air Force History; Chicago: University of Chicago Press, 1950.

Craven, Wesley Frank and Cate, James Lea. *The Army Air Forces in World War II, Volume 5. The Pacific: Matterhorn to Nagasaki, June 1944 to August 1945*. Washington, DC: Office of Air Force History; Chicago: University of Chicago Press, 1953.

Craven, Wesley Frank and Cate, James Lea. *The Army Air Forces in World War II, Volume 6. Men and Planes*. Washington, DC: Office of Air Force History; Chicago: University of Chicago Press, 1955.

Craven, Wesley Frank and Cate, James Lea. *The Army Air Forces in World War II, Volume 7. Services around the World*. Washington, DC: Office of Air Force History; Chicago: University of Chicago Press, 1958.

Davis, Richard G. *Carl A. Spaatz and the Air War in Europe*. Washington, DC: Smithsonian Institution Press, 1992.

Dexter, David. *The New Guinea Offensives. Australia in the War of 1939–1945*. Canberra: Australian War Memorial, 1961.

Director of Statistical Services, Headquarters United States Air Force. *United States Air Force Statistical Digest, Fiscal Year 1953*. Washington, DC: Comptroller Headquarters, United States Air Force, 1953.

Dorr, Robert. *Air Combat: An Oral History of Fighter Pilots*. New York: Berkley, 2006.

Eisenhower, Dwight D. *Crusade in Europe.* New York: Doubleday &
    Company, 1948.
Eisenhower, Dwight D. *At Ease: Stories I Tell to Friends.* Garden City, New
    York: Doubleday & Company, 1967.
Fuller, J. F. C. *The Decisive Battles of the Western World, and their Influence
    upon History* (Volume 3). London: Eyre & Spottiswoode, 1956.
Futrell, Robert F. Various articles in: Craven, Wesley Frank and Cate,
    James Lea. *The Army Air Forces in World War II, Volume 4. The Pacific:
    Guadalcanal to Saipan, August 1942 to July 1944.* Washington, DC: Office
    of Air Force History; Chicago: University of Chicago Press, 1950.
Futrell, Robert F. *United States Air Force Operations in the Korean Conflict,
    25 June–1 November 1950. USAF Historical Study No. 71.* Maxwell AFB,
    Alabama: Air University Press, 1951.
Futrell, Robert F. Various articles in: Craven, Wesley Frank and Cate,
    James Lea. *The Army Air Forces in World War II, Volume 5. The Pacific:
    Matterhorn to Nagasaki, June 1944 to August 1945.* Washington, DC:
    Office of Air Force History; Chicago: University of Chicago Press,
    1953.
Futrell, Robert F. *The United States Air Force in Korea, 1950–1953.*
    Washington, DC: United States Government Printing Office, 1997.
General Headquarters, United States Army Forces in the Pacific. *Downfall:
    Strategic Plan for Operations in the Japanese Archipelago.* Manila: General
    Headquarters United States Army Forces in the Pacific, 1945.
General Headquarters, United States Army Forces in the Pacific, Military
    Intelligence Section, General Staff. *Estimate of the Enemy Situation with
    Respect to Kyushu.* Manila: General Headquarters, United States Army
    Forces in the Pacific, 1945.
Giangreco, D.M. "Casualty Projections for the US Invasions of Japan,
    1945–1946. Planning and Policy Implications." In *The Journal of Military
    History.* Lexington, Virginia: Society for Military History, George C.
    Marshall Library, Virginia Military Institute, 1997.
Goldstein Donald M. *Ennis C. Whitehead, Aerospace Commander and
    Pioneer.* Denver: University of Denver, 1971.
Griffith, Thomas E., Jr. *MacArthur's Airman: General George C. Kenney and
    the War in the Southwest Pacific.* Lawrence, Kansas: University Press of
    Kansas, 1998.
Herman, Arthur. *Douglas MacArthur: American Warrior.* New York: Random
    House, 2016.
Jose, Ricardo Trota. "The Philippine National Guard in World War I."
    In *Philippine Studies*, Vol. 36, No. 3. Quezon City: Ateneo de Manila
    University, 1988.

Jose, Ricardo Trota. *The Philippine Army 1935–1942*. Quezon City: Ateneo de Manila University, 1992.

Kenney, George C. *General Kenney Reports: A Personal History of the Pacific War*. Washington, DC: Office of Air Force History, US Air Force, 1987.

King, Ernest J., and Walter Muir Whitehill. *Fleet Admiral King: A Naval Record*. New York: W. W. Norton, 1952.

Lankov, Andrei. *From Stalin to Kim Il Sung: The Formation of North Korea, 1945–1960*. New Brunswick: Rutgers University Press, 2002.

Leahy, William. *I Was There*. New York: Whittlesey House, 1950.

LeMay, General Curtis E. and Bill Yenne. *Superfortress: The B-29 and American Airpower in World War II*. New York: McGraw Hill, 1988; Yardley, Pennsylvania: Westholme, 2006.

MacArthur, Douglas. *Reminiscences*. New York: McGraw Hill, 1964.

Manchester, William. *American Caesar: Douglas MacArthur 1880–1964*. Boston: Little, Brown and Company, 1978.

Masuda, Hiroshi. *MacArthur in Asia: The General and His Staff in the Philippines, Japan, and Korea*. Ithaca, NY: Cornell University Press, 2012.

Matloff, Maurice and Edwin M Snell. *Strategic Planning For Coalition Warfare 1943–1944*. Washington, DC: Center of Military History United States Army/US Government Printing Office, 1990.

Maurer, Maurer. *Air Force Combat Units of World War II*. Maxwell AFB: Office of Air Force History, 1983.

Mitchell, William L. *Winged Defense: The Development and Possibilities of Modern Airpower Economic and Military*. New York: G. P. Putnam's Sons, 1925.

Morison, Samuel Eliot. *History of United States Naval Operations in World War II, Volume VI. Breaking the Bismarcks Barrier*. Boston: Little Brown and Company, 1950.

Morison, Samuel Eliot. *History of United States Naval Operations in World War II, Volume V. The Struggle for Guadalcanal, August 1942– February 1943*. Boston: Little, Brown and Company, 1958.

Morison, Samuel Eliot. *History of United States Naval Operations in World War II, Volume III. The Rising Sun in the Pacific*. Boston: Little Brown and Company, 1984.

Mortensen, Bernhardt. Various articles in: Craven, Wesley Frank and Cate, James Lea. *The Army Air Forces in World War II, Volume 4. The Pacific: Guadalcanal to Saipan, August 1942 to July 1944*. Washington, DC: Office of Air Force History; Chicago: University of Chicago Press, 1950.

Mortensen, Bernhardt. Various articles in: Craven, Wesley Frank and Cate, James Lea. *The Army Air Forces in World War II, Volume 5. The Pacific: Matterhorn to Nagasaki, June 1944 to August 1945*. Washington, DC: Office of Air Force History; Chicago: University of Chicago Press, 1953.

Morton, Louis. *United States Army in World War II, The War in the Pacific, The Fall of the Philippines.* Washington, DC: Center of Military History, 1953.

Murray, Williamson and Allan Reed Millett. *A War To Be Won: Fighting the Second World War.* Cambridge and London: The Belknap Press of Harvard University, 2000.

Nemenzo, Eldon Luis G. and Guillermo A. Molina Jr. *The Philippine Air Force Story.* Quezon City: Kaunlaran Trading and Printing Co., 1992.

Office of Statistical Control, Headquarters USAAF. *Army Air Forces Statistical Digest, World War II.* Washington, DC: Headquarters, USAAF, 1945.

Porter, Catherine. "Preparedness in the Philippines." In *Far Eastern Survey*, Vol. 10, No. 6. New York: Institute of Pacific Relations, 1941.

Quezon, Manuel. *Second Annual Report of the President of the Philippines to the President and the Congress of the United States Covering the Calendar Year Ended December 31, 1937.* Washington, DC: United States Government Printing Office, 1939.

Sakai, Saburo. *Samurai! The Autobiography of Japan's World War II Flying Ace.* New York: E.P. Dutton and Company, 1957.

Schnabel, James. *United States Army in the Korean War* (four volumes). Washington, DC: US Government Printing Office, 1961.

Stratemeyer, George (edited by William T. Y'Blood). *The Three Wars of Lt. Gen. George E. Stratemeyer: His Korean War Diary.* Washington, DC: Air Force History and Museums Program, 1999.

Supreme Command of the Allied Powers. *Final Report: Progress of Demobilization of the Japanese Armed Forces.* Tokyo: Supreme Command of the Allied Powers, 1946.

Toland, John. *The Rising Sun: The Decline and Fall of the Japanese Empire 1936–1945.* New York: Random House, 1970.

Truman, Harry S. *Memoirs: Year of Decisions.* Garden City, New York: Doubleday & Company, 1955.

Truman, Harry S. *Memoirs: Years of Trial and Hope.* Garden City, New York: Doubleday & Company, 1956.

Truman, Harry S. (edited by Robert H. Ferrell). *The Autobiography of Harry S. Truman.* Columbia, Missouri: University of Missouri Press, 2002.

United States Strategic Bombing Survey. *Interrogations of Japanese Officials* (multiple volumes). Washington, DC: US Government Printing Office, 1946.

US War Department. *Handbook of Japanese Military Forces, TM-E 30-480* (Reprint). Baton Rouge and London: Louisiana State University Press, 1991.

Villamor, Jesus A. and Gerald S. Snyder. *They Never Surrendered: A True Story of Resistance in World War II*. Quezon City: Vera-Reyes, 1982.

Wamock, A. Timothy, editor, Air Force Historical Research Agency. *The USAF in Korea: A Chronology 1950–1953*. Maxwell AFB, Alabama: Air University Press, 2000.

Watson, Richard L. Jr. *USAAF Historical Study No. 17: Air Action in the Papuan Campaign, 21 July 1942 to 23 January 1943*. Washington, DC: USAAF Historical Office, 1944.

Watson, Richard L. *USAAF Historical Study No. 113: The Fifth Air Force in the Huon Peninsula Campaign*. Washington, DC: Historical Office, Headquarters, US Army Air Forces, 1946.

Watson, Richard L. "The Battle of the Bismarck Sea." In Craven, Wesley Frank and Cate, James Lea. *The Army Air Forces in World War II, Volume 4. The Pacific: Guadalcanal to Saipan, August 1942 to July 1944*. Washington, DC: Office of Air Force History; Chicago: University of Chicago Press, 1950.

Watson, Richard L. "The Papuan Campaign." In Craven, Wesley Frank and Cate, James Lea. *The Army Air Forces in World War II, Volume 4. The Pacific: Guadalcanal to Saipan, August 1942 to July 1944*. Washington, DC: Office of Air Force History; Chicago: University of Chicago Press, 1950.

Weintraub, Stanley. *MacArthur's War: Korea and the Undoing of an American Hero*. New York: Simon & Schuster, 2000.

Willoughby, Charles, editor. *Japanese Operations in the Southwest Pacific Area. Reports of General MacArthur* (two volumes). Washington, DC: US Government Printing Office, 1966.

Yenne, Bill. *Aces High: The Heroic Saga of the Two Top-Scoring American Aces of World War II*. New York: Berkley/Caliber, 2009.

Yenne, Bill. *Hap Arnold: The General Who Invented the US Air Force*. Washington, DC: Regnery, 2013.

Yenne, Bill. *The Imperial Japanese Army: The Invincible Years 1941–42*. Oxford, UK: Osprey Publishing, 2014.

Yenne, Bill. *Eight Men Who Led the Eighth Air Force to Victory over the Luftwaffe*. New York: Berkley/Caliber, 2015.

Zhang, Xiaoming. *Red Wings over the Yalu: China, the Soviet Union, and the Air War in Korea*. College Station, Texas: Texas A&M University Press, 2002.

Index

Page numbers in **bold** refer to maps.

About the Author

Bill Yenne is the author of more than three dozen nonfiction books, mainly on military and historical topics. He received the Air Force Association's Gill Robb Wilson Award for his "most outstanding contribution in the field of arts and letters." He was commended for his "work of over two dozen airpower-themed books and for years of effort shaping how many people understand and appreciate airpower."

Yenne's book *Hit the Target: Eight Men Who Led the Eighth Air Force to Victory over the Luftwaffe*, selected for the Chief of Staff of the Air Force Reading List, discussed American airpower in the European Theater. In *MacArthur's Air Force*, Yenne turns his attention to the Pacific.

Yenne's previous Pacific Theater books have included *The Imperial Japanese Army: The Invincible Years*, and *Aces High: The Heroic Story of the Two Top-Scoring American Aces of World War II*, which was described by pilot and best-selling author Dan Roam as "The greatest flying story of all time."

Yenne has appeared in documentaries airing on the History Channel, the National Geographic Channel, the Smithsonian Channel, ARD German Television, and NHK Japanese Television. His book signings have been covered by C-SPAN.

Surrounded by remarkable children and grandchildren, he and his wife live in San Francisco. Visit him on the web at www.BillYenne.com.